MANAGING THE STRUCTURED TECHNIQUES

STRATEGIES FOR SOFTWARE DEVELOPMENT IN THE 1990's

EDWARD YOURDON

MANAGING THE STRUCTURED TECHNIQUES

STRATEGIES FOR SOFTWARE DEVELOPMENT IN THE 1990's

Third Edition

YOURDON Press
1501 Broadway, New York, N.Y.   10036
15/17 Ridgemount St., London WD1E 7BH, England

Library of Congress Cataloging-in-Publication Data

Yourdon, Edward.
  Managing the structured techniques.

  Includes bibliographies and index.
  1. Electronic data processing — Structured techniques.
2. Computer software — Development. 3. Electronic data
processing departments — Management. I. Title.
QA76.9.S84Y68 1986   005.1'13   85-29484
ISBN 0-917072-56-1

Printed in the United States of America

Library of Congress Catalog Number

ISBN: 0-917072-56-1

This book was set in Times Roman by YOURDON Press, 1501 Broadway, New York, N.Y., using a PDP-11/70 running under the UNIX*
operating system.

─────────────
*UNIX is a registered trademark of Bell Laboratories.

Cover design by George Armstrong

To Toni

ACKNOWLEDGMENTS

The previous edition of *Managing the Structured Techniques* was published in 1979; much has happened in the seven years that have passed. Structured systems development techniques now are widely used and accepted in organizations around the world. We also have seen the emergence of personal computers, fourth generation programming languages, programmer/analyst workstations, and a host of other technological developments.

This new edition reflects these changes and is based largely on both the successes and failures that my colleagues and I, as well as the many organizations that YOURDON inc. works with, have experienced. Consequently, I would like to express my appreciation to all of my co-workers and to our many clients and students for their ideas, support, and suggestions.

Within YOURDON Press, it is a pleasure to acknowledge the dedication and hard work of Carol Crowell, Teresa Ridley, and Gerry Madigan; their efforts have succeeded in making this an even better book than the second edition.

As usual, my family gets the largest vote of thanks for tolerating many long evenings and weekends that I spent hunched over my personal computer, typing the material for the book.

New York City
November, 1985.

CONTENTS

MANAGING THE STRUCTURED TECHNIQUES

STRATEGIES FOR SOFTWARE DEVELOPMENT IN THE 1990's

Chapter One:

Introduction

1.1 The structured revolution

If you were a successful data processing manager, chances are that you wouldn't be reading this book. If your customers smiled and applauded when you delivered a new system, if your programmers wrote code that worked correctly the first time, if your systems ran year after year with no bugs or failures, if your maintenance programmers complained only that their job was boring because it was so easy — if all of these things were true, you probably would be spending your days sipping mint juleps at your villa in the Mediterranean. Or, maybe you'd be spending your time trying to determine how your computers could *really* do something effective for your users.

But you are reading this book. Conclusion: Your customers grumble and complain when you deliver new systems to them; your programmers spend inordinate amounts of time writing relatively small pieces of code; your systems crash, abort, and produce garbage output with disconcerting regularity; and maintenance is such a dirty word in your organization that you assign the task to trainees and misfits.

This description could continue. Your programmers quit after a year in your organization, and they always wait until the final stages of a critical project to resign. The documentation that you finally forced them to write turns out to be unreadable and completely inaccurate — so you're told by the new programmer, who promptly throws the old coding and documentation into the wastebasket and begins anew. And on and on.

Sound familiar? It should. Indeed, these problems are almost universal. As a consultant and educator, I've visited hundreds of organizations around the world for the past twenty years, and everyone is having the same problems. It doesn't matter whether you're using IBM or Burroughs computers, programming code in COBOL, FORTRAN, or assembly language, or writing documentation in English, French, Japanese, or Norwegian. Things just aren't what they ought to be.

For the remainder of the 1980's and 1990's, this phenomenon will have both national and international economic consequences. In 1985, the information processing industry represented 8 percent of the GNP of the United States; by the early 1990's, it will represent 15 percent or more. Furthermore, software represents more than 50 percent of the cost of an information processing system. Thus, the *quality* of our information systems and the *productivity* of the people building those systems is now every bit as important as quality and productivity were in the steel industry in the 1960's and the automobile industry in the 1970's. Just as American dominance in many of the traditional "smokestack" industries came under heavy attack from Europe, Japan, Asia, and various Third World countries, so the American computer industry, both hardware and software, is coming under attack from those same countries today.

Because these problems are so prevalent, there has been a strong interest in structured techniques — that is, the collection of procedures and concepts that generally will double the productivity and effectiveness of a data processing department. The elements that make up this structured revolution include the following:

- **Structured analysis**. A collection of guidelines and graphical communication tools that allows the systems analyst to replace the classical functional specification with a new kind of specification that users actually can read and understand.

- **Top-down design and implementation**. The strategy of designing a system by breaking it into major functions, and then breaking those into smaller pieces, and so on, until implementation can be expressed in terms of program statements.

- **Structured design**. A set of guidelines and techniques to help the designer distinguish between "good" design and "bad" design at the modular level.

- **Structured programming**. An approach to programming that proposes that all program logic can be constructed from combinations of three basic forms and that reasonable programs can be written with little or no use of the GOTO statement.

Associated with these techniques are the following aids to implementation:

- **Chief programmer teams**. The concept of building a team of EDP specialists around a "super-programmer," who can code ten to twenty times faster than the average programmer.

- **Program librarians**. A programming secretary who relieves the programmer of the clerical aspects of programming and who also controls access to source programs, listings, and other documents.

- **Structured walkthroughs**. The use of peer group reviews in which an entire programming team walks through the code produced by one of its members.

Much discussion and controversy has arisen about each of these techniques, as we will see later in this book. Some of the methods are more controversial than others; some are more effective than others in certain situations. Indeed, some of the techniques may not work at all in your organization.

In general, though, the new techniques *do* work. They double the productivity of the average programmer, increase the reliability of his code by an order of magnitude, and decrease the difficulty of maintenance by a factor of two to ten. Finally, they substantially improve the chances that you will deliver a system that your customers will accept.

No one can promise that structured techniques will improve your sex life or decrease the incidence of cavities among your programmers and analysts, but what the techniques can do is impressive. Chances are that if you use the techniques, you'll be sipping your mint julep in your Mediterranean villa before long. If you don't use the techniques, well, chances are you'll be replaced by someone who does.

1.2 Management implications

At this point, a bit of cynicism may be expected. "Hrumph! My analysts, designers, and programmers have been doing these things for years. I don't see what the big fuss is all about."

The entire world has not been ignorant of the structured techniques for the past decade. Some managers have been implementing the methods for years in their departments, and some programmers have been writing structured code since the early 1960's. However, most data processing professionals have not been using the techniques, even if they thought they were.

These comments raise important questions. If the structured techniques are so wonderful, why weren't they universally adopted years ago? Why are they just now gaining strong support? These questions are particularly relevant because most of the structured development techniques have been discussed in the literature and among academic EDP professionals for more than a decade, but only have been introduced into commercial organizations during the past four or five years.

During the 1960's and 1970's, limitations in computer hardware technology and systems software made adopting the structured techniques difficult. Expensive, inefficient hardware, and restrictive programming languages and inadequate compiler limitations were common resistances offered by programmers and systems analysts. In the 1980's, a new technological constraint has become widespread: many programmers and systems analysts lack the automated tools (such as "programmer's workbench" or "analyst's workbench") that make it possible to develop and maintain the graphical models of structured analysis and design efficiently. This problem will have disappeared by the beginning of the 1990's so that just as no one complains about inefficient computer hardware or unsophisticated programming languages any more (except people burdened with maintaining old systems!), eventually no programmer or systems analyst will be without the automated tools needed to practice the structured techniques effectively.

While these technical concerns have been important, an even more fundamental reason exists for the long delay: management. The introduction of top-down implementation requires a change in the sequence in which programmers test their code (necessitating a revision to standards manuals), and a change in the manner in which the system is delivered to the customer. These changes often create a management problem. Furthermore, the introduction of chief programmer teams can be interpreted to mean (as we will discuss in a later chapter) that you should fire your analysts and your current staff of "average" programmers, replacing them all with a few carefully chosen super-programmers to whom you pay $100,000 per year, and I respectfully suggest that *that* action will lead to a few additional management problems. Finally, the introduction of structured analysis usually introduces management problems, for it introduces a whole new method of communication between the end-user and the systems analyst.

To what does all this point? I maintain that the structured techniques work with extremely impressive results; that the theory underlying the techniques has been known for a decade or more; that now hardware/software technology has improved to the point at which employing the techniques is practical in most organizations; and, most important, that many of the problems in implementing the techniques will be *management* problems.

1.3 Competing Religions

Unfortunately, many MIS organizations treat the structured techniques as a highly political, indeed, almost religious, issue. Hence, the question of whether the organization should endorse the structured techniques becomes almost as sensitive as the issue of whether one should endorse the Catholic religion or the Republican party.

The controversy has become more intense during the early and mid-1980's with the emergence of several new trends:

- the widespread use of personal computers.

- The emergence of powerful, user-friendly fourth-generation programming languages.

- The emergence of application prototyping packages that allow systems analysts and programmers to implement quickly a rough approximation of the user's requirements and operate it on a computer so the user can observe it.

- The growing recognition of data modeling or information modeling as an important discipline.

Advocates of these new trends often remark, rather loudly, in many cases, that the structured techniques are "the techniques of the 1970's" and that they should be replaced in favor of personal computers or prototyping or one of the other new trends. Indeed, some are even beginning to suggest that these "new" techniques are obsolete, and that they will soon be replaced by *fifth* generation computer systems containing artificial intelligence-based "expert systems."

My position on this "religious" argument is rather simple: there are some techniques that certainly will be replaced by new methods and technologies (for example, as the practice of building systems in assembly language was replaced by COBOL and FORTRAN), *but the major philosophical concepts used to build reliable, maintainable information systems, which is what the structured techniques are all about, can continue to embrace new technologies without destroying the concepts themselves.*

Thus, fourth generation programming languages are often a better alternative for coding than current third generation languages like COBOL or PL/I, but the major philosophical concerns for developing well-organized, well-documented maintainable code doesn't change. Application prototyping packages may provide an alternative to the top-down implementation technique discussed in Chapter 4; but it doesn't replace the concept of providing the user with a visible, tangible model of a working system as early as possible.

As we will see throughout this book, most of the "new" techniques of the 1980's, as well as those to be introduced in the 1990's, are consistent with the structured techniques that began to emerge in the mid-1970's and which continue to evolve. Fourth generation languages, prototyping packages, and personal computers are not competitors of the structured techniques; they are complementary techniques that help implement the structured techniques more and more effectively.

1.4 Objective

The objective of this book is to make it possible for you, as a data processing manager, to implement the structured techniques with a minimum of problems.

The first task will be to discuss how to *sell* the techniques to and within your organization. Usually, there will be some resistance, either from the management above you, the management below you, or from the analysts, designers, and programmers themselves. The nature of this resistance is predictable, and Chapter 2 presents some techniques for dealing with it.

Chapters 3 through 10 deal individually with the eight aspects of the structured revolution described in Section 1.1. The intent is to provide a sufficient technical overview of each technique with a suggested limited bibliography for further reading so that you won't be bamboozled by your staff or by your computer vendor. More important, though, specific management problems that have resulted from each technique are addressed and, wherever possible, specific solutions are recommended.

The next five chapters of the book discuss other practical management issues involved in implementing the structured techniques. Chapter 11 discusses the problem of deciding which specific technique should be introduced first in your organization. Chapter 12 presents the concept of a pilot project as a formal experiment in structured analysis, structured design, and structured programming. Chapter 13 deals with the problem of revising your programming standards in light of the new techniques. Chapter 14 explores the impact of the new classical budgeting/scheduling/control activities of project management. Chapter 15 examines the most practical subject of all: What can you expect to go wrong when you implement some or all of the structured techniques?

The last five chapters discuss the "competing religions" that were introduced in the early 1980's as possible replacements for the structured techniques, but which this book regards as complementary enhancements to the structured techniques. Chapter 16 addresses the phenomenon of personal computers in major organizations, particularly PC's in the user organization and under the user's direct control. In many such situations, the user is developing systems himself without guidance from the MIS organization or other programmers or systems analysts; how does this affect the use of structured techniques? Chapter 17 discusses the use of fourth generation languages, such as FOCUS, RAMIS, and ADR/IDEAL. Chapter 18 examines the use of application prototyping packages and their impact on the structured techniques. Chapter 19 discusses the role of information modeling, a concept that in the 1970's often was regarded as separate from and perhaps even opposed to the structured techniques. Finally, Chapter 20 addresses the future of structured techniques, that is the developments that we can expect for the remainder of the 1980's and into the 1990's.

Chapter Two:

How to Sell the Structured Techniques

2.1 Introduction

It is convenient for me to assume that you already have been convinced of the virtues of structured analysis, top-down design, and structured design and that your only problem is to convince the rest of your organization that the techniques are something more than a plot by the computer vendor to sell more memory or disk packs.

These assumptions may be unnecessarily pessimistic. Both you and the other members of your organization already may have been sold on the new techniques. If so, skip the rest of this chapter and begin reading in Chapter 3 about the specific management problems associated with structured analysis.

On the other hand, these assumptions may be slightly optimistic. Perhaps you are unconvinced, and the rest of your staff has not even heard of the structured techniques. If so, the balance of this chapter serves a double purpose: While giving you suggestions about how to sell your organization on the advantages of the methods, it should be possible for *me* to sell *you.*

The remainder of this chapter addresses the various concerns of this selling stage. We first must ask whether your MIS organization, as well as the kind of projects it undertakes, is the right environment for the structured techniques, a topic of heated discussion during the mid-1980's. Then we can ask whether it is necessary to sell structured development techniques through the art of gentle persuasion. Are there other approaches that would work as well? If we assume that friendly persuasion is the best approach, it then becomes important to ascertain who in your organization needs to be sold: top management, middle management, first-level project leaders, or the people who actually write the programs? Finally, let's examine the selling approach itself. How do we convince someone that the structured techniques — or anything that does what they purport to do — are desperately needed in today's data processing environment? The following pages provide some answers.

2.2 The environment for structured techniques

No company is entirely like another, nor are any two MIS organizations exactly alike. Nor are the end-users in one company the same as the end-users in another, nor are the MIS systems they want built the same as the MIS systems that are necessary in other organizations. While the structured techniques discussed in this book can be used in almost any company, they make far more sense in some companies than in others.

In general, the structured techniques will be most successful in the following kind of environment:

- *An MIS organization that does a significant amount of applications development work.* Some organizations spend 97 percent of their MIS budget maintaining systems that were developed ten years ago. While some of the documentation techniques in Chapter 7 and the walkthrough technique in Chapter 10 may be useful, such topics as structured analysis and structured design will not evoke much enthusism in the MIS organization. Also, if the MIS organization spends most of its time installing packaged software — which makes sense in some new companies where user policies can be developed from the beginning to be compatible with the quirks of a particular commercial application package — then many topics in this book may not seem crucial (although one could argue strongly that structured analysis is appropriate to define user requirements in order to determine which commercial package should be obtained, and that the data modeling concepts discussed in Chapter 19 are also important).

- *Systems being developed are large, complex, and vital to the success of the organization.* If the MIS organization is in the fortunate position of writing primarily tiny systems, then many topics in this book may not seem very important. For example, an organization may have developed a comprehensive data model for the enterprise and installed a fourth generation language for fast implementation of user-requested reports and *ad hoc* inquiries into a database. This scenario means that (a) the data modeling techniques discussed in Chapter 19 (which are also a part of the structured analysis techniques discussed in Chapter 3) must have been employed; and (b) the organization already must have successfully implemented the standard transaction processing systems — such as payroll, inventory, general ledger, and order entry — that will continue to feed the organization's database and keep it up to date.

- *An organization that is accustomed to organizing its large, complex projects with a project life cycle that breaks the project into recognizable phases or activities.* In a few organizations, projects still are done on an *ad hoc* basis, with communication between users, MIS projects managers, programmers, and systems analysts occurring on an informal, verbal basis. For example, this informality may exist in some research organizations and in some personal computer companies where the software is developed by "wunderkind" programmers. In such organizations, anarchy prevails; the structured techniques are the antithesis of anarchy and thus would not be welcomed. The easiest way to determine whether or not the organization is ready for structured analysis and structured design is simply to ask whether there is an official project life cycle.*

- *Management, end-users, and the MIS organization all are concerned about issues of productivity of MIS personnel and the quality of the systems they produce.* If nobody cares, then the structured techniques will almost certainly not be imple-

---

* — Brian Dickinson's *Developing Structured Systems* (YOURDON Press, 1981) and Ed Yourdon's *Managing the Systems Life Cycle* (YOURDON Press, 2nd edition, 1985) offer two views of a typical project life cycle in an MIS organization using structured techniques.

mented successfully. The same is true if only the technicians — the programmers and systems analysts — in the
MIS organization are concerned. If the MIS organization is
concerned, but end-users and top management isn't, then it
will be difficult to achieve the commitment and support to
implement the structured techniques successfully. The rest
of this chapter is concerned with the techniques for obtain-
ing that support.

2.3 Introducing the structured techniques within your organization

Not too long ago, a major insurance company in New York City
was introduced to structured analysis and the related techniques by its
computer vendor. Assorted levels of EDP management were assembled for a one-hour sales pitch, to which they all listened quietly and
politely. At the end of the presentation, after the vendor's representa-
tive had been thanked for his efforts and excused from the meeting,
the managers talked things over. After a lively exchange of views, one
manager summarized the feelings of a majority of people in the room:
"It seems to me that the problem is to find out how we can *avoid* using
these new techniques. If we can manage to stall for a year or two, all
of this surely will disappear — just like decision tables."

This reaction is one way of dealing with the structured revolution:
pretending that it doesn't exist. You can sympathize with the management of this organization. They were worried about the new standards
manual they would have to write, the training that would be necessary,
and all of the other organizational changes that certainly would accom-
pany the new techniques.

While you and your organization probably won't adopt this head-
in-the-sand attitude, you might adopt other equally extreme approaches
to the introduction of the structured techniques. Some of the more
common approaches include an edict from the boss, the "sheep-dip"
approach, and sending out a scout.

The first of these approaches typically is the least successful. The
edict often is passed down from the top data processing manager (who
usually is totally unfamiliar with data flow diagrams, nested IF statements in COBOL, highly cohesive modules, and the other technical issues of structured systems development), and it frequently is expressed
in such hard-line terms as "Troops! Thou shalt not GOTO! Thy
modules shall be highly cohesive! Thou shalt draw many bubbles and
make many data flow diagrams!" One such edict in a large military or-

ganization caused a great deal of scurrying around in the lower levels of the organization, for no one had any idea what the new techniques were all about.

Of course, some degree of management persuasion, perhaps in the form of an edict, may be necessary to shake the troops out of their rut. But if the programmers' first introduction to structured programming is a dictatorial memo from a high-level manager whom they never have seen and who they suspect never has written a line of code on anything more modern than an IBM 1401, their reaction will be predictable: resistant and subversive in one form or another.

Next, there is the manager who believes in the "enlightened" approach to the new techniques, which usually takes the form of mass training, or what Gerald Weinberg* likes to call the sheep-dip approach.

My consulting firm frequently receives phone calls from data processing managers who say, for example, "I'd like to put every one of my three hundred programmers, designers, and analysts in a class for a day, and have you teach them everything there is to know about structured programming, structured design, top-down implementation, structured analysis, and all of those other things. Then, as soon as they get back, we can cut their schedules in half — after all, they'll be at least twice as productive as they were!"

We usually find that some progress is made by this approach, but not much. The confusion, the misunderstandings caused by superficial exposure to new concepts, and the unrealistic management expectations sometimes exceed the positive benefits of using the new techniques.

Then there is the approach of sending a scout to evaluate the new techniques. Whether or not management formally recognizes the phenomenon, there is usually one person or group of people who is the first to become aware of new hardware/software technologies. The scout(s) in your organization probably began reading about structured programming in the literature in 1972 to 1973, or possibly as early as 1968. He or she first heard about structured design in 1974 to 1975, and probably explored the ideas of structured analysis in 1976 to 1977. Now that scout probably is trying to introduce the techniques to members of your staff who never read any literature, never attend any conferences, and never are exposed to any new ideas.

---

*Weinberg, whose work you should know, is author of *The Psychology of Computer Programming* (New York: Van Nostrand Reinhold, 1971), which laid the groundwork for the structured walkthrough concept discussed in Chapter 10.

The trouble is, as is true in many other fields, nobody wants to listen to the scout. Everyone else is too busy. As one manager put it, "We're too involved in patching the old programs to listen to any ideas about how to develop the new programs." In addition, nobody really trusts the scout: In the past, he's brought back a few ideas that didn't work. Personality problems may further complicate matters: The scout may be too inarticulate or too arrogant to communicate his ideas effectively.

You may argue that these examples are exaggerated and that they wouldn't occur in *real* organizations. Or, you may argue that the problems outlined above are the result of incompetent management and that you never would make such silly mistakes. Perhaps so, but we should remember that what begins as a good, common-sense idea in the mind of a manager sometimes is translated into something quite ridiculous when it is communicated to the rest of the staff. The examples discussed earlier did occur in organizations that generally conducted their data processing in a levelheaded way, but that began doing rather silly things with the new techniques.

In summary, it is important to recognize that first, the brute force approach is risky; second, there is some resistance to new techniques in any MIS organization, so it probably will be necessary to sell the new techniques to a rather dubious audience; and third, the new techniques will be most effective if they are introduced slowly, gently, and with a healthy dose of diplomacy.

2.4 Who needs to be sold?

Before we can address effective methods of selling the structured development techniques, we have to identify our audience. Whom are we trying to convince that structured analysis is the greatest invention since peanut butter? Although every organization is different, we usually can identify several categories of people, each of which must be sold in a slightly different manner:

1. Top management
    a. Corporate management not involved in MIS
    b. Top MIS management, usually without a programming background, such as from accounting department

2. Middle management
   a. First-level managers, or team leaders
   b. Second-level managers, third-level managers, and so forth

3. Technicians
   a. Veterans, six or more years' experience
   b. Junior programmers, one to five years' experience
   c. Trainees, just out of school
   d. Maintenance programmers

2.4.1 Selling top management

My experience is that top management is relatively easy to sell. Two points should be considered:

1. Top MIS management often knows nothing about the technical details of programming, design, and systems analysis. They couldn't tell you, for example, whether or not the GOTO statement should be removed from COBOL. Consequently, they're not likely to argue with any suggestion.

2. Top MIS management usually is interested in the overall economics of data processing in their organization. If they're told that structured analysis and the related techniques will double the productivity of their people, they'll be sold. However, an interesting point illustrates how top management is likely to perceive the value of everything the MIS organization does: as of 1985, an organization is not allowed to show its corporate data, such as the customer database, as an asset on the balance sheet. A manager who is concerned only with the bottom line is likely to conclude that data has no value, and thus MIS systems that produce data must also have no value.

Fortunately, the economic importance of high-quality MIS systems and highly productive MIS personnel is attracting the attention of top managers of American companies. However, top management in most organizations will not commit the entire data processing staff to a new technique without the concurrence of their middle-level managers.

Hence, the question of who needs to be sold involves what middle management thinks of the new techniques. Must they be sold?

2.4.2 Selling middle management

Surprisingly, middle management frequently has resisted the new techniques. When the Vice President of Data Processing asks the Manager of Systems for his opinion of structured programming, he's likely to get one or any combination of the following reactions:

- "We've been doing that for years. All of these new structured techniques are really just the same as modular programming.

- "It'll never work. We tried these ideas a couple of years ago, and they didn't work then, so they won't work now."

- "Are you suggesting that I've been doing my job wrong for the past ten years? I resent that. Our current methods work just fine."

These objections are similar to those made by the people who design, code, and test programs. There's a reason for the similarity: Many middle-level MIS managers rose from the ranks of programming and systems analysis and thus react to new technological concepts as if they were still technicians.

This reaction is particularly true of the "We've been doing it for years" reaction from the middle-level manager. Indeed, maybe he and his staff have been using structured analysis, structured design, structured programming, and the related techniques for the past ten years without telling anyone, but it's unlikely from what I have seen in the average American and European data processing organization. It's possible that the manager sincerely thinks his staff is using structured techniques.* The organization's standards manuals may even dictate some-

---

*The Peter Principle also may be involved. Years ago when the manager was programming, he may have been a *super* technician and used structured programming. Because he was a good technician, he was promoted until he reached his level of incompetence. The mediocre programmers who had reached their levels of incompetence were left to design and code unstructured, unreliable, unmaintainable programs.

thing resembling structured programming and structured design. But that doesn't mean anyone actually is doing it.

Let's imagine a somewhat more optimistic scenario: Once upon a time, when the manager was a technician, he designed and coded good programs. Now that he's a manager, he has tried to pass on his experiences and ideas to his staff, a staff composed of intelligent programmers, designers, and systems analysts who are trying to do a good job. Everyone thinks that he is designing good, modular programs that are easy to debug, maintain, expand, and modify.

Unfortunately, each programmer/analyst has a slightly different interpretation of the design/coding philosophies espoused by the manager; after all, phrases in the standards manual such as "All programs should be designed in terms of functionally independent modules with a single entry and a single exit" leave a lot to the programmer's imagination. The result has been a non-uniform, informal, sloppy implementation of the basic philosophies that the manager had practiced diligently ten years earlier, particularly if the organization is not using the walkthrough techniques discussed in Chapter 10. Consequently, the programs written by today's staff are not so easy to maintain and not so easy to expand and modify.

This consideration brings us to the third middle-manager reaction, the one characterized by "Whaddya mean with this structured stuff? Our old way of doing things is just fine!" Generally, it would be more accurate for the manager to say that he hasn't had any obvious disasters in his department, that things are relatively stable, and, therefore, that the old way of doing things must be satisfactory. Later in this chapter, we'll discuss statistics taken from the data processing industry that will indicate the old way is *not* satisfactory.

I don't suggest that middle-level managers are ignorant or that they should be ignored when they react negatively to the new techniques. They've survived vendor hardware that was too small and too inefficient to permit many of the structured philosophies to be implemented practically; they've survived several generations of vendor software that didn't meet expectations or that didn't work at all, and they've survived a couple of decades in which the major problem was not the complexity of the application but the reliability of the hardware and software.

However, today things are different. Technology is radically different from that of ten years ago, so we can afford to do things differently. Users' applications are more complex, so it's no longer sufficient to lock one brilliant programmer in a room for six months and expect him to develop a perfect system.* Also, our problems are different. Reliability is more important, maintenance costs are a greater consideration, hardware costs generally are lower, and programmers and systems analysts are more expensive.

Whether or not these comments are sufficient to convince the middle-level manager to abandon his current approach and begin using the new techniques, usually middle management does have to be sold.

2.4.3 Selling the technicians

Finally, there is the question of selling the people who actually create the programs: senior programmers, designers, systems analysts; junior programmers; trainees; maintenance programmers. A few brief comments are in order:

1. The senior programmers, designers, and systems analysts often display much the same reaction to the structured techniques as do the middle-level managers. Although many of their specific objections and complaints are discussed in later chapters, let us note here that they seem to fall into general categories: "It'll never work," or "My old way of doing things is just fine," or "I've been writing structured programs for years and years."

2. Junior technicians tend to be less negative. Although converting them from their training may not be easy, they usually do not have strong opinions about the technical aspects of the new techniques, and they usually have fewer bad habits to break.

3. Trainees don't have to be sold. By definition, they know nothing about programming and systems analysis, and they are perfectly happy to learn good techniques or bad techniques. Indeed, leading American, Canadian, and European universities now introduce structured programming and structured design in first-year programming courses, and the students have no problems.

---

* It may be possible if the programmer has a fourth generation language; but then there is a different set of problems. See Chapter 17 for more details.

4. Maintenance programmers do not need to be convinced that the current method of designing and writing programs is unsatisfactory. They are the ones who have to debug and patch the mess.

Occasionally, subtle political problems make the selling job more difficult. For example, trainee programmers can be taught how to design and code programs using all the new techniques; but what do they do if their first project requires them to work with or under senior programmers who persist in using the old unstructured techniques?

What about the maintenance programmer who agrees that current programming techniques are unsatisfactory, and who would like to use as an example the program he is maintaining, except that the program was designed and coded years ago by a person who is now his manager? Obviously, it's impolitic to suggest that a system that is the full-time occupation of a whole department, a system that built the manager's career and reputation, is a bad system.

Or, a maintenance programmer agrees that classical programming techniques are terrible, but his first structured program turns out to be even more difficult to maintain than the old programs. We discuss this problem further in Chapter 6 when we look at structured programming: A program that *appears* to be structured may not actually *be* structured and, in fact, may be worse than a classical program.

2.4.4 Some final comments on selling the organization

Throughout this section, I've suggested that top management may have a different reaction to the new techniques than middle management, and that programmers and systems analysts may respond differently depending on whether they are trainees or veterans.

Accordingly, I recommend that the organization be sold on the structured techniques from the top down. I've seen organizations in which structured programming was introduced at the grass-roots level, only to be stymied by suspicious middle-level managers and ignored by top-level management. Management commitment is essential *before* any significant effort should be made to sell the approach to the technicians themselves.

There are exceptions, as for example, when top management immediately turns to middle managers for a technical opinion. In this case, initial selling of the structured techniques may have to begin with middle managers. They can convince top management of the favorable economic aspects, as well as persuade the programmers of the strong technical arguments in favor of the techniques.

2.5 How to sell the new techniques

Having discussed other aspects of the selling of structured development techniques, we still are left with one fundamental question: How do we convince a dubious audience (whether programmers, designers, systems analysts, or managers — that the new techniques are worth exploring?

The most effective approach is the double-whammy. First, convince your audience that the current techniques leave much to be desired. Second, convince them that the new techniques are demonstrably better than any of the methods currently in use.

To do this properly, you need ammunition: some statistics, case studies, and documented evidence that the current techniques generally are bad and that the new techniques generally are good. The remainder of this chapter provides you with useful statistics, beginning with those figures describing the current EDP industry.

2.5.1 The average application programmer is not very productive

On the average, an application programmer can produce ten to fifteen debugged program statements per day; for systems programs, particularly large operating systems, the number drops to as few as two or three debugged statements per day. Given the salary of today's programmers, that means that every statement in a new system costs somewhere between five and fifty dollars.

This figure of average programmer productivity is documented in *The Mythical Man-Month*, by Fred Brooks.* What makes the figure so interesting is that it seems to be invariant over a long period. IBM first observed the productivity statistics on projects in the late 1950's. They were confirmed over and over again in major projects throughout the 1960's and 1970's, and they continue to be valid today.

The productivity figures seem to be both machine independent and language independent. That is, the available statistics strongly suggest that the average application programmer can generate ten to fifteen debugged statements per day regardless of whether he programs on an

---

*Frederick P. Brooks, Jr., *The Mythical Man-Month* (Reading: Addison-Wesley, 1975).

IBM, a Honeywell, a Burroughs, or any other computer. Similarly, it appears that the programmer will write approximately ten statements per day regardless of whether he programs in COBOL, FORTRAN, PL/I, assembler, or any of the other major languages.[†]

Controversy arises with the definition of programmer productivity, particularly when it is expressed in terms of debugged statements per day. Some of the commotion is made by programmers, who always remember that wonderful day when they wrote six hundred lines of code. What they usually forget, and what the figure of ten to fifteen statements per day is drawn from, is the tremendous amount of time required to design, debug, and possibly even document the code.

Most of the controversy surrounding the measurement of productivity, though, is of a somewhat more philosophical nature and can be summarized as follows:

- *The Hawthorne Effect may become significant when measuring programmer productivity.* Proponents of this philosophy fear that if a programmer knows that he will be judged by the number of lines of code he writes, then he automatically will write more lines of code, but they be trivial lines of code. That which could have been programmed with a simple loop is transformed into a thousand in-line instructions. Thus far, my experience has been that programmers do not react in this fashion because they know that their salary will not increase proportionally to the number of lines of code that they write.

- *There can be extreme variations in productivity, from project to project, from programmer to programmer (as discussed in the next section), and from day to day.* Most of

---

[†]Since one can *accomplish* much more with ten COBOL statements than with ten assembly language statements, a programmer is much more productive when he programs in COBOL (or any other high-level language). However, writing ten assembly language statements represents approximately the same level of intellectual complexity as writing ten COBOL statements. The same argument is now used in the mid-1980's to promote the use of fourth generation programming languages; this is discussed in more detail in Chapter 17.

the published statistics on productivity have been taken from relatively large projects with several programmers; thus, the overall productivity figures represent a smoothing effect that might not be seen on a one-person project involving two hundred lines of code.

- *People measure productivity differently.* Does one include only the coding and unit-test activities, or should one also include the time spent designing, documenting, and system-testing? In calculating productivity for a project, does one count only the programmers, or should one include analysts, managers, and clerical staff? The lack of agreement in this area means that productivity reported by Company A may appear radically different from that reported by Company B. Obviously, consistency within an organization is important.

The rest of this book could be devoted to a discussion of the subtleties of measuring productivity, but I would prefer to leave that to others.* It is sufficient to observe that productivity, no matter how crudely measured, is not very high, and programmer productivity can be substantially improved with the use of the structured techniques.

2.5.2 There is a substantial variation in programmer abilities

Things would be bad enough if all programmers wrote ten debugged COBOL statements every day. What is more disturbing is that ten statements is an average, and the variation between high productivity and low productivity is staggering.

This point was first made in a paper by Professor Harold Sackman, et al., in 1968.† Sackman reported about a study in which he found that some programmers could design, code, and test a program twenty-five times more quickly than others. Similarly, he found that some programmers produce code that is nearly ten times more efficient than the code produced by others.

---

* — See, for example, Tom DeMarco's *Controlling Software Projects* (YOURDON Press, 1982), or Barry Boehm's *Software Engineering Economics,* (Prentice-Hall, 1982).

†H. Sackman, W.J. Erickson, and E.E. Grant, "Exploratory Experimental Studies Comparing Online and Offline Programming Performance," *Communications of the ACM,* Vol. 11, No. 1 (January 1968), pp. 3-11.

What makes Sackman's experiment so interesting is his observation that there was no significant correlation between programming performance and years of experience, and no correlation between programming performance and scores on programming aptitude tests.* This is no surprise to many programming managers, who know that a programmer with ten years of experience may have had one year of real experience, repeated nine times.

As with the statistics concerning programmer productivity in the preceding section, there is much dispute about the Sackman statistics. It may be argued, for example, that Sackman studied only a small sample of programmers (approximately one dozen people), and that universal conclusions about the entire programming industry cannot be drawn from the sample. One also might argue that the programmer who takes a long time to design and code a program may require substantially less time to test it; similarly, one could expect that a programmer whose program occupies a large chunk of memory would have written it in such a way as to require less CPU time and vice versa.

Although these comments are valid, there still is the strong impression that some programmers may be substantially better than their colleagues. An equally distinct impression is that a high IQ and ten years of experience may not be sufficient qualifications to make a really good programmer.

If this is the case, what should we do? Should we identify those programmers who are an order of magnitude better than their colleagues, and then fire everyone else? The Sackman statistics provide a slightly more civilized solution: the chief programmer team concept discussed in Chapter 8.

Others propose that we examine what makes the "good" programmers so good, and then teach those skills to the average programmer. Indeed, this approach provides much of the motivation for structured programming and structured design. Some programmers are successful largely because of their *instinctive* ability to break a large system into small independent modules, and then code those modules with well-organized (that is, well-structured) statements.† The technologies

---

*Actually, this comment is true only of the *experienced* programmers. Sackman found that, for trainee programmers, there *was* a correlation between programming performance and scores on aptitude tests.

† This has also been observed with young children who, in many schools, are now learning to program in a language like LOGO. Some children instinctively follow a top-down problem-solving approach, while others develop monolithic programs. It should be noted

of structured programming and structured design might be regarded as an attempt to capture in words what a few of these programmers have been doing by instinct for years.

In the meantime, you as a manager should recognize that you have a potential problem. If you have a staff of ten or twenty programmers, and if there is an order-of-magnitude difference in their abilities, then *your* ability to schedule, manage, and budget projects is seriously impaired. This difficulty is compounded by the probability that you don't know precisely how good or bad your programmers are in the areas of designing, coding, testing, and writing efficient programs.

Sackman was able to do something most programming organizations *never* do: he had a dozen programmers working on the same programming problem. In the real world, Charlie works on program A, while Susy works on program B, and since program A and program B are intrinsically different, it is difficult to determine whether Charlie codes faster than Susy, and whether Charlie's code is more efficient than Susy's code.

Sackman's experiments thus confirm what we could only guess at before: There are substantial variations in programmer abilities. This knowledge should give us motivation to try some of the new structured technologies to be discussed in subsequent chapters of the book.

2.5.3 The average programmer spends very little time programming

One reason for the low productivity of programmers is that we don't give them enough of an opportunity to program. In a typical organization, a programmer spends a significant portion of his time attending meetings, filling out reports, walking downstairs to the computer room to pick up his output, walking across the hall to discuss some esoteric programming issue with another programmer, and so on.

A study published by George Weinwurm* indicates that the average programmer spends only 27 percent of his day doing something that could be interpreted as programming — writing instructions on a coding sheet, looking at a listing, debugging. The remainder of the

---

noted that children of seven and eight can be easily taught the concept of top-down design, and that with a language like LOGO, they easily learn the concept of procedures (subroutines), the notion of passing arguments (parameters) to procedures, and even the concept of recursion.

*George F. Weinwurm, ed., *On the Management of Computer Programming* (Philadelphia:

programmer's working day is spent performing basically clerical duties or duties that have nothing to do with programming.

To see whether this statistic is relevant in your organization, you might spend a few hours *watching* your programmers as they carry out their normal duties. Then ask yourself: How many of their activities really require a bachelor's degree in computer science, six months of on-the-job training, and a $20,000 annual salary? How much of the programmer's activities could be done by an intelligent clerk?

As you might have anticipated, Weinwurm's study provides some motivation to apply the program librarian concept, discussed in Chapter 9 and for automating much of the clerical work done by programmers and systems analysts, which we will discuss at various points in the subsequent chapters.

2.5.4 Testing typically occupies 50 percent of a programming project

One-third of the time, energy, and money expended in a programming project is for design; roughly one-sixth is spent on coding; and the remaining half is spent trying to make the thing work!* Indeed, it has been known for so long that testing consumes half the time allotted to a project that everyone seems to accept it as a law of nature. That it is *not* a law of nature has become painfully apparent in some recent programming projects in which the code virtually worked correctly the first time it was run.

In other words, we spend so much time on testing primarily because the programmers make so many unnecessary mistakes. With the use of structured analysis, structured design, structured programming, and structured walkthroughs, we can cut the number of unnecessary bugs almost to zero. Thus, if you're spending 50 percent of your resources in a programming project on testing, you're probably wasting a substantial amount of money.

In addition, the way we conduct testing causes trouble. The current approach in most organizations roughly is as follows: First, test all the modules in a stand-alone fashion; then, combine modules into programs, and carry out program testing; next, combine the programs into subsystems and conduct subsystem testing; finally, combine the

---

Auerbach Publishers, 1970).
*An excellent source for such statistics is Philip Metzger's *Programming Project Management* (Englewood Cliffs: Prentice-Hall, 1975).

subsystems into a system, and do system testing. Largely as a result of this approach to testing, many projects encounter the following problems:

- There is little tangible evidence of progress during the testing phase. It is largely during this period of time that programmers remark that they are 98 percent finished or that there is only one more bug to find.

- The worst bugs — interface bugs — most often are found at the end of the testing phase, while trivial bugs, for example, local logic errors within a module, are found at the beginning. If they had their choice, most programmers would like to reverse the sequence, finding the major bugs first and cleaning up the trivial bugs last.

- Deadlines frequently are missed, and since the classical approach to testing usually means that nothing works until it *all* works, the project can become politically vulnerable. When the deadline arrives, the user is not impressed with fifty thousand lines of code that have passed the module test phase, but that don't do anything as a system.

- The user discovers that he doesn't like the system, the fault of the current approach to testing, since the user doesn't see anything until he sees the entire system in operation.

We deal with each of these problems in Chapter 4 in the sections on top-down implementation. At this point, it is sufficient to recognize that the current method of doing things is fraught with problems.

2.5.5 Bugs last forever in large systems

One of the most interesting statistics of recent years came from an employee of IBM, who remarked at a software engineering conference that every release of IBM's OS/360 operating system had a thousand bugs.*

---

*See the republished proceedings of the NATO conference in *Software Engineering, Concepts and Techniques,* J.M. Buxton, P. Naur, and B. Randell, eds. (New York: Petrocelli/Charter, 1976).

Obviously, IBM is not unique in this area, nor is this a phenomenon restricted to operating systems. Large programs or systems have a number of residual bugs that never will be eliminated completely. Indeed, there is increasing evidence to suggest that large programs — whether payroll programs, order-entry programs, compilers, operating systems, or air defense systems — behave in the manner shown in the following graph.

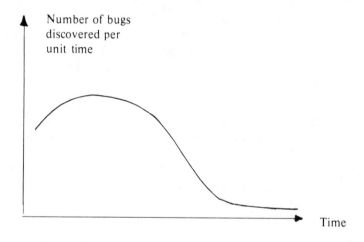

During the first few months of a system's use, more and more bugs will be discovered. There are various reasons for this: The users become increasingly experienced with the system and thus push it harder. The volume of processing builds up, exposing bugs that were in the code all the time, but which did not come to light during the early use of the system.

At some point, the bug-discovery curve turns downward (otherwise, the system will be discarded by the users). Each month, the users find fewer and fewer bugs. Eventually, though, the curve levels off and then remains relatively constant over a long period. In the case of IBM's operating system, the curve apparently leveled off at a thousand bugs per release. For a medium-sized payroll system, we might measure this as one bug (requiring a rerun of the system) every third payroll run. However we measure it, one fact remains clear: *The system may never be bug-free.*

In fact, if we wait long enough, the curve probably will turn up again; that is, there gradually will be more bugs discovered per unit time. This usually occurs with old systems, which have been so heavily patched and modified that nobody understands them. In such a situation, every time the programmer fixes one old bug, he introduces two new ones into the system.

Another way to assess the reliability of a system is by considering the total number of bugs discovered during its lifetime. Currently, classical methods of developing computer programs turn up an average of three to five bugs per one hundred statements, bugs that appear *after* the program has been tested and put into production. Thus, if we develop a payroll system with ten thousand COBOL statements, we should expect to find between one hundred and five hundred bugs in production during the five-to-eight-year expected lifetime of the system. Obviously, the majority of those bugs will be found during the first few months of production, but they will continue to appear even after five years of use.

Again, all I am suggesting at this point is that the unreliability of our present systems is a problem. This is particularly true when typical American code is compared with, say, typical Japanese code, where there are typically three to five bugs per *ten thousand* lines of code. In later chapters, we'll see how we can improve the reliability of our computer systems.

2.5.6 *Bugs are more critical in today's computer systems*

As we pointed out in the preceding section, most current computer systems have a substantial number of bugs, a phenomenon that has been with us ever since the first programmer wrote the first program. The problem is not that programmers today are less knowledgeable or sloppier than that first programmer, but that the methods now used are outdated.

In addition, the bugs matter more today than they did in the early days of programming. We are beginning to appreciate that it is expensive to put bugs into a program and then go through the laborious process of finding and removing them. We are realizing that it is considerably cheaper to avoid bugs in the first place.

A more serious reason for being concerned about bugs is that our customers, our companies, and the rest of society are becoming less tolerant of buggy programs. Twenty years ago, a computer bug often was the source of an amusing newspaper article, as for example, when a billing program produced an invoice for $ 0.00, or, even worse, *minus*

$ 0.00, and sent nasty dunning letters to the customer who refused to pay. True, such events were considered an irritation and a public relations problem, but a small price to pay for the marvels of the electronic computer.

Today, however, we are faced with a somewhat different situation. Consider the consequences of a bug in a payroll system for 100,000 people. I saw one wildcat strike that was triggered by a payroll system's failure to pay correct overtime wages. Or, imagine the effects of a bug that shuts down a nationwide on-line order-entry system, or an airline's reservation system.

At an even more serious level are the potential repercussions of a bug in any of the computerized telephone switching systems being installed worldwide: A software bug could leave an entire city without telephone service until a programmer could figure out how to eliminate the problem. Even more disastrous would be a failure in a computerized air traffic control system: A software bug could lead to mid-air collisions, with substantial loss of property and life.

Or, consider the results of a malfunction in an air defense system, or in any of the sophisticated military command-and-control systems under development today.*

The moral is simple and clear: We can't afford bugs — *any* bugs — in the systems being designed. Nor can we afford to continue to introduce bugs into our current systems.

2.5.7 *Programmers are not very good at fixing bugs*

To further complicate matters, once bugs are discovered, programmers are not very good at fixing them. A study by Barry Boehm† indicates that, at best, a programmer has approximately a 50 percent chance of successfully eliminating a bug on his first attempt if he modifies only five to ten lines of code. If he changes more lines of code, his chances of success drop. If, for example, the bug requires fifty lines of code to be changed, the programmer's chance of success drops to approximately 20 percent.

---

* — For a rather alarming list of errors in such "critical" systems, see "Some Computer-Related Disasters and Other Egregious Horrors," by Peter G. Neumann in the January 1985 issue of *ACM SIGSOFT Software Engineering Notes,* (Volume 10, Number 1).
†B.W. Boehm, "Software and Its Impact: A Quantitative Study," *Datamation,* Vol. 19, No. 5 (May 1973), pp. 48 - 59.

Interestingly, if the programmer modifies fewer than five to ten lines of code in his attempt to correct the bug, his chances of success also drop, though only slightly. Although this might seem surprising at first, it probably can be explained by human psychology. One tends to be overconfident when changing a single line of code to correct a trivial bug. If the bug is serious enough to require several lines of code to be changed, one tends to be more careful.

Obviously, some of the problems associated with correcting bugs are human problems: keypunching errors, coding mistakes, psychological errors, and so forth. However, many problems are of a different sort: We may successfully fix a bug in subroutine X, only to find later that the supposed fix has introduced a new bug in subroutine Y. This phenomenon is becoming more troublesome, particularly in regard to larger systems having many modules with which the programmer is unfamiliar. It is even more impossible for him to be aware of the subtle interactions between the modules.

Largely because of this problem, interest has grown in the techniques of structured design, which attempt to minimize the interdependencies between modules. We will discuss this at length in Chapter 5.

2.5.8 Maintenance is becoming too expensive

A survey in the October 1972 issue of *EDP Analyzer** indicated perhaps for the first time that most EDP organizations were spending about 50 percent of their budgets on maintenance. More recently, a book entitled *Software Maintenance Management,* by B. P. Lientz and E. B. Swanson (Reading: Addison-Wesley, 1980), confirmed these figures. Indeed, many large organizations spend 75 percent or even perhaps as much as 80 percent of their data processing budgets on maintaining existing systems.

Nobody is suggesting that maintenance could be eliminated altogether, but 80 percent, or 75 percent, or even 50 percent is too much to be spending on existing programs. Consider how we currently are spending our maintenance money:

- ongoing debugging

---

*Richard G. Canning, ed., "That Maintenance 'Iceberg,'" *EDP Analyzer,* Vol. 10, No. 10 (October 1972).

- changes required by new hardware, new versions of vendor operating systems, new compilers, and so on
- expansions, changes, and new features requested by users

The first two points are possible to control. As suggested earlier, *any* money spent on debugging is too much; Lientz and Swanson report that the typical organization spends approximately 12 percent of its maintenance budget on "emergency" debugging and another 9 percent on "routine" debugging. We should be able to code programs with virtually no bugs. Similarly, we should be able to write programs that can run essentially unchanged whenever the vendor upgrades his operating system or compiler. The fact that we spend a great deal of money in these two areas suggests there is a problem.

The third category in our maintenance list — new features for the user — never can be eliminated; indeed, Lientz and Swanson report that the average organization spends 41 percent of its maintenance budget on such enhancements. However, the cost for these changes could be minimized if our computer systems were easier to change. A rule of thumb to follow is that if a modification or a new feature to a system can be explained easily by a user, then it *should* be easy to introduce into the computer system. If it is not easy, then the system probably was designed inadequately.

2.6 Statistics supporting use of the structured techniques

Thus far, we have understood that the current approach to program design and coding is not as successful as we would like. It is fair to offer criticism only if we can suggest something better, raising the obvious question: Why should we believe that things will improve with the use of structured programming, structured design, structured analysis, and the other techniques?

Some people argue that using the techniques is simply a matter of common sense, for example: "It makes *sense* to use structured programming because of increased productivity, fewer bugs, and easier maintenance, among other reasons." Indeed, we already have used such arguments in this chapter, and we will repeat them in subsequent chapters.

Unfortunately, common sense and rational arguments are not always sufficient to convince data processing managers. Perhaps that's because DP managers already have been promised too many miracles in the form of fourth generation languages, virtual memory, relational database systems, distributed systems, and goodness knows what else. Or, perhaps it's because the common-sense sales pitch makes structured analysis sound like just another brand of toothpaste or dog food, and we all have grown a little cynical and skeptical about *that* kind of selling.

From my experience, the most convincing arguments have been based on real experiences, or case studies in which people actually have used structured programming, chief programmer teams, librarians, walkthroughs, or some other aspect of the structured techniques, with documented results. Fortunately, the number of such case studies is growing: At least one more is described at each computer conference, and virtually every issue of *Datamation, Infosystems, Computer Decisions,* or *Computerworld* contains some kind of we-tried-it-and-it-worked testimonial. These and other popular computer journals are a good source from which to build your own file of testimonials to convince skeptical members of your data processing department.

The only problem with using case studies is that they all measure their results differently, thus making comparisons and generalizations difficult. As we pointed out in our earlier discussion of productivity, some organizations include system testing and documentation in their productivity measures, while others do not; some organizations include analysts, managers, and clerical staff in their measurements, while others count only the programmers.

One early set of statistics provided data on fifty-one different programming projects carried out by IBM's Federal Systems Division; all of the projects used one or more of the structured techniques discussed in this book. The results of the survey were published in the January 1977 issue of the *IBM Systems Journal* * and are summarized below.

As Table 2.1 indicates, the scope of projects included in the survey is enormous, ranging from tiny 900-line programs to immense systems of 712,000 lines. However, the same questions were asked of each project manager, such as, "Did your project make significant use of the Chief Programmer Team concept? of Structured Coding?" The results are summarized in Table 2.2.

From the study, it appears that the customer is the most significant influence on a project's success. Also, the experience and qualifications of the programming personnel seems to have a significant

---

*C.E. Walston and C.P. Felix, "A Method of Programming Measurement and Estimation," *IBM Systems Journal,* Vol. 16, No. 1 (1977), pp. 54 - 73.

impact on productivity, confirming, in a somewhat less dramatic way, the results of the Sackman experiment.

In addition, the figures in this study indicate that employing structured techniques improves programmer productivity by a factor of 1.5 to 2.0. It is unfortunate that IBM did not include structured design or structured analysis as distinct methodologies in this study, although both may be interpreted as being part of top-down development. In any case, other experiments have suggested that structured design by itself also has the effect of increasing productivity by a factor of 1.5 to 2.0.

Table 2.1
Range of Projects in IBM Survey

	Low	High	Median
Size of system (lines of code)	900	712,000	21,000
Manpower (months)	3	11,760	60
Duration of project (months)	1	68	10

Table 2.2
Effect of Structured Techniques

	Use of Concept		Factor[‡]
	Low*	High	
Chief programmer team	219[†]	408	1.9
Structured code	169	301	1.8
Top-down development	198	321	1.6
Code reviews (walkthroughs)	220	339	1.5
Customer interface complexity	500	124	−4.0
Personnel qualification and experience	132	410	3.1

---

*In this survey, "low" meant a low or negative response to a particular question. Thus, the low category for chief programmer team means that the project manager either did not use the chief programmer team concept at all, or that he used it minimally.
†This figure represents the average productivity of projects that gave a low response to a particular question. Productivity is expressed in "lines of delivered, debugged source code per man-month," a measure that included all of the people and all of the time (for designing, coding, testing, documenting, and so on) charged on the project. Thus, the

Unfortunately, neither this study nor most similar studies comment on increased program reliability achieved with the new techniques. However, other IBM experiments (notably the New York Times system and the Skylab system), as well as projects conducted by other organizations, have shown that the structured techniques enable us to write programs with an average of one to five bugs per ten thousand statements, that is, programs that are roughly one hundred times more reliable than those programs produced by classical techniques.

Finally, the IBM study, as well as most similar studies, did not provide quantitative data on the improved maintainability of a system produced with the structured techniques. Obviously, if the system is one hundred times more reliable than it would have been if developed with classical techniques, the maintenance effort is reduced. But what about the ease of adding new features to the system? Thus far, virtually everyone who has used the structured techniques has agreed that the resulting systems are *qualitatively* easier to maintain and modify, but I have not yet seen any organization reporting that their maintenance effort has been reduced from, say, 50 percent of the overall budget to 37.54 percent. Since the structured techniques still are relatively new, and since it takes time for maintenance savings to be realized, we may have to wait to see statistics.

Thus far, only a few tentative results have been reported that show that maintenance costs may be reduced by as much as a factor of ten. One measure is "Mean Time To Repair" for software maintenance, which indicates how long it takes to fix a bug. Another approach counts the number of "trouble reports" waiting to be resolved at any given time. Still another way is to measure the number of lines of code for which a maintenance programmer can assume responsibility without suffering a nervous breakdown.

Because of the difficulty of comparing the results of two projects, much work has been done recently in the area of developing standardized data for software engineering environments; among the leaders in

---

subset of the 51 projects that did *not* use or minimally used the CPTO concept had an average productivity of 219 lines of delivered (that is, actually given to the customer, as opposed to test and support code that ultimately was thrown away), debugged source code per man-month; those projects that *did* use the chief programmer team project had an average productivity of 408 lines of delivered, debugged source code per man-month.
[‡]This column represents the productivity ratio between the projects that used structured techniques and those that did not.

this work is Professor Victor Basili and his team at the University of Maryland. Two excellent papers that summarize his approach are "A Methodology for Collecting Valid Software Engineering Data," *IEEE Transactions on Software Engineering,* November 1984, by V. Basili and D. Weiss, and "Evaluating Software Development by Analysis of Changes: Some Data from the Software Engineering Laboratory," *IEEE Transactions on Software Engineering,* February 1985, by D.M. Weiss and V.R. Basili.

Chapter Three:

Structured Analysis

3.1 Introduction

Perhaps the most important of the structured disciplines discussed in this book is structured analysis. As the term implies, structured analysis is the first phase of an EDP systems development project, when the user's requirements are defined and documented.

To understand why structured analysis is so important, examine the steps that usually occur in classical systems analysis. The analyst prepares a document describing the proposed system. The document, which may contain hundreds and even thousands of pages of technical jargon and terms, is submitted to the user for review. In most cases, it might as well be written in a language foreign to the user because most users have neither the time nor the technical knowledge to wade through and understand the implications of the proposed system. In contrast, structured analysis recognizes that with classical systems analysis, the user does not have a good understanding of what the data processing people are going to develop for him on anything other than a trivial EDP project.

The user's inability to interpret classical analysis documents comes as a rude shock to many systems analysts, who complain, "But we gave the user a detailed functional specification, and he signed off on it!" Many systems analysts sincerely believe that signing off on a thousand-page functional specification guarantees that the user knows what kind of EDP system he is getting. Unfortunately, this assumption isn't valid. Most users acknowledge that they never read functional specifications in detail because they're too long and too technical. Moreover, I maintain that if they did read the specification, they probably wouldn't understand it.

The reasons for the user's difficulty with classical functional specifications can be summarized as follows:

- They're *monolithic* and must be read from beginning to end. A user cannot easily find information about a particular part of the proposed system without searching the entire document.

- They're *redundant,* giving the same information in numerous locations throughout the document, but without benefit of cross-reference.

- They're *difficult to modify* and *difficult to maintain.* A simple change in the user's requirements may necessitate changes to several different parts of the functional specification — and, because the document is monolithic, it's exceedingly painful to change. Consequently, the specification may not be kept current.

- They're often *physical* instead of *logical,* in that they describe the user's requirements in terms of either the physical hardware or the kind of physical file structure that will be used to implement the system. Such information often muddles the discussion about *what* the user wants his system to do by giving details about *how* the system will do things.

- They are *not a useful target* for ongoing development of the system; indeed, as one of my company's clients said, the classical functional specification is "of historical significance only." As a result, the system that is designed may differ considerably from the system that was specified.

Two other drawbacks should be stressed about functional specifications. Because they usually are long narratives, they tend to be boring. It's extremely difficult to read through a thousand pages of narrative text without feeling the urge to assume the fetal position and fall fast asleep! Since our society increasingly is video-oriented, there's less and less of a chance that users actually will spend time poring over hundreds of pages of prose.

There is an additional problem connected with the length of the functional specification. Because the specification is so long and monolithic, feedback between user and analyst typically takes weeks or even months. Thus, if the user does read the specification, and if he does find something that he wants changed, the time that elapses before he sees the modified specification may be so great that he will have forgotten what he wanted changed.

As analysis continues, all these problems become compounded, causing the classical analysis phase of most large projects to be painful and time-consuming. Typically, everyone involved feels desperate to end the analysis phase as soon as possible, and few people ever go back to re-examine or revise the functional specifications. Once classical analysis is done, it's done forever — to the relief of both the users *and* the analysts.

3.2 The tools of structured analysis

What, then, is *structured* analysis? Basically, structured analysis is the use of graphic documentation tools to produce a new kind of functional specification — a structured specification. The primary documentation tools of structured analysis include the following items:

- Data flow diagram
- Data dictionary
- Process specifications
- Entity-relationship diagrams
- State transition diagrams

Data flow diagrams provide an easy, graphic means of modeling the flow of data through a system, any system, whether manual, automated, or a mixture of both. Figure 3.1 shows the basic elements of a data flow diagram: sources (or sinks) of data, data flows, processes, and data stores.

A typical system requires several levels of data flow diagrams. For example, an overview of the system might be provided in a data flow diagram such as the one shown in Figure 3.2.

Each of the processes shown in Figure 3.2 can be defined in terms of its own data flow diagram. For example, Process #3 in the "parent" diagram (Figure 3.2) can be exploded into Figure 3.3.

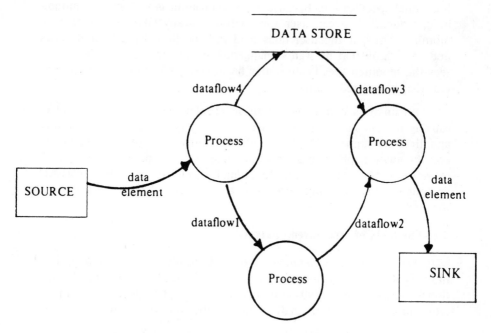

Figure 3.1. The elements of a data flow diagram.

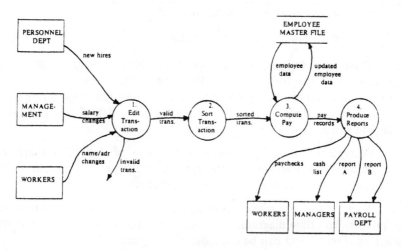

Figure 3.2. An overview data flow diagram.

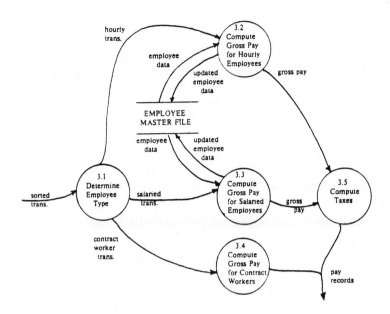

Figure 3.3. A detailed data flow diagram.

Note that this detailed data flow diagram, or "child," is a replacement for its parent, having the same net inputs and outputs.

The second major tool of structured analysis is the *data dictionary*. A data dictionary is an organized collection of logical definitions of all data names that are shown on the data flow diagram. In a typical system, there are likely to be several thousand such data definitions. For example, the data element shown on the data flow diagram in Figure 3.1 might be called CUSTOMER-ORDER and defined in the data dictionary as follows.

```
CUSTOMER-ORDER =    CUSTOMER-NAME
                 +  ACCOUNT-NUMBER
                 +  [SHIPPING-ADDRESS | "TAKE-AWAY"]
                 +  (SALESPERSON)
                 +  {ITEM-ORDERS}
```

For the most part, this data definition can be read without any explanation once the mathematical operators, or notations, are understood. These are defined as follows:

NOTATION	MEANING
x = a+b	x consists of data elements a and b
x = [a | b]	x consists of either a or b
x = (a)	x consists of an optional data element a
x = { a}	x consists of zero or more occurrences of a
x = y{ a}	x consists of y or more occurrences of a
x = { a}z	x consists of z or fewer occurrences of a
x = y{ a}z	x consists of between y and z occurrences of a

Thus, the data element description at the top of the page tells us that a CUSTOMER-ORDER consists of a CUSTOMER-NAME, together with an ACCOUNT-NUMBER, together with either a SHIPPING-ADDRESS or the literal string TAKE-AWAY, together with an optional SALESPERSON description, together with zero or more ITEM-ORDERS.

Just as with a data flow diagram, the data dictionary can present a top-down definition of a complex data element. For example, having defined CUSTOMER-ORDER, it behooves us to provide an appropriate description of some of its component data elements. Thus, the data dictionary probably also would contain a definition for ITEM-ORDERS:

ITEM-ORDERS =   PART-NUMBER
         + (PART-NAME)
         + QUANTITY
         + UNIT-PRICE
         + {DISCOUNT}

Indeed, a proper job of systems analysis requires that every data element eventually be defined, down to the lowest level of detail. At the lowest level, we might define QUANTITY as QUANTITY = 3{digit}3 to indicate that QUANTITY is a three-digit number.

The third major tool of structured analysis is the *process specification*. The purpose of the process specification is to allow the analyst to describe, rigorously and precisely, the business policy (but *not* the implementation tactics) represented by each of the bottom-level processes in the bottom-level data flow diagrams. At the same time, the description is intended to be comprehensible to the average user. These bottom-level process descriptions often are referred to as "mini-specs," since each one is a miniature functional specification. The process specification can be written in a variety of forms: formulas, graphs, decision tables, or — as I prefer — in a form known as "structured English," consisting of a limited set of verbs and nouns organized to represent a compromise between readability and rigor.

For example, a bottom-level process entitled CARRY-OUT-BACK-BILLING might have associated with it the structured English shown on the following page. In its most extreme form, structured English consists only of the following elements.

- A limited set of action-oriented verbs, such as find or print.

- Control constructs borrowed from structured programming — for example, IF-THEN-ELSE, DO-WHILE, CASE, and so on.

- Data elements defined in the data dictionary.

STRUCTURED ENGLISH FOR CARRY-OUT-BACK-BILLING

1. IF the dollar amount of the invoice times the number of weeks overdue is greater than $10,000 THEN:
   a. Give a photocopy of the invoice to the appropriate salesperson who is to call the customer.
   b. Log on the back of the invoice that a copy has been given to the salesperson, with the date on which it was done.
   c. Refile the invoice in the file for examining two weeks from today.

2. OTHERWISE IF more than four overdue notices have been sent THEN:
   a. Give a photocopy of the invoice to the appropriate salesperson to call the customer.
   b. Log on the back of the invoice that a copy has been given to the salesperson, with the date on which it was done.
   c. Refile the invoice in the file to be examined one week from today.

3. OTHERWISE (the situation has not yet reached serious proportions):
   a. Add 1 to the overdue notice count on the back of the invoice (if no such count has been recorded, write "overdue notice count = 1")
   b. IF the invoice in the file is illegible THEN type a new one.
   c. Send the customer a photocopy of the invoice, stamped "Nth notice: invoice overdue. Please remit immediately," where N is the value of the overdue notice count.
   d. Log on the back of the invoice the date on which the Nth overdue notice was sent.
   e. Refile the invoice in the file for two weeks from today's date.

As noted, other methods can be used to document the business policy for the bottom-level processes in the data flow diagrams. Depending on the application, decision tables, mathematical formulas, graphs, or even narrative English might be appropriate. The key point is that each mini-spec describes only one small piece of the system.

Also, a mini-spec, if properly written, tells *what* the process has to accomplish without saying *how* the process eventually will be built.

The next major tool of structured analysis is the *entity relationship diagram.* An example of an entity-relationship diagram, often abbreviated as E-R diagram, is shown in Figure 3.4.

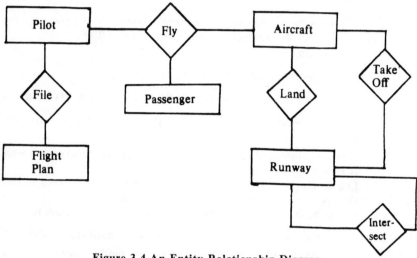

Figure 3.4 An Entity-Relationship Diagram

The purpose of an E-R diagram is to highlight the major objects or entities of stored data that the system must deal with, as well as to highlight the relationships among those objects. Many of the earlier books and articles on structured analysis did not include E-R diagrams as a modeling tool, but it has become evident that in most information processing systems, the information modeled by the E-R diagram is just as important as the processing that is modeled by the data flow diagram.

It is also important to note that the DFD and the E-R diagram highlight two different aspects of the same system; consequently, there are one-to-one correspondences that the system analyst can check to ensure that he has a consistent model. Specifically, each data store shown in a DFD, for example, the Employee Master File shown in Figure 3.2, should correspond to one object in the E-R diagram.

There is one last modeling tool that is important for the class of systems characterized as real-time systems; Examples of such systems are process control systems, telephone switching systems, command-and-control systems for many defense applications, and patient monitoring systems in hospitals. In these, the time-dependent behavior of the system is important: the end-user has business policy requirements concerning the sequence of activities, the response time required to respond to various external signals, and so on. To help highlight these aspects of the system, we use a *state transition diagram*, such as shown in Figure 3.5.

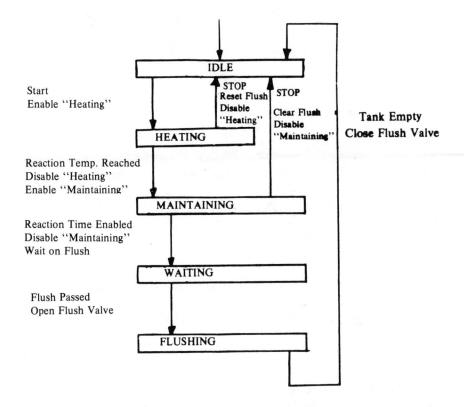

Figure 3.5 A state transition diagram

In this diagram, each of the rectangular boxes represents a "state" in which the system may reside from time to time; the arrows indicate the conditions which cause a change of state, as well as the actions that take place upon a state change.

State transition diagrams, sometimes abbreviated as STD diagrams, usually are associated with a modified form of the standard data flow diagram, a modification that allows the systems analyst to show control signals as well as data flowing from one process to another. A typical real-time DFD is shown in Figure 3.6.

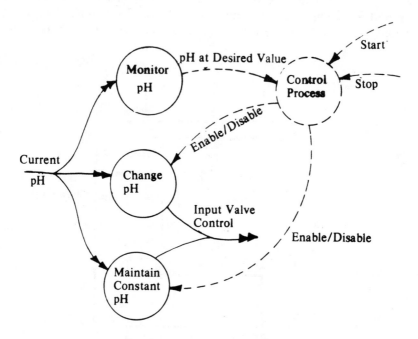

Figure 3.6 A data flow diagram for real-time systems

In such a modified data flow diagram, one of the processes is a control process, which synchronizes the activities of the other processes. The STD diagram represents a process specification for the "inside" of that control process.

Once again, there is a way of checking the consistency of these diagrams: each of the inputs to the control process should correspond to a state change condition in the STD diagram, and each of the outputs from the control process should correspond to a state change action in the STD diagram.

Even though the discussion of the major tools of structured analysis has been brief, you should see that a structured specification resulting from these graphic tools has a number of desirable characteristics, summarized as follows:

- It is partitioned, rather than monolithic.

- It is graphic, consisting largely of pictures rather than words.

- It is top-down, presenting a description of the system at progressively detailed levels.

- It is logical, depicting an implementation-independent model of the system that will be developed for the user.

3.3 Applying the tools of structured analysis

The previous section presented an overview of the graphic tools that can be used to develop a top-down partitioned model of a data processing system. This section shows how the tools of structured analysis can be applied to the typical project's systems development life cycle.

In most EDP projects, the systems analysis phase is preceded by a brief feasibility study, or project survey. The major purpose of the survey is to determine whether a proposed EDP project warrants the investment of significant amounts of time and money. The output of the survey may be called the project charter and usually consists of three parts.

- *a project abstract,* specifying the name of the project and of the responsible user, the starting date of the project and the target delivery date, the original budget allocation, and any other suitable information

- *a statement of goals and objectives,* listing functions to be implemented, deficiencies to be remedied, and features to be added to or modified in the present system

- *schedule constraints,* including key dates and deadlines and usually presented in PERT format

This project charter is input to the activity of systems analysis, shown in more detail in Figure 3.7. Note that the systems analysis activity is represented as a data flow diagram and not as a flowchart. Aside from the obvious artistic differences between a flowchart and a data flow diagram, there is an additional, very important difference: the strong implication in Figure 3.7, and in all data flow diagrams, that all the processes shown in the bubbles could be taking place at the same time; that is, it is not necessary for step number one to be completed before step number two begins. In addition, there may well be feedback from step number two to step number one. But, as we have seen in the previous section, control signals typically are not shown on a DFD (except for real-time systems, where we want to highlight the synchronization and time-dependent behavior of the system).

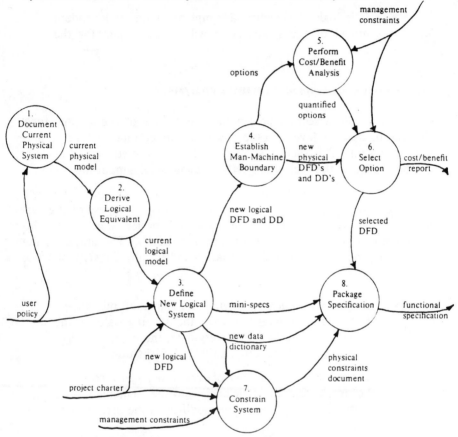

Figure 3.7. Systems analysis activity.

Before we examine the components of Figure 3.4, two assumptions need to be mentioned that are true of most projects. The user often enters into a project believing that the analyst is totally ignorant of the user's business. In truth, the analyst generally *does* begin a project ignorant to some degree of the user's business operation, although he may possess some superficial knowledge.

The second assumption is that the analyst usually is engaged in specifying the details of a new system that will replace an existing system. The existing system may be manual, automated, or a mixture of both. The new system as well may be a mixture of manual and automated processing. But regardless of the details, the user normally wants to take his existing system and (a) modernize it, (b) enhance it, (c) make it cheaper, (d) make it more reliable, (e) add features, (f) eliminate functions that are no longer required, (g) make it faster, or (h) some combination of the above.

Keeping the two assumptions in mind, let's examine Figure 3.4 more closely by taking a look at each of the eight bubbles.

Bubble 1: Document Current Physical System

Because the new system probably will bear some resemblance to the existing system, it makes sense to begin the analysis process with a study, a *model*, of the present system. It's usually best to begin with a model of the existing physical system, since that's the only one the user and analyst can be certain that they understand completely.

If the user's existing system is automated, documenting the current physical system can be relatively simple. It may consist simply of gathering existing documentation, such as run books, system flowcharts (which can be thought of as physical data flow diagrams), program listings, and the like. Assembling program listings may seem a trivial step, but it often is crucially important. As we have discussed, the functional specifications of existing systems usually are obsolete, so the code displayed in the program listings may provide the only *written* documentation that pertains to the business policy of the existing system.

If the user's existing system is manual, a significant amount of work will be required to document it. Many of the details pertaining to the user's business policy may exist only in the user's head. However, it is important to note that the same tools of structured analysis can be used to document the existing manual system. The differences are that the bubbles in the data flow diagram typically will consist of individuals (or departments of people) rather than functional processes; and the data elements that flow back and forth will be described in physical terms — for example, scraps of paper, photocopies of purchase orders, or carbon copies of invoices.

While the documentation of the user's current system is often quite important, it is also a source of some danger, as we will see in the next section: the systems analysts may become mired, as authors McMenamin and Palmer point out in *Essential Systems Analysis* (YOURDON Press, 1984), in "the current physical tarpit." It is important to spend only as much time modeling the current physical system as is necessary for (a) the systems analysts to become acquainted with the user's environment, and (b) to give the users a sense of confidence that the systems analysts actually know what they're doing.

Bubble 2: Derive Logical Equivalent

After modeling the user's existing physical system, the analyst next describes the system in logical terms. This usually means substituting functional names in place of people's names in the data flow diagram, a surprisingly complicated task in many instances, since an individual person may carry out several functions or portions of several functions. In addition, "logicalizing" the model usually requires the analyst to describe physical data elements in logical terms; that is, the analyst becomes less interested at this point in a data element known as "the blue copy of the invoice," and more interested in the data contained on that blue copy.

In most cases, the analyst requires several iterations before he is able to remove all physical characteristics from his model, thereby reducing it to a completely logical model. When he is finished, he has a description of today's system as it must be, rather than a description of today's system as it happens to be.

Bubble 3: Define New Logical System

Defining the new logical system is at the heart of the analysis activity, for it is at this stage that the analyst, working with the user, decides where new features will be added, which old functions will be deleted, and on down the line of user requirements. However, note that the analyst still is working with a logical model, a model that communicates as little as possible about the ultimate implementation of the system.

In the ideal case (as perceived by the analyst), the new logical system may be identical to the old logical system. That is, if the user were to say, "I like my system. It provides all the functions I need. The only thing wrong is that it's too slow, too unreliable, and too expensive," then he's complaining about the physical attributes of his system, not the logical attributes, and the two logical systems would be identical.

However, it is unlikely that the new logical system will be exactly identical to the old logical system. In most cases, the user will want some new features in the new system, and the analyst will hear the classic request, "Gee, as long as you're computerizing everything, I've always wondered if it would be possible to . . . ." At this stage, while on the subject of changes, the analyst may be able to convince the user to eliminate some of the features of the old system; for instance, production of many copies of a report that are distributed to seventeen different branch offices, but that are never read.

In most cases, the analyst can expect at least a 75 percent overlap between the old system and the new system, and it's extremely hard to determine where the new features fit if one doesn't have a good model of the old system.

Bubble 4: Establish Man-Machine Boundary

If the analyst has done a good job in defining the new logical system, his model will allow for different man-machine boundaries. That is, by deriving a totally *logical* model, the analyst can provide the user with a variety of choices: a totally manual system, a totally automated system, or any one of a number of partially automated systems in which some of the activities are carried out by people and some by a computerized process.

In order to establish the man-machine boundaries, the analyst might provide a scenario of options, but there usually are factors that need to be considered one of the options can be chosen.

Establishing the man-machine boundary could be regarded as an *implementation* decision: it determines not so much what the system must do, but rather a portion of how the system will be implemented (by people or by machines, or both). Since it is an issue that the end-user is quite naturally concerned with, we normally include it in the phase of the project known as systems analysis. As we will see in Bubble 7, there are usually other implementation constraints imposed by the end-user in addition to the fundamental choice of the man-machine boundary.

Bubble 5: Perform Cost/Benefit Analysis

One important activity associated with the development of a man-machine boundary is a cost/benefit analysis of the options. A totally automated system might cost $10,000,000 and a totally manual system might cost $1.39 or just the opposite.

The analyst should not choose one of the options at this point. Instead, he simply should generate the appropriate cost/benefit data, which then can be used in the ultimate selection process.

Bubble 6: Select Option

Choosing a particular man-machine boundary often requires political input, as well as the apolitical data about costs and benefits. Management in the user organization (or above the user organization) may have strong feelings about the extent to which automation is acceptable. For example, they may be trying to avoid eliminating jobs and the consequent labor problems, or they may be trying to resist automation as a matter of principle, or they may be taking into consideration other subtle aspects of employee morale.

Thus, it should not be the analyst who makes the decision at this point. He certainly can provide the options, and he may wish to offer recommendations, but it is extremely important that the user (or management, in the broadest sense of the word) make the choice.

Bubble 7: Constraint System

Much of the activity indicated in the previous bubbles — 2 and 3, in particular — should be expressed in completely logical terms. However, there inevitably will be some aspects of the new system that are physical in nature and that the user feels strongly enough about to force them to be placed into the functional specification. Some examples follow:

- "The system must be able to run in an environment that is not air-conditioned and in which temperatures can exceed 102 degrees."

- "It must be small enough to fit into a broom closet because we're running out of space."

- "It must be something we can lease because we don't have enough cash to buy anything."

- "It can't be a Brand X Widget computer because we've heard from reliable sources that they're about to go bankrupt."

Constraints of this sort are important, but they should be considered separately from those affecting the logical model of the system. We suggest that such user requirements be combined to form a physical constraints document, which would comprise one part of the overall functional specification.

Bubble 8: Package Specification

The last step, packaging the specification, is primarily a clerical activity: assembling the various pieces of the specification — data flow diagram, data dictionary, structured English, mini-specs, and the physical constraints document; ensuring that the terminology and format of the documents are consistent; adding a table of contents, an introduction, and an overview, if appropriate, and so on.

The final document, the structured specification, is the output of the entire analysis activity and becomes input to the design activity. The process of design, discussed in Chapter 5, makes considerable use of the documents prepared by structured analysis.

3.4 Management problems with structured analysis

In the systems development field, like all other activities in life, we are finally beginning to learn that there's no such thing as a "free lunch." Or, to put it another way: You never get something for nothing. According to an informal survey conducted in 1983 by YOURDON inc., structured analysis is currently used by approximately 50 percent of the MIS organizations and is considered to be quite successful in most of those organizations. *But*, there have been some problems, and there will probably be problems for your organization when it first begins to introduce structured analysis. The problems most likely to arise are as follows.

1. Fears that structured analysis may not work. Structured analysis did not begin to attract serious attention until the late 1970's and was not widely used until the early to mid-1980's. Hence, you may still encounter a reaction similar to that which accompanied the introduction of structured programming and structured design in the 1970's: "How do we know that this stuff is going to work? It sounds like black magic."

There are various ways of responding to such comments, but your answer should depend on whether the comments come from your boss, the end-user, or the systems analyst on your project. Depending on the situation, your response might be:

- *Direct confrontation.* To the person who asks, "How do you know that structured analysis will work?" you might respond, "How do you know it won't? Could it be any worse than what you have now?" Often, your boss and your systems analysts will agree that the problems listed at the beginning of Section 3.1 are true. You'll all agree that the end-user rarely reads the voluminous specifications currently being produced and that such documents generally are obsolete and unmaintainable by the time programming begins. If everyone agrees that the current technology for producing functional specifications is a disaster and that there is no alternative approach, then all parties may be willing to accept structured analysis.

- *Common sense.* To the person who expresses further doubts about the new techniques, you might response, "But structured analysis is just common sense!" This kind of comment is best made if you can say it while looking utterly innocent, as if to say, "But, gee, isn't this the way we've been doing it all along?"

- *Testimonials.* Perhaps the most convincing way of dealing with these fears is to find a similar project in a similar organization or perhaps another division of your own company that has tried the structured analysis techniques discussed in this chapter. You should be able to find case studies in a recent issue of the popular computer journals that your staff reads; if not, feel free to contact me at YOURDON inc. (1501 Broadway, New York, NY 10036) and we'll happily put you in touch with organizations similar to yours who are using structured analysis.

These suggested ways for presenting the concepts of structured analysis work well in most organizations. However, if yours is particularly conservative, you may need to employ more political methods.

Indeed, it's extremely important for you to realize that the introduction of structured analysis necessitates a much more political approach than do the concepts of structured design and structured programming discussed later in this book. After all, nobody, except perhaps the programmer responsible for a piece of code, knows how the code is written, or whether it is good or bad, so you won't be required to present the implementation rationale to nontechnical people when you begin to introduce new technologies in the design and programming area. But analysis clearly involves the end-user, who may have extremely strong views on the subject and who undoubtedly will ask for an explanation. In addition, the format and organization of the analysis product may be subject to various external constraints. For example, an aerospace vendor may find that the "statement of requirements" for a system built for the U.S. Department of Defense has to obey strict rules for format, substance, and organization.

Further, the output of systems analysis may be visible to levels of management outside the MIS area itself. So, it is important to be prepared to explain the merits of structured analysis to nontechnical people, clearly a political situation. If you're faced with this kind of situation, it could be better for you to begin with structured programming and structured design, and when you've demonstrated that these newfangled techniques actually work, then you might try to sneak structured analysis into the organization.

2. Fears relating to the amount of time spent on analysis. Managers and users often act as if *any* time spent on analysis (or design, for that matter) is just a way for the technical staff to rest up before they get to the real work of the project — programming. This attitude has been around for a long time, perhaps because coding has long been viewed as the only tangible activity of systems development. Structured analysis seems to intensify this suspicion, particularly because roughly 30 percent of the total project manpower should be allocated for systems analysis and another 20 percent for design.

There are rational arguments for devoting a substantial effort to properly defining the user's requirements. Indeed, there have been studies (including one by Barry Boehm published in *IEEE Transactions on Software Engineering*)* that have documented that a systems analysis error often is two orders of magnitude more expensive to correct if it is not discovered until acceptance testing. More recently, James Martin has pointed out in *An Information Systems Manifesto* (Englewood Cliffs: Prentice-Hall, 1984) that approximately 50 percent of the number of errors, and 75 percent of the cost of error correction in operational systems is attributable to errors of systems analysis.

But you probably know all of these arguments. The problem is getting doubting users and skeptical non-MIS managers to believe them. There is no definite way to convince the skeptics other than testimonials and showing them that the methods work. A small pilot project that demonstrates the virtues of structured analysis, as well as all the other structured techniques, is worth a try at this point. (Pilot projects are discussed in detail in Chapter 12).

---

* B. Boehm, "Software Engineering," *IEEE Transactions on Software Engineering,* Volume C-25, No. 12 (December 1976).

3. Needs to justify analysis of the current system. Managers and users frequently ask, "Why should we spend so much time studying the current system if we're about to throw it away?" Studying the current system and environment can take a considerable amount of time (indeed, it often takes as much time as you're willing to allow the systems analysts to spend!) and the time consumed adds to the frustration and impatience felt by the non-MIS personnel. However, there are usually some very important reasons for studying the user's old system:

- You cannot tell what kind of new system the user needs if you don't understand what he's doing now.

- Even if *you* think you can design a new system for a user without studying his old system, you probably cannot convince the user of that. Most users will express irritation at having an outsider, such as the systems analyst, tell them how they should be running their business, especially if it becomes evident that the outsider doesn't even know how they actually are running it currently.

- Many end-users are not accustomed to thinking in abstract terms; if they are to discuss their business policy, they must begin by describing things in familiar terms — for example, familiar paper forms of data, familiar descriptions of processes carried out by human processors. Then they can begin discussing their system in more abstract terms, as they and the systems analyst explore the essence of their system, the things the system must do *regardless* of the technology that's available.

Notwithstanding these good reasons for doing some current physical modeling, you should listen carefully for this complaint because it may indicate that (a) your users and managers have little patience and will want the activity to be done as quickly as possible, or (b) your systems analysts have a proclivity for over-doing the current physical model.

4. Reluctance to recognize the techniques as anything different. Resistance to structured analysis may take the following form: "Isn't this just the same old stuff that we've been doing for years?" This is a question that you'll hear repeatedly, and it will be asked equally frequently about structured design, structured programming, and virtually every one of the other topics in this book. The simplest reply to such a question is, "Well, perhaps you have been doing it all along. Let's take a look at one of your functional specifications . . . ."

At this juncture, the we've-been-doing-it-all-along person will probably say something like, "Ahhh, actually, well, errrr . . . . ummmm, we really don't have any functional specifications lying around that I can show you. They're all marked **TOP SECRET**." Or, if this person does produce a sample specification for you to look at, he might say, "Actually this one was produced in an awful hurry, so it's kind of sloppy. We didn't get around to doing the data dictionary, but that seemed like a lot of low-level work, and we figured we would get the programmers to do it. And I have to admit that most of it *is* a monolothic narrative document, but — see, right here on page 509, there's a detailed flowchart, and that's not too much different from a data flow diagram anyway. I mean, we've got the *idea* of structured analysis; it's just that we don't use all the fancy words, and we're not quite so formal about it."

Of course, that's just the point. The *idea* of structured analysis has probably been in a lot of people's heads for a very long time, but organizing, formalizing, and giving names to the ideas is what distinguishes a formal discipline from an apple-pie-and-motherhood set of fuzzy attitudes.

The urge to freeze the specifications. One of the advantages of the graphic, partitioned specification produced by structured analysis is that it can be modified very easily if the user's needs change during the analysis phase, or even during the design and programming phases of the project. Indeed, the specification continues to be maintained and modified, along with the code, for the ten-to-fifteen-year life cycle of the system.

Unfortunately, many MIS organizations are convinced that the specification has to be frozen at a relatively early stage in the development phase, with no more consideration given to user changes until after the code has been completed. Perhaps this was appropriate for conventional specifications, in which a minor change to the requirements often created enormous amounts of clerical work, but it is a dangerous practice. If anyone is going to freeze the specifications, it should be the user. In particular, the user who bears the cost of the changes (cost, in this context, may mean money, manpower, and delays to the schedule) has the right to *insist* on change, making it unrealistic and unwise to freeze the specification. Rather than abolishing changes, one must learn to *control* them. Structured analysis facilitates such control.

6. *The difficulty of maintaining graphical models.* As we have seen, structured analysis depends heavily on pictures: data flow diagrams, entity-relationship diagrams, and state transition diagrams. Despite the comments above about allowing changes from the user, many systems analysts complain that it is tedious and time-consuming to continue redrawing a diagram that may have required an hour or more of manual labor; this problem is compounded in a large system that has a hundred or more data flow diagrams, as well as dozens of E-R diagrams and STD diagrams.

Until the mid-1980's, the only solution to this problem was the program librarian concept discussed in Chapter 9; after all, systems analysts are not hired for their talents as draftspeople and artists. If that kind of talent is required, the MIS organization should hire specialists to do the work. More recently, though, there has been a more attractive solution: *analyst workbenches* that allow the systems analyst to compose and revise DFD's, E-R diagrams, and STF diagrams, as well as the associated textual material in data dictionaries and process descriptions, on a graphics-oriented personal workstation. The future development of such workbenches is discussed in Chapter 20.

7. *Fear that users won't look at structured analysis models.* As we discussed earlier, it's best to meet this fear head-on: you won't know whether users will look at the graphical models of structured analysis until you try.

Sometimes, though, the fear is well-founded: occasionally users will not look at data flow diagrams. If this happens, check carefully to see how the models have been presented to the user. If your systems analyst says, "This is a top-down third normal form balanced data flow diagram, which I learned about last month while studying for my Masters Degree in Computer Science, and it represents the very latest software engineering approach to defining the logical essence of your system," then you shouldn't be surprised if the user faints or throws the systems analyst out of his office. If, on the other hand, the systems analyst says, "This is a picture that I drew to show you my understanding of what goes on in your department," then resistance by the user is a more serious matter.

Indeed, this latter situation is a good argument for an approach known as *prototyping,* which also involves developing a model of user requirements. But the model appears to be more "real" because it actually runs on a computer, with "live" inputs and "real" outputs. Prototyping is discussed in more detail in Chapter 18.

8. Concern that the modeling techniques may not apply to real-time systems. Many of the early books and articles on structured analysis concentrated on "business" systems, such as payroll, inventory, and general ledger. In such systems, any attempt to show interrupts or signals in the statement of requirements was usually a terrible mistake; at best, it represented an intrusion of implementation details in the statement of what the system had to do. Hence, these books abolished all efforts to show signals, interrupts, timing sequences, and so forth, much to the consternation of people building real-time systems, for whom such issues are of paramount importance.

We saw in Section 3.1 that the structured analysis model now includes the state transition diagram as a vital component; it also has a provision for showing control and signals in the data flow diagram. For more detail, see the three-volume set of books entitled *Structured Development for Real-Time Systems,* by Paul Ward and Steve Mellor (YOURDON Press, 1985).

9. What about users with personal computers? They don't want to do any analysis! This, of course, has become a concern in the mid-1980's, as personal computers have begun springing up like mushrooms in many organizations.

We will deal with this question in more detail in Chapter 16. The short answer is that *all* complex systems need to be modeled, regardless of who implements the system and regardless of whether it operates on a central mainframe or a remote stand-alone personal computer. Remember the assumptions at the beginning of Chapter 2: if your organization does nothing but build trivial systems (each of which, in the extreme case, runs once and is then thrown away) then you don't need any structured techniques. But if you're reading this book, it's presumably because you or your users are building more complex systems.

10. The myth of the perfect specification. To conclude our discussion of typical problems, we introduce a slightly pessimistic but realistic note: The structured approach is not perfect, nor can it produce a perfect specification, mainly because people are not perfect.

Communication between two human beings always involves some risk of a misunderstanding of one sort or another. This potential is important to recognize because management in some MIS organizations believes that if one spends enough time, and enough money, and if one plays enough games, then one can do a *perfect* job of systems analysis.

Playing the game right politically can provide the manager trying to introduce the structured techniques with a significant edge. Effective ways to play the game are given below:

- Put a user on the project team. (This will keep *both* parties honest.)

- Transfer the development team into the user's department. (Team members will be very responsive to user requirements if they know who's paying their salaries.)

- Write a formal contract between the user and the development team. (If each page of the specification must be signed in blood by both parties, you can be more confident that the misunderstandings will be minimal.)

Under the right circumstances, each of these games has some value, but even these ploys won't guarantee that you will do a perfect job of capturing the user's requirements. Indeed, even if you do, these requirements probably will change before the coding is completed because, during the one to two years it takes to write the code, the technology will have changed, the business and economic climate will have changed, and the government regulations will have changed. Most dramatic of all, the user himself may have changed: You may end up delivering your system to a person other than the one who requested it.

Bibliography

1. DeMarco, T. *Structured Analysis and System Specification.* New York: YOURDON Press, 1978.

2. Gane, C., and T. Sarson. *Structured Systems Analysis: Tools and Techniques.* New York: Improved System Technologies, Inc., 1977.

3. Ross, D.T., and K.E. Schoman, Jr. "Structured Analysis for Requirements Definition." *IEEE Transactions on Software Engineering,* Vol. SE-3, No. 1 (January 1977).

4. Weinberg, V. *Structured Analysis.* New York: YOURDON Press, 1978.

5. Ward, P. *Systems Development Without Pain.* New York: YOURDON Press, 1984.

6. McMenamin, S., and J. Palmer. *Essential Systems Analysis.* New York: YOURDON Press, 1984.

7. King, D. *Current Practices in Software Engineering.* New York: YOURDON Press, 1984.

8. Keller, R. *The Practice of Structured Analysis.* New York: YOURDON Press, 1983.

9. Ward, P., and S. Mellor. *Structured Development for Real-Time Systems.* (Volumes 1-3). New York: YOURDON Press, 1985.

10. Dickinson, B. *Developing Structured Systems.* New York: YOURDON Press, 1981.

Chapter Four:

Top-Down Design and Testing

This chapter deals specifically with two related techniques: top-down design and top-down testing. The format of the chapter is simple: First, a brief overview of the technical concepts behind the top-down approach; second, a review of the management-oriented benefits of the approach; and third, a discussion of the problems and difficulties that as a manager you are likely to encounter when implementing the top-down approach in your organization.

4.1 An overview of the top-down approach

Top-down design and top-down testing have been practiced instinctively by many programmers for years. In academic circles, the top-down approach has been referred to as "systematic programming," "stepwise refinement," "levels of abstraction," and a variety of other names. The phrase "top-down," however, today seems to dominate the other buzzwords.

The purpose of this section is to provide you with enough of an understanding of these important concepts of design and implementation to enable you to discuss them intelligently with your technical people and with other EDP managers. This chapter is not intended to make you an expert on top-down design and certainly doesn't cover everything about the subject. If you and/or your programmers require a more detailed discussion of the top-down approach, the references at the end of this chapter should be helpful.

Many EDP people use the phrase top-down loosely. For reasons that are largely historical, top-down design and structured programming have long been discussed together. Indeed, you'll notice that many of the references at the end of this chapter emphasize structured programming, but that few include top-down in the title. There is nothing wrong with the association, but you should make sure that when you are discussing top-down design with one of your colleagues, he or she is not thinking about structured programming. The two are not synonymous, as you will see in our discussion of structured programming in Chapter 6.

Also, when you are discussing the top-down approach with a colleague, make sure that you're both discussing the same aspect of the top-down approach. We can identify three related, but distinct, aspects of top-down:

- *Top-down design:* a design strategy that breaks large, complex problems into smaller, less complex problems and then decomposes each of those smaller problems into even smaller problems, until the original problem has been expressed as some combination of many small, solvable problems.

- *Top-down coding:* a strategy of coding high-level, executive modules as soon as they have been designed and generally before the low-level, detail modules have been designed.

- *Top-down testing* or *top-down implementation:* a strategy of testing the high-level modules of a system before the low-level modules have been coded and possibly before they have been designed.

What a perfectly simple idea! Indeed, what more does one need to say to introduce the top-down approach? Perhaps a simple example would be useful to illustrate the top-down aspects of design, coding, and testing. Let us take as our example that most universal of all commercial data processing systems, the payroll system.

A few years ago I participated in the development of a payroll system. We began the project by breaking the entire system into an edit, an update, a sort, and several print routines. ("What's so special about that?" you ask. "We've been doing that sort of thing for years!" That's just the point: Many organizations have followed some form of top-down design all along.) Having identified the edit, update, and print levels as top-level modules and having determined the next few levels of modules beneath them, we wrote code for the top-level modules in many cases, writing code to call lower-level modules that we had not yet designed.

Our primary reason for writing this code was to make it possible to test — or exercise, as we preferred to call it, since the testing was not exhaustive — a preliminary version of the payroll system, but one that was, in a sense, a *complete* payroll system. Approximately six weeks after beginning the project, we produced what we referred to as "Version 1:" a payroll system that accepted input transactions and a master file and that produced paychecks.

Of course, our Version 1 payroll system had a few minor limitations. The user was required to provide error-free transactions, for our payroll system made no attempt to validate them. In addition, the user was required to provide transactions that already had been sorted, as our system was too lazy to do the sorting. Furthermore, our system was unwilling to allow the user to hire new employees, fire existing employees, give any employee a salary increase, or, for that matter, make *any* change to an employee's current status.

Worse, our payroll system uniformly paid everyone a salary of one hundred dollars per week and withheld a uniform fifteen dollars in taxes from everyone's paycheck. It insisted that all employees be paid by check, instead of allowing the convenience of being paid by cash or having one's paycheck deposited directly into a bank account. The final indignity: It printed all of the paychecks in octal.

Not a very exciting payroll system. On the other hand, it did involve all of the top-level modules. What made the system so primitive was the fact that all of the lower-level modules existed as "stubs," or "dummy routines." For example, the top-level module in the update portion of the system called a module to compute an employee's salary. For the Version 1 system, that module simply returned an output of one hundred dollars. Similarly, the top-level module in the edit part of the system called a module to determine the validity of a specific transaction. For Version 1, that module simply returned with an indication that the transaction was valid, without going to any effort to actually validate the transaction.

Subsequent versions of the payroll system merely involved adding lower-level modules to the existing skeleton of top-level modules. A second version of the system, for example, allowed the user to hire and fire employees. It also sorted the transactions, and in a few very simple cases, it actually computed an employee's gross pay. However, Version

2 still made no attempt to validate the input transactions. In most cases, it still paid employees one hundred dollars per week. In all cases, it withheld fifteen dollars in taxes and printed paychecks in octal. Subsequent versions rectified these limitations, until a final version produced output that was satisfactory to the user.

That process in a nutshell is the top-down approach. The concept of top-down design is simple and has been around for a long time. Indeed, one could argue that it is just a variation of Julius Caesar's "divide and conquer" strategy. Most intelligent programmers would argue that they've been doing top-down design all along, and most serious data processing managers would insist that they always have enforced top-down design in their departments.

However, my visits to several hundred organizations around the world during the past dozen years suggest otherwise. Many managers promote good design strategies in their standards manuals, but fail to enforce them. Many programmers follow such a sloppy, informal version of top-down design that they are unable to take advantage of its benefits. Some programmers attempt to practice bottom-up design; that is, they first try to identify all of the bottom-level modules that will be required, and then try to figure out how to put them together. Finally, the majority of programmers do *no* design, but rather begin coding as soon as they have been given specifications.

Still, it probably is fair to say that many organizations attempt to practice top-down design. In contrast, very few organizations make any conscious attempt at top-down testing. The small number of organizations that have a formal test plan unfortunately advocate a bottom-up strategy, as follows: First, the bottom-level modules are tested in isolation. Then, these are combined with modules at the next higher level to form programs, which are tested in isolation. Next, the programs are combined with modules at the next higher level to form subsystems, which are tested in isolation. Finally, all of the subsystems are combined to permit a system test.

So, if your programmers tell you that they already practice top-down design and top-down testing, beware! Look more closely at what they *really* are doing. For example, could they provide you with a payroll system that paid all employees one hundred dollars in octal shortly after the beginning of the project?

4.2 The benefits of the top-down approach

The benefits of top-down design should be immediately obvious. Most problems, whether in the data processing field or elsewhere, are too complex to be grasped in their entirety. Top-down design provides an organized method of breaking the original problem into smaller problems that we can grasp and solve with some degree of success.

The benefits of top-down testing are not so immediately apparent, particularly in organizations that have followed the bottom-up approach for the past ten or twenty years. Those benefits are summarized in the following sections.

4.2.1 Major interfaces are exercised at the beginning of the project

In the brief sketch drawn earlier of the payroll system, Version 1 demonstrated that to a limited extent the edit subsystem could communicate with the update subsystem, which was capable of communicating with the sort subsystem, which in turn could communicate with the various print routines.

In any major computer system, one usually can identify subsystems and interfaces between the subsystems. Those interfaces may be implemented in the form of a magnetic tape file, or a disk file, or data passed from module to module through memory. Typically, the interface will be documented by the designer(s) on paper: some documentation of the file layout, the intermodule calling sequence, or something of that nature. Unfortunately, individual programmers may interpret the interface documents slightly differently. They may code bugs into that portion of their program that passes information through the interface. The interface document may be blatantly incorrect (a common occurrence with certain information supplied by computer vendors!); or the interface document may be incomplete, failing to describe certain conditions, exceptions, or special situations.

What we are saying, then, is that the interface between modules and the interface between subsystems are common places for bugs to occur. In the bottom-up approach, major interfaces usually are not tested until the very end, at which point, the discovery of an interface bug can be disastrous. The presence of the interface bug may require that several modules be recoded; even worse, it often occurs the day before the final deadline — or the day after the final deadline.

By contrast, the top-down approach tends to force important, top-level interfaces to be exercised at an early stage in the project, so that if there are problems, they can be resolved while there still is the time, the energy, and the resources to deal with them. Indeed, we usually find that as we go further and further in the project, the bugs become progressively simpler — that is, the interface problems become more and more localized.

We should emphasize that interface problems occur not only at the interfaces between major pieces of an application system, but also at the interfaces between the vendor's hardware and your applications, and between the vendor's software and your applications. Thus, one of my clients found that Version 1 of an on-line system represented a major test of a CRT terminal with which they had no prior experience, a new modem, newly installed telephone lines, a recently acquired telecommunications monitor from a major software firm, a newly acquired database management system from a different software firm, the vendor's operating system, and several major application subsystems.

You can imagine the sort of things that were discovered in Version 1: The vendor's terminal worked, but the programming manual for the terminal left out key details that would have caused major problems if their absence had not been detected at the outset. The modem had the nasty habit of dropping bits of data at random intervals. The telephone lines actually worked, but the telecommunications monitor gobbled up all available memory in the computer, fragmented the memory into small pieces, and then shut down the system because it could not obtain enough big chunks of memory. The database management package worked fine, but could only carry out one disk access at a time, a fact which would have caused major throughput problems if it had not been discovered at an early stage. All of the application subsystems had a variety of interface bugs. It was a wonder the client ever got Version 1 working at all, but when he did, it worked relatively smoothly from there on.

4.2.2 Users can see a working demonstration of the system

Perhaps the single most important advantage of the top-down approach is that one can demonstrate a skeleton version of a system to a user at an early stage, *before* the programmers have wasted time coding from fuzzy, inaccurate specifications.

This point brings up one of the most serious philosophical problems in the computer field today: the myth of perfect systems analysis, a point discussed briefly in the previous chapter. This is the belief that if one spends enough time talking to the user, or if one puts a user on the analysis team, or, conversely, if one makes the programmers work in the user department, or if one gets the user to formally sign and accept the functional specification, and if a few other well-intentioned gimmicks are implemented, then it will be possible to get *perfect* specifications from which we can write perfect code that will make the user perfectly happy.

Humbug! In a few cases, this approach has worked to some degree, but it usually is an exercise in futility. First, in any new, sophisticated computer system, the user does not know what he wants, and he *won't* know what he wants until he begins to see something more tangible than a stack of paper.

Second, communication problems between the user, the analyst, and the programmer are inevitable. The user will explain what he wants in a language that is incomplete, ambiguous, and imprecise. The analyst and the programmer will misinterpret the user's wishes in subtle ways. Even with the improved graphic tools of structured analysis discussed in Chapter 3, misunderstandings still can arise. Furthermore, the less experienced the user and the more complex the system, the more likely the misunderstandings.

Finally, today things often change more quickly than we can develop computer systems. Systems have been specified in 1983 and scheduled to be installed in 1985, but by 1985, major premises upon which the systems were based had changed. The business had changed, the economy had changed, the technology had changed, the competition had changed. Even the user had changed. Thus, the "ultimate system" was delivered to a person other than the one who originally had ordered it.

All of these phenomena argue strongly for a top-down approach. Even if the user seems to know what he wants, implement a top-level skeleton first, and make him look at it. Chances are, he'll want something deleted from or added to the original specifications. In general, it is easier to make changes *before* coding. In many cases, one can avoid the frustrating experience of writing beautiful code, only to throw it away because the user changed his mind!*

---

* — An alternative is to use prototyping tools that also can demonstrate a rudimentary version of a system to the user at an early stage. For more discussion of these tools, see Chapter 18.

4.2.3 Deadline problems can be dealt with more satisfactorily

Although this book is aimed at managers and their problems, it is not about project management. Projects still are typically behind schedule and over budget. Indeed, a 1984 survey of roughly two hundred large organizations by Capers Jones indicates that the typical project is one year behind schedule and 100 percent over budget. Why? Partly because deadlines reflect political pressures more than a manager's sober, rational judgment. The reason a deadline is January 1 is that someone insisted that the system must be operational by the beginning of the new year, regardless PERT charts.

Unforeseen events also cause deadline problems. If the bubonic plague strikes the programmers, the project will be late; if a tornado demolishes the computer room, projects definitely will fall behind schedule.

Yet many of us persist in drawing neater, more accurate PERT charts, hoping that users and top management will allow us to schedule projects on a rational basis. Also, many of us continue to assume that neither tornadoes nor epidemics will strike.

Thus, when the deadline arrives, the classical bottom-up approach usually leaves us in a vulnerable position. Typically, we find that the design has been completed, most or all of the code has been written, and most, possibly all, of the modules have been tested individually. Unfortunately, when the modules are assembled, they don't work. When the deadline arrives, we are in the middle of system testing, with twenty thousand lines of code that don't *do* anything. Try to explain that to a user who doesn't know the difference between a BASIC statement and a football. Even worse, try to explain it to a user who *has* written a few lines of BASIC — they are often under the impression that any amount of code can be written in an afternoon.

Also, try to explain to top managers who have been getting status reports all along indicating that things are on schedule. Chances are, you've been fooled, too. Your programmers probably began telling you on the second day of the project that they were 95 percent done, and on "deadline day," they *still* are 95 percent done! Sure, they reached the milestone of "design completed" on schedule, but what does that mean? They reached the milestone of "all modules coded" on schedule, but what does that mean?

Compare these developments with the top-down approach, but be sure to recognize that there is no magic. Whether one works top-down or bottom-up, there still will be deadline problems. The system still may not be finished when the deadline arrives, and the users still will be irritated, even if you never committed your staff to meeting the deadline.

However, you undoubtedly will be in a *much* stronger political position than you would be with the bottom-up approach because you will have a skeleton version of the system that performs some demonstrable processing. Of course, this advantage must be viewed in the proper perspective, for if we present a payroll system that produces octal paychecks, the user is unlikely to be impressed with the effort and might well send us off to the slave labor camps in Siberia. Consider the following dialogue, and you will see what I mean:

User: Good morning. Today's the deadline. Where is my payroll system?

DP Manager: I'm sorry to say that we're not finished.

User: What? That's ridiculous! We agreed that you would be finished by January 1.

DP Manager: Actually, *you* agreed that it would be done on January 1. I told you all along that that date was optimistic. However, I do have a Version 3 payroll system that works and can be put into operation today.

User: Version 3? What does that mean?

DP Manager: Well, it's a payroll system that pays everyone by check; it won't pay anyone in cash, or by direct bank deposit. And if anyone works double overtime on a national holiday, the system still will pay one hundred dollars per week. And the system does not validate transactions that *decrease* salary, which means that an employee's salary might accidentally be reduced below zero. But, other than those minor details, the system works.

User: That's ridiculous! That's unacceptable! I want the whole thing! I asked for the whole payroll system to be working by January 1.

DP Manager: I know, but we didn't make it. In the meantime, you should be able to live with these minor restrictions. We'll have them fixed in another two weeks.

User: Grumble, grumble . . . well, I suppose it's better
                    than nothing.

4.2.4 Debugging is easier

One of the advantages of the top-down approach involves a technical process that shouldn't concern you as a manager, but that nevertheless is a factor you should be aware of: The process of debugging is easier when the top-down approach is used.

To explain, the distinction between testing and debugging needs to be defined. Loosely speaking, *testing* is the process one goes through to demonstrate the correctness or incorrectness of a program or system. It usually consists of supplying known inputs to the system and verifying that the outputs are correct. *Debugging*, on the other hand, is the black art of tracking down a bug once its existence has been discovered. The existence of a bug usually is learned from a controlled test procedure; hence, testing and debugging are considered by most programmers to be almost synonymous. But when a production program blows up in the middle of the night, and the computer operator calls the responsible programmer, it's debugging that the sleepy programmer is doing, not testing.

Given that distinction, we maintain that debugging is easier in a top-down testing environment because top-down testing tends to be incremental. That is, it usually consists of adding one new module to an existing skeleton of modules, and then observing the behavior of the new system. If the new system misbehaves, common sense tells the programmer that the problem must be located in the new module or in the interface between the new module and the rest of the system. Indeed, if the programmer becomes desperate, he always has the option of a strategic retreat; he can remove the new module, re-insert the dummy, or stub, in its place, and retreat to his office to contemplate the mystery of the bug.

In contrast, the bottom-up approach tends to be phased. That is, one usually finds geometrically increasing numbers of modules being combined for the first time, any one of which (or any combination of which) may contain a bug. This problem is particularly evident during system testing, when hundreds or even thousands of modules are combined for the first time, and one of those modules contains a bug that ultimately destroys the entire system. Even worse, a bug in module A combines with a bug in module B to produce a subtly incorrect output that the programmer finds impossible to relate to any single module; or a bug in module A cancels the effect of a bug in module B, thus leading to correct output, until the maintenance programmer innocently fixes the bug in module A.

4.2.5 Requirements for machine test time are distributed more evenly throughout a top-down project

In many projects, the requirement for machine time rises almost exponentially toward the end of the project. However, the requirement for machine time in a top-down project remains fairly constant during the lifetime of the project.

The differences between the two approaches can be shown graphically as follows:

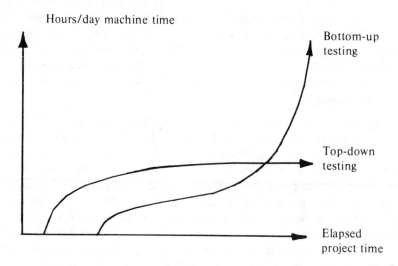

You should be able to anticipate the reasons for these two curves from what we have said about the top-down approach. The bottom-up approach generally does not begin using computer test time until the project is well underway, simply because the approach involves designing and coding most or all of the system before testing begins. Once testing does begin, the requirement for machine time rises rapidly as modules are combined into programs, programs into subsystems, and subsystems into systems.

In contrast, the top-down approach begins using machine time earlier because one begins writing code before the design is finished. Normally, the requirement for test time reaches a certain point and then levels off, remaining relatively constant for the duration of the project. The reason for the constant requirement for test time is fairly simple: The incremental nature of the testing involves adding one new module to the system each day and running roughly the same set of test data through the system. It should be noted that early use of machine time can cause some problems, which are discussed in Section 4.3.2.

4.2.6 Programmer morale is improved

A minor advantage of the top-down approach — but one that should not be ignored — is that the programmers are usually happier and better motivated. Why? For the same reasons that users and managers like the top-down approach: They can see tangible results of progress at an earlier stage. The morale boost of seeing an early version of a system is particularly effective in avoiding the "mid-project slump" found in most projects that continue for two or three years.

This boost can be significant. Programmers, for the most part, *do* like to program. They do *not* like to write detailed specifications, they do *not* like to prepare flowcharts, they do *not* like to become engrossed in the paperwork that is characteristic of the early stages of a typical project. However, when they begin the programming and testing — the fun part — they begin to work the sixteen-hour days on which we have come to depend.

With the top-down approach, the programming usually begins much earlier in the project, so that the programmer begins, at an earlier stage, doing what he really enjoys doing. In addition, he has the tremendous morale boost of seeing a Version 1 system actually work. It doesn't matter that the Version 1 payroll system is trivial and that it only produces octal paychecks. It is a real program that accepts real inputs and produces real outputs. That progress alone probably is sufficient to motivate the programmer to work sixteen-hour days to produce Version 2 of the system.

4.2.7 Top-down testing eliminates the need for test harnesses

Finally, there is a characteristic of top-down testing that is basically technical in nature, although it has some management overtones.

The classic bottom-up scheme usually requires the presence of a test driver, or test harness; that is, a program that can read test data from a file, pass the test data to the module being tested, capture the output from the module, and print the output on a suitable output device. A few organizations are disciplined enough to require their programmers to make use of a general-purpose test driver, along with a general-purpose test data generator, perhaps, but most organizations don't bother. In most companies, each programmer writes a quick-and-dirty test driver for each module being tested.

The top-down approach eliminates the need for drivers, since the existing skeleton system can serve as a natural test driver for a new detail module being added to the system. On the other hand, the top-down approach *does* require the use of stubs, or dummy routines. Such routines are substitutes for detailed modules that have not been coded yet, and their implementation usually consists of the following:

1. Immediate exit, with no processing

2. Returning constant output, that is, returning one hundred dollars in the dummy version of the salary computation module in the payroll system example

3. Returning a random number within some range

4. Printing an output message, to inform the programmer that the dummy module was executed

5. Executing a timing loop to consume N micro-seconds in a controlled fashion (useful in some real-time systems)

6. Providing a primitive quick-and-dirty implementation of the *real* function of the module

7. Asking for help from an on-line terminal (in which case a human being does the work that the module was supposed to do)

Although there is nothing fundamentally wrong with test drivers, dummy routines usually are simpler to code than a corresponding driver routine. In the best case, the dummy routine consists of one statement: EXIT.

4.3 Management problems with the top-down approach

Based on the preceding discussion, you might be tempted to issue a memo to your programmers that says: "Troops! Starting tomorrow, I want all of you to design and test your systems in a top-down fashion!" Or maybe you should send all three hundred of your programmers to a one-hour class on top-down implementation, and *then* issue the edict.

As stated in Chapter 2, such an approach may lead to confusion. Indeed, even if you ease into top-down implementation slowly, gradually, and diplomatically, you may experience confusion. The troops, even with the best of intentions, are likely to do some silly things in the name of top-down implementation.

What sort of things? Companies vary, but the sort of problems that I have seen include the following:

- A misunderstanding of radical top-down implementation versus conservative top-down implementation

- Lack of sufficient test time

- Lack of hardware for top-down testing

- Staffing problems

- Programmers' fears that changes to low-level modules will propagate to high-level modules

- Common tendency to practice top-down *program* testing, combined with bottom-up *system* testing

- Communication problems in multi-team projects

- Difficulty in visualizing top-down versions

- Difficulty in getting the user involved

- Unwillingness to renegotiate schedules and budgets

A brief discussion of each of these potential problem areas follows.

4.3.1 Misunderstanding between radical top-down and conservative top-down

You may well be wondering, "What's conservative top-down? What's radical top-down?" Indeed, these concepts have not been discussed, but they cause many organizations trouble when they first attempt the top-down approach.

We could describe the radical top-down approach in the following manner: First, design the top level of a system; that is, recognize that the payroll system mentioned earlier will have a top-level edit module, a top-level update module, and a variety of top-level print modules. Having done this much design, *immediately* write the code for those modules, and test them as a Version 1 system. Next, design the second-level modules, those modules a level below the top-level modules just completed. Having designed the second-level modules, next write the code and test a Version 2 system, and so forth.

The conservative approach to top-down implementation consists of designing all the top-level modules, then the next level, then all third-level modules, and so on until the entire design is finished. Then code the top-level modules and implement them as a Version 1. From the experience gained in implementing Version 1, make any necessary changes to the lower levels of design, then code and test at the second level, and on down to the lowest level.

Thus, the radical approach and the conservative approach represent the two extreme points on a spectrum. There are an infinite number of compromise top-down strategies that you can select, depending on your situation. You may decide, for example, to finish 75 percent of the systems analysis and design, and then begin top-down coding and testing of those modules that you have designed. Or you might decide to design 25 percent of the system, and then, with 75 percent of the system still fuzzy, start coding and implementing.

There is no single right answer. I cannot tell you whether the radical approach is better than the conservative approach for all possible projects. However, I *can* identify the primary factors that will help you decide just how radical or conservative you will want to be:

- *User fickleness.* If the user has no idea of what he wants or has a tendency to change his mind, opt for the radical approach. Why waste time designing detailed logic that will be thrown away? On the other hand, if the user knows precisely what he wants, attempt a complete design.

- *Design quality.* Committing oneself to code too early in the project may make it difficult to improve the design later. All other things being equal, we prefer to finish the entire systems analysis and design (see Section 4.3.5 below).

- *Time pressures.* If you are under extreme pressure from users or higher levels of management to produce some tangible output quickly, go for the radical approach. If your deadline is absolutely inflexible, for example, if it is a case of "you bet your job," go for the radical approach. If you are not under much pressure, and if the deadline is flexible, go for the conservative approach.

- *Accurate estimates.* If you are required by your organization to provide accurate, detailed estimates of schedules, manpower, and other resources, then you should opt for the conservative approach. How can you estimate how long it will take to implement the system until you know how many modules it will contain?

All of this makes sense, at least, it *should* make sense. The reason that problems have occurred is that some programmers, managers, and users have interpreted the top-down approach as a religion, and all three parties tend to interpret that religion differently.

To the user community, top-down means that they should have a working system with a perfect design on the second day of the project. The programmers sometimes interpret the religion as an official license to begin writing code on the second day of the project, which unfortunately degenerates into coding without *any* design!

In practice, hardly anyone follows the extreme radical approach described earlier. Most designers instinctively explore at least half of the design before committing themselves to code, even if much of that design is subconscious and undocumented. Unfortunately, many projects do seem to follow the extreme conservative approach, and while it may lead to better technical designs, it fails for two reasons: (a) on a large project, the user is incapable of specifying the details with accuracy; and (b) on a large project, users and top management increasingly are unwilling to accept two or three years of effort by the MIS department with no visible, tangible output. Hence, the movement toward the radical approach.

There are several important things that you as a manager should be cautious about. Don't let the users intimidate you into taking a radical approach in situations in which that approach seems inappropriate. Don't let your project management textbooks convince you to follow the conservative approach in developing the perfect design when you know that the user really is uncertain about what kind of system he wants. Finally, *don't ever* let the programmers bamboozle you into thinking that top-down implementation means that they are automatically at liberty to begin generating code on the first day of the project.

4.3.2 Lack of sufficient machine time

In some of the organizations I have visited, the programmers have complained (sometimes privately, so that the boss wouldn't become irritated) that they get only one test shot a day. In other words, they have to wait twenty-four hours to see the output of any test run that they have submitted. In a few organizations, the programmers complain that they may get as little as one test shot a week.

In addition, the programmers sometimes state that they can't get *any* machine time when they need it. As we observed previously, the top-down approach requires machine availability earlier in the project life cycle than is traditional, causing problems in organizations in which the assumption always is that programmers do not need machine time until a project has been underway for six months.

In most organizations in which this problem has occurred, the programmers have abandoned top-down testing partially or completely, often without even knowing it. Instead of adding only *one* new module to an existing skeleton and testing the system incrementally, the programmers begin adding *all* of the modules at a particular level (for example, all of the second-level edit modules in the payroll system) and testing them *en masse*. In the worst case, the programmers will retreat to the bottom-up approach with which they are more familiar.

So, ensure that your programmers have enough machine time to indulge in the top-down approach, at least for their first few projects, when they occasionally may be tempted to slip back into their old ways.

How *much* machine time should you allocate? Should one expect to use more machine time with the top-down approach than would have been used with the bottom-up approach? The honest answer is that I don't know. You probably will be safe if you allocate roughly as much test time as you would have allocated with your classical bottom-up techniques; and then use the experience of your first few pilot projects (a concept discussed in more detail in Chapter 12) to refine your estimates.

My experience has been that the amount of machine time is somewhat less important than the frequency of test shots. If the programmer knows that he is going to have only one test shot a week, he is tempted to throw all of his modules into the machine at once and hope that they'll all work. On the other hand, if he knows that he'll get two or three test shots a day, he will be more inclined to follow the incremental approach of testing one new module at a time.

One reason for the inability to predict the amount of machine time needed in a top-down project is that very few projects use *only* top-down implementation. Most organizations use top-down implementation, plus structured design, plus structured walkthroughs, and so on. Generally, the result is much less machine time. If your programmers write code with no bugs, then they will need a modest amount of machine time to verify that they have no bugs, but, they will need no debugging time, and they will need no computer time for re-compiling and re-testing their programs.

4.3.3 Lack of hardware for testing

Not getting enough machine time for testing is one problem. Not getting *any* machine time for testing is a qualitatively different problem. The most extreme form of this phenomenon occurs in projects that have no available computer hardware during the system development phase. While this is not a very common problem in large organizations with many years of accumulated MIS experience, it does sometimes happen.

Consider the organization trying to build a large *on-line* system for a department of end-users who currently do their work manually. In order to carry out top-down implementation, the programmers require access to terminals, modems, multiplexors, and communications lines, in addition to the conventional central site hardware. If this is the department's *first* on-line system, the terminals and communications equipment may not exist; and management frequently is reluctant to install the communications equipment until the last possible moment.

The result? Bottom-up development, in one form or another. A great deal of application software will be written and tested in a batch environment, or, at best, in a simulated on-line environment, and an attempt will be made, sometimes on the day before the deadline, to interface all of this software with the newly arrived teleprocessing hardware/software.

The reason for management's reluctance is obvious: The teleprocessing equipment is expensive, and management is concerned that it will be idle for a substantial portion of the development phase of the project. However, my experience has been that the equipment will be idle anyway, while the programmers try to find their bugs. The only question is whether you would prefer to have the equipment installed and idle before the deadline or after the deadline.

Obviously, compromises are possible. If an on-line system eventually will have one thousand terminals, we could expect to carry out a reasonable form of top-down implementation with three or four terminals and one or two communications lines. If certain pieces of hardware simply are *not* available, then simulator software is better than none.

4.3.4 Staffing problems

Some organizations assign a full complement of programmers, designers, and analysts to a programming project on the first day of the project. Sometimes this assignment is the result of contractual and billing procedures, particularly in dealings between a software consulting organization and a separate user organization. Sometimes, however, the problem is more mundane. As a manager, for example, you know that you'll need Fred and Susy in the middle of the project. Unfortunately, if you don't grab them at the beginning of the project, they'll be occupied with something else when you need them. Rather than lose them, you may decide to bring them into your project, even though there is nothing for them to do.

The result of this kind of management decision should be obvious. In an attempt to keep Fred and Susy busy, someone will invent some bottom-level modules and hope that they will be needed later. Fred and Susy then will be sent off to code these modules, and the rest of the team will continue to work on the top part of the system.

Subsequent design work may show that nobody really needs Fred's module after all and that the interface that was specified for Susy's module is completely impractical. That's the risk one runs when combining top-down design with bottom-up design.

Two things should be observed about staffing. First, it often is practical to have several programmer/analysts working on the top portion of the system, even if they function only as coders, reviewers (as in a structured walkthrough, discussed in Chapter 10). Thus, Fred and Susy might be very useful as participants in the top-level design, *more* useful, perhaps, than sending them off to code bottom-level modules that may never be needed.

Second, it is a good idea to complete all, or most, of the system's design before trying to figure out how many Fred's and Susy's will be required to code the individual modules. Thus, the normal problems of staffing and resource planning often provide a strong argument for the conservative top-down approach.

4.3.5 Programmers' fears that changes to low-level modules will propagate up to the top-level modules

Relatively few programmers object to the top-down approach, but those who do frequently mention one major concern: Implementing bottom-level modules late in the project may cause problems in top-level modules that already have been designed, coded, and tested.

This concern usually is exaggerated. Yes, the implementation of bottom-level modules may suggest or even require changes to some of the higher-level modules, but this is usually fairly minor. It is *possible* that the implementation of the last bottom-level module will uncover design flaws that will be propagated throughout the rest of the system, but it's rather unlikely.

If it appears that this may be a serious problem on your project or something that is going to bother your programmers, then opt for the conservative top-down approach. Finish the entire design before writing any code. This way, you'll be able to anticipate almost all of the potential design problems with bottom-level modules.

At the same time, note that this problem is identical to the one frequently observed in a bottom-up project. At the very end of the pilot, when two major subsystems are linked together for the first time, we find that the interface isn't right; subsystem A is passing the wrong kind of data to subsystem B (usually because someone misread or misunderstood the interface documentation). Correcting that interface problem may have a ripple effect all the way down to the bottom-level modules. My experience has been that problems of this sort are *much* worse than the problems discovered in the top-down approach.

Also, remember that many of the problems will come from the user, and this is an argument for using a more radical top-down implementation. There is no point in finishing the entire design and letting the programmers reassure themselves that all of the interfaces are proper and that the design is perfect, only to have half of the entire effort thrown out because the user changed his mind.

4.3.6 The mistake of combining top-down program testing and bottom-up system testing

This problem is characterized by the following kind of dialogue at the beginning of a project:

Boss:	OK, troops, let's break the system into individual programs.
Troops:	Right, boss.
Boss:	Fred, you take program #1. Susy, you take program #2. Charlie, you take program #3. And then I want all of you to use top-down testing, structured programmming, and the rest of that stuff.
Troops:	Right, boss.
Boss:	And when you're done, let's all get back together, and then we'll merge the programs into a system.

As one might expect, this approach has many of the same problems as the original bottom-up approach. Fred, Susy, and Charlie find that their individual programming projects are quite easy, but problems occur when they are reunited. They find that Fred decided to change the interface specifications without telling anyone; Susy's program doesn't work with Charlie's program, and so forth.

In most cases, this problem is the result of a misunderstanding of the top-down concept. Sometimes, it is the result of other problems, such as lack of sufficient computer time.

Depending on the size of the project, this combination of top-down program development and bottom-up systems development may or may not be serious. If Fred, Susy, and Charlie are writing small programs that require only a day's effort, then their systems integration difficulties should be manageable. But if this situation occurs with fifty programmers who each spend a year developing their individual programs, chaos will reign.

4.3.7 Communication problems in multi-team projects

On very large projects, the programming group is usually broken into smaller teams, each being responsible for a program, or a subsystem, or some other unit of work. At that point, Mealy's Law* takes over: The eventual structure of the system reflects the structure of the

---

*So named after George Mealy, one of the architects of IBM's OS/360.

organization that builds the system. For example, if two teams have difficulty communicating with each other because of personality clashes or political problems, then their subsystems probably will have difficulty communicating.

In particular, each team tends to isolate itself from other teams. Early integration of the top-level skeleton of one team's subsystem with the top-level skeleton of another team's subsystem often is regarded as a hassle, and both teams avoid it. As a result, they use the approach discussed in the previous section: top-down program development and bottom-up systems integration.

Why is it a hassle interfacing two subsystems at an early stage? Because the interfaces are fuzzy! Team A hasn't defined precisely what data it requires from team B, and as a result, it's difficult to put the two subsystems into the machine and make them communicate. But that is exactly what the top-down approach is trying to accomplish: *forcing* the precise definition of major interfaces and forcing those interfaces to be coded and exercised in a computer to ensure that they work.

In other words, you should *expect* problems in this area. The larger your project, the more problems there will be. Rather than avoiding the problems, you should confront them directly. This is what the top-down approach is all about.

4.3.8 Difficulty visualizing top-down versions

Visualizing systems versions proves to be a common and serious problem. Many people, particularly programmers, have a confused notion of the sequence of implementation in a top-down project.

In our example of a payroll system, many programmers think that top-down implementation means the following: Version 1 of the system will do all of the editing, but nothing else; Version 2 will combine all of the editing and all of the update logic (and thus all of the salary computations, tax calculations, and so forth); Version 3 will combine the editing, the update logic, and the sorting; and Version 4 will throw in the printing.

It is puzzling that some programmers have had such difficulty visualizing a skeleton version of a *complete* system, for example, visualizing a payroll system that incorporates the top-level logic of the edit, the update, and the printing. Regardless of why, this problem does occur and should be watched.

4.3.9 Difficulty getting the user involved

One of the major objectives of top-down testing is to involve the user in the early skeleton versions of the system. If something is wrong with the system from the user's point of view, it is better to discover the problem as early as possible. Unfortunately, sometimes the user is too busy to participate in early versions of the system. He may say, in effect "Leave me alone! I'm swamped with work — that's why I need a new system! Don't talk to me until you've got the entire system finished!"

Such a user deserves what he gets, just as a customer who refuses to look at a custom-built house until it's finished deserves what he gets. Unfortunately, the MIS project manager (or the architect) often is blamed even if the customer is wrong.

The moral: Make an extra effort to involve your user in early versions of your system, even if he thinks that it's a waste of time. He'll thank you for it later.

4.3.10 Unwillingness to renegotiate schedules and budgets

It's likely that when the user sees Version 1 of his new MIS system, he will want major changes. He may decide that certain processing capabilities that he never mentioned in the functional specification are now essential. Features that he previously considered essential now are deemed useless. Still other features of the system may be modified drastically.

Thus, it's likely to be a whole new ball game. When Version 2 of his system is demonstrated to the user, the game may change again. Indeed, each version of a top-down system may bring changes to the specification.

Unfortunately, the user, as well as the MIS project manager, sometimes fails to appreciate that these changes require a re-evaluation of the timetable, the manpower staffing plan, and the budget for the project. Further, the user may be reluctant to agree to any changes in the project schedule or budget. "Why, these are just small changes," he'll say. "You should be able to work these into the system without any real fuss or bother." Or, if he's clever, your user may say to you, "I thought all this top-down development stuff was supposed to make it easier for me to get what I want, and easier to make changes. Now you're telling me that you can't make any changes!"

In fact, you *can* accommodate minor changes to the original specifications without changing the schedule or budget, the increased productivity associated with the structured techniques helps you in that respect. But if it's a major change that the user wants, it's obvious that something will have to give.

More important, it's a mistake to let the user think that he can arbitrarily change the specifications for his system without having to worry about the additional time and money it may cost. So you should go through the negotiation process even if you can accommodate the change with no extra work.

Bibliography

1. Baker, F.T. "Chief Programmer Team Management of Production Programming." *IBM Systems Journal,* Vol. 11, No. 1 (January 1972), pp. 56 - 73.

    This classic article on the so-called New York Times System gives an illustration of top-down design as well as of several other important structured techniques.

2. Dahl, O.J., E.W. Dijkstra, and C.A.R. Hoare. *Structured Programming.* Englewood Cliffs: Prentice-Hall, 1972.

    Another formal, scholarly view of top-down design.

3. Dijkstra, E. "Structured Programming." *Software Engineering, Concepts and Techniques.* eds. J.M. Buxton, P. Naur, and B. Randell. New York: Petrocelli/Charter, 1976.

    One of the first discussions to refer to top-down design as levels of abstraction.

4. McGowan, C.L., and J.R. Kelly. *Top-Down Structured Programming.* New York: Petrocelli/Charter, 1975.

    A discussion of structured programming and top-down design, discussed primarily in terms of PL/I.

5. Mills, H.D. "Top-Down Programming in Large Systems." *Debugging Techniques in Large Systems.* Englewood Cliffs: Prentice-Hall, 1971.

    Mills is one of IBM's foremost advocates of top-down design, top-down implementation, and other related structured techniques.

6. Wirth, N. *Systematic Programming.* Englewood Cliffs: Prentice-Hall, 1973.

    A more theoretical and academic view of the "stepwise refinement" (Wirth's phrase for top-down design) process by one of the world's leading computer science scholars.

7. Yourdon, E. *Techniques of Program Structure and Design.* Englewood Cliffs: Prentice-Hall, 1975.

    Chapter 2 of this book discusses the top-down approach, in terms meant to be understood by programmers, designers, and analysts.

8. _____, and L.L. Constantine. *Structured Design: Fundamentals of a Discipline of Computer Program and Systems Design.* Englewood Cliffs: Prentice-Hall, 1979.

    Chapter 20 discusses top-down implementation in great detail.

Chapter Five:

Structured Design

Having discussed top-down design, we now turn to a related topic: structured design. As in Chapter 4, we begin with an overview of the technical concepts of structured design, followed by a discussion of the problems you are likely to experience in attempting to implement structured design in your organization.

5.1 An overview of structured design

The term *structured design* was introduced by IBM in an article in the *IBM Systems Journal* in 1974.* Prior to that article, the various concepts discussed in this chapter were referred to as *modular design*, *logical design*, *composite design*, or the *design of program structure*.

That last phrase best describes the idea. What concerns us here is the architecture, organization, and structure of computer programs and of systems of programs. Structure is a concept that people have talked about for years, but have only recently formalized. The references at the end of this chapter constitute most of the major writing on the subject. Note that all of the articles have been published since 1974.

Structured design is not the same as top-down design. Solving a large, complex problem using top-down design generally is preferable to employing bottom-up design, random design, or no design. However, it does not guarantee creation of a good design. In fact, we quite easily can design a terrible system in a top-down fashion. A good system, in the context of this discussion, is easy to implement, easy to debug, and

---

*Stevens, W.G., G.J. Myers, and L.L. Constantine, "Structured Design," *IBM Systems Journal,* Vol. 13, No. 2 (May 1974), pp. 115-39.

easy to maintain. A terrible system is one that, for some reason or another, is expensive to develop and maintain.

This really should not come as a surprise. As stated in Chapter 4, top-down design does not actually tell us *how* to break a large system into smaller pieces. In addition, it does not indicate what kind of inter-module interfaces are preferable. In general, it lacks the formal guidelines that enable us to design systems so that we can debug, maintain, or modify one module without having to know anything about other modules and certainly without having to modify the code in any other modules.

This is not to suggest that top-down design is *bad*. Indeed, some people have designed very good systems using nothing more than the informal guidelines of top-down design. There are two reasons for their success: First, top-down design certainly is preferable to using *no* design, which is the common situation in many organizations today; and second, some programmers and designers instinctively produce a *good* top-down design, without realizing that they have done so.

Structured design can be thought of as a collection of five related concepts, two of which are discussed in other chapters of this book, as noted:

- *Documentation techniques* — graphic tools that emphasize the structural, or hierarchical, aspects of a system rather than the procedural (loops and decisions) aspects. These tools, including HIPO and structure charts, are discussed in Chapter 7.

- *Evaluation criteria* — guidelines that help us distinguish between good and bad systems at the modular level

- *Heuristics* — rules of thumb, which are useful when evaluating the "goodness" of a particular design, but which certainly should not be followed religiously

- *Design strategies* — strategies that allow us to systematically derive good solutions to common types of data processing problems; top-down design could be thought of as one such strategy, although it usually is considered less useful than some of the other available ones

- *Implementation strategies* — plans that dictate the order in which to code and implement modules, including bottom-up implementation

We do not have the opportunity in this book to discuss all of the technical theory, heuristics, and design strategies in detail; consult the references at the end of the chapter for more information. However, we can illustrate the philosophy behind structured design with a short example and then briefly define some of the technical concepts.

Put yourself in the position of a management consultant. Suppose that you were asked to render an opinion of a company with an organizational chart as shown in Figure 5.1. Most likely, you would comment that Vice-President A, Manager X, and Manager Y all have trivial jobs, since their responsibility seems to consist solely of managing one subordinate. Being a cynic, you probably would suggest that all of the work in that department is being done by Worker Z and that all of the managers should be fired!

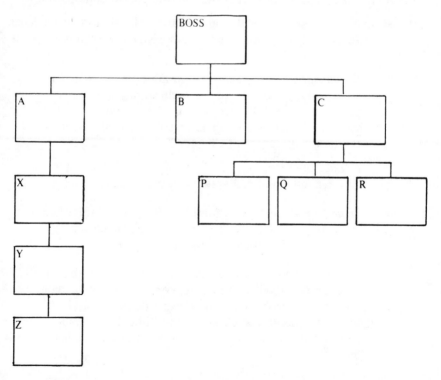

Figure 5.1. Representation of organizational chart for Company 1.

Similarly, suppose you were asked to evaluate a company having an organizational chart like that in Figure 5.2. Chances are that you would predict trouble: The boss is a prime candidate for a heart attack; at the very least, one would expect him to make mistakes, simply because he manages too many people.

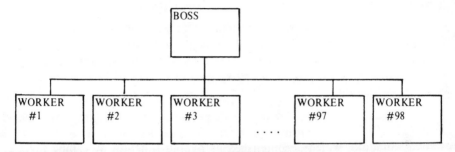

Figure 5.2. Representation of organizational chart for Company 2.

Finally, suppose you saw the organizational chart in Figure 5.3. Each manager supervises an appropriate number of immediate subordinates — a reasonable span of control — and the entire organization seems properly balanced. While there may be other problems in this company, at least the architecture indicated by the organizational chart is realistic.

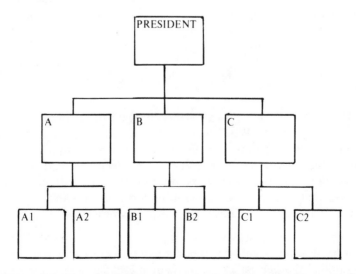

Figure 5.3. Representation of organizational chart for Company 3.

Of course, all good companies do not require exactly three vice-presidents, nor perfect symmetry. Just because Vice-President A has two immediate subordinates, we do not suggest that Vice-President B also must have two immediate subordinates. But, Figures 5.1 and 5.2 show evidence of structural problems and Figure 5.3 does *not* show similar evidence.

Program structures and system structures can be discussed in a similar way. Figures 5.1, 5.2, and 5.3 might well be structural representations of three different programs or three different systems, since the distinction between programs and systems is largely artificial at this level of abstraction.

Thus, we can make some *structural* criticism of the program/system shown in Figure 5.1. It consists of a top-level "executive" module, which accomplishes its overall function by calling upon three "vice-president" modules. Our concern, of course, is with module A: From Figure 5.1, we suspect that it consists of a single instruction, a subroutine call to module X. Similarly, we deduce that module X contains only one instruction: a call to subroutine Y. Also, we conclude that module Y is a one-instruction module that does nothing but call module Z. Hence, module Z is where all the work is being done.

These deductions must be kept in a certain perspective. Although we suspect that modules A, X, and Y are trivial, we don't know their importance unless we look at the code. Also, we recognize that there is nothing disastrously wrong with a series of one-instruction subroutines doing nothing but calling a lower-level module. It's just that such a structure is . . . well, what should we call it? trivial? bureaucratic? inefficient? In short, there probably is a better alternative to Figure 5.1.

Obviously, Figure 5.2 represents the opposite extreme: an excessive span of control. We should be concerned about it in a software environment for the same reason that it concerns us in a management environment: extreme complexity. Our executive module probably has too many loops and decisions and too much management logic, in the sense that it cannot be properly understood by either the maintenance programmer or the development programmer.

What we have just illustrated is a heuristic — a rule of thumb that should be used as a guideline, but not interpreted as a religious rule. For example, the heuristic seen in Figures 5.1, 5.2, and 5.3 is known as span of control, a phrase borrowed from the management field. Other concepts of structured design are the following:

- *Coupling* — a description of the strength of association between different modules in a system; in other words, coupling is a name for a generally bad characteristic of a system. My former colleague Larry Constantine describes coupling as the taffy that sticks modules together, so that an innocent attempt to modify or debug one module might result in the programmer tangling with another module. We can identify design practices that increase coupling between modules (bad news), as well as those that decrease the coupling between modules (good news).

- *Cohesion* — a term borrowed from sociology and social psychology, describing the strength of association of the elements *inside* a module, the philosophy being that the elements of a module all should be strongly associated (highly cohesive) and all involved in performing the same task. On a more practical level, cohesion is a way of talking about the rationale that programmers use to form modules. We can identify several useful levels of cohesion, some of which are good and others bad. The ultimate objective of cohesion is to show programmers how to form good modules, all of whose instructions are essential to the performance of one, and only one, task.

- *Pathological connection* — one of the strongest forms of coupling between modules, occurring when one module refers to the "insides" of another module. Pathological connections can be avoided if a subroutine executes only when it is called formally by a superordinate; the subroutine operates only on data given to it by its superordinate; the subroutine receives only those data essential to the performance of its task; and the subroutine delivers all of its outputs, or results, to its superordinate.

- *Transform-centered design* — one of several design strategies that helps the designer/programmer to systematically derive good solutions to common types of applications. Transform-centered design requires the designer to study the flow of data through the system as the basis for determining which modules will be required and how they will be organized hierarchically. Other design strategies, such as those proposed by J.

D. Warnier, K. T. Orr, and M. Jackson,* require the designer to study the structure of the input and output data to determine the program structure.

- *Packaging* — a term useful for describing the decisions that the designer ultimately must make to shoe-horn his logical modules into the physical environment provided by the computer hardware, the vendor's operating system, and the programming language. An important precept of structured design is that packaging should be delayed for as long as possible, partly because it obscures the basic nature of the design problem, and partly because it leads to gross inefficiencies if completed too early.

5.2 Management problems with structured design

Since I have provided only the briefest overview of structured design, I strongly suggest that you provide your designer/programmers with much more detailed information before you realistically can expect them to put the idea into practice.[†]

Even with a reasonable amount of training and study, designer/programmers may experience some problems with their first few attempts to use structured design; fortunately, this is becoming less of a problem because 75 percent of the MIS organizations in the United States now are using some form of structured design, and most colleges are teaching structured design to computer science students. The most common problems seem to be as follows:

1. Designer's inability to grasp abstract design philosophies and concepts

2. Conflicts between the old classical design philosophies and the new structured philosophies

3. Difficulty enforcing formal design disciplines within small or medium-sized projects

---

*See the references listed at the end of the chapter.
[†]Edward Yourdon and Larry L. Constantine, *Structured Design: Fundamentals of a Discipline of Computer Program and Systems Design* (Englewood Cliffs: Prentice-Hall, 1979).

4.   Complaints of inefficiency

5.   Difficulty defining the proper roles of analyst, designer, and programmer.

Each of these problems is discussed in a subsection below.

5.2.1 Designer's problems grasping abstract design philosophies

The overview presented earlier in this chapter may have made structured design seem like a simple concept. Don't be fooled: Many of your programmers and designers will find the discipline quite difficult to comprehend. Perhaps this is as it should be: Design *is* hard, and it never will be trivial to design a large system.

Nevertheless, structured design techniques do work, and they can be used by those possessing a reasonable degree of intelligence. This requirement may pose a management problem, however: You may find that using structured design requires more talented people than those currently doing your design.

This comment is not meant to be snide or cynical. I have no intention of insulting you or your staff. My comment is based on observing several thousand programmers, designers, and analysts to whom I have tried to teach top-down design, structured design, and structured programming. Most grasp top-down design and structured programming without too much trouble, but for many, the concept of structured design is incomprehensible.

Part of the problem may be the terminology. Structured design introduces the terms *cohesion, coupling, pathological connections, heuristics,* and *transform-centered design,* for example. A more thorough discussion of the subject would add more buzz-words: afferent and efferent modules, and temporally and procedurally cohesive modules, among others. Perhaps, for this reason, we should not be surprised to see designers despair and walk away from structured design!

The terminology poses a dilemma: On the one hand, we don't want to introduce buzzwords in a field already overloaded with them. On the other hand, we *do* need words to describe technical aspects of computer systems design never described before, and we do not want to use words that have vendor-dependent meanings (for example, the word "task" means something different depending on the programming language, operating system, and hardware used). In fact, most of the buzzwords in structured design are not new, but rather have been borrowed from other fields.

Apologies aside, we do expect computer people to have a basic vocabulary. Unfortunately, this assumption may be erroneous for, during the course of a training session, a substantial number of designers have asked me, "By the way, what's a heuristic? I've never heard of the word." Providing all programmers and designers with a dictionary definition of the word heuristic, or simply substituting *rule of thumb* or *guideline*, still would not solve the problem. Why? Primarily because most programmers and designers feel an incredible urge to define everything in terms of sacred principles. Even a simple guideline, like span of control, becomes a religious rule.

Indeed, some MIS organizations insist that all programs have the kind of symmetrical structure shown in Figure 5.3. Thus, the designers in such situations are told that every system *must* contain one top-level module; that it *must* have exactly three second-level modules, whose names will be input, process, and output; that if the input second-level module has two immediate subordinates beneath it, then the process and output modules also must have two immediate subordinates.

In the same fashion, we find designers who interpret the concepts of coupling, cohesion, pathological connections, and transform-centered design in terms of ultimate good and evil. Hence, modules with low cohesion must be evil, and those with high cohesion must be good. Pathological connections must be bad, and so forth.

The only advice is the obvious: Hire intelligent people, who will read the available literature on the subject. Send them to conferences, symposia, workshops, or training sessions to learn the techniques. Make them trade ideas with their colleagues, and teach them that structured design is common sense, not a new religion.

5.2.2 Conflicts between design philosophies

Even if your programmers understand structured design, your organization probably has design standards that seriously conflict with the structured design philosophies. For example, some companies have outlawed the use of subroutine calls, PERFORM statements, CALL statements, procedure calls, and BALR instructions in IBM assembly language. Clearly, structured design is difficult to institute with these strictures.

More commonly, problems arise in applying the concepts of cohesion, packaging, and pathological connections. The organizational standards may dictate, for example, that every program have a "general-purpose edit module" and a "general-purpose error routine." While the standards obviously are well-intentioned, structured design would argue against such modules because they represent classic examples of "logical cohesion."* Similarly, the organizational standards may require the programmer to develop a "master-file-control" module for his program, that is, a module that, depending on the nature of a flag passed to it, either will open, close, read, or carry out any of a number of other similar functions on the master file. Structured design would reject that standard, too, on the ground that the module represents a classic example of "communicational cohesion."†

As a manager, be aware that many such standards were created at least five to ten years ago, often for the sake of machine efficiency, a consideration that is largely irrelevant today (see Section 5.2.4). So, what should you do? Be prepared for some conflicts and scrap some of your obsolete standards.

5.2.3 Difficulty enforcing structured design on small projects

After trying it once or twice, your designers no doubt will tell you that a proper application of cohesion, coupling, transform-centered design, and all the rest of structured design *takes a lot of time.*

To appreciate this, imagine how your designers would react if you asked them to develop a simple sequential file update program of two- or three-hundred COBOL statements. Now suppose that you have decided to enforce the following "religious rules" of structured design:

1. The update program must be broken into modules, no one of which can be longer than one page of a listing.

2. All modules must be invoked with a CALL statement. PERFORM statements are not allowed.

3. No module is allowed to "remember" anything from one execution to the next. This means do not use "first-time" switches, or internal state maintenance.

---

*A logically cohesive module contains many similar functions, which is quite different from a module that performs one function. The concern is that the code for those similar functions may become so intertwined that a subsequent attempt to modify one of the functions inadvertently will damage or destroy another function in the same module.

†Communicational cohesion occurs when all elements of one module process the same input and/or produce the same output.

4. No manager module is allowed to do any work; that is, any module that is not at the bottom of the hierarchy must consist only of CALL statements imbedded within loops and decisions.

Actually, these rules are quite reasonable for medium-sized and large projects, but you can imagine how your designers and programmers would squawk if you imposed such rules on a two-hundred-statement COBOL application.

Obviously, only you or the standards department can decide how formal you want to be. If your programmers work individually on small programs that require only a day or two of work, then some of the principles of structured design may be useful, but I wouldn't address the formality. For medium-sized projects requiring two or three programmers for a few months, some of the formality of structured design is appropriate. On big projects, one should be a fanatic.

Be careful of one thing: Programming projects may *appear* to be one-person projects, when in fact they are small pieces of a large, integrated system. Many organizations for years have believed in the theory that a big system can be broken into small pieces, each of which can be coded by individual programmers as if each comprised an independent project. While that theory is absolutely valid, we must recognize that the principles of structured design dictate *how* to break a system into small independent pieces (modules) such that they later can be integrated successfully into a whole system.

Also, consider that the maintenance costs of numerous small programs eventually will add up. Even if it does take considerably longer to develop a small program with the formality of structured design, it may be worth the effort in terms of easier maintenance.

5.2.4 Complaints of inefficiency

Many programmers and managers still think in second-generation terms, when every microsecond was important and each byte of memory was to be cherished as a precious national resource. To such people, certain aspects of structured design may be anathema. For instance, the extensive use of subroutines suggests some inefficiency; the emphasis on highly cohesive modules points to even more inefficiency; and the guideline that data be passed through a parameter list instead of being placed in a globally accessible area usually raises howls of anguish from programmers, designers, and managers alike.

Efficiency is essential in some cases, as in real-time systems or in systems with high volumes of processing; and clearly nobody wants a grossly inefficient system. Nevertheless, we usually can argue that most of the hue and cry about efficiency is irrelevant in today's computer systems.

As a manager, keep the following points regarding efficiency in mind:

1. In most cases, neither you nor the computer operations manager knows whether or not your computer systems are efficient. More significantly, nobody really cares. If your programmer writes a program that consumes one minute of machine time, for example, does anybody know whether it could have been written so as to consume only thirty seconds of CPU time? Does anybody care?

2. Efficiency seems to be influenced more by the quality of the programmer than by any specific techniques of structured design. Recall the Sackman experiment described in Chapter 2: Picking a capable programmer can improve the efficiency of your systems by a factor of ten.

3. Most informal surveys have suggested that diligent use of structured design adds an overhead of about 10 percent to the CPU time and memory requirements of a program. (The reason we refer to surveys as informal is that few people have attempted the kind of study that Sackman undertook. Indeed, to determine the precise cost of structured design, we would need to have a pair of identical twins with identical training work on the same problem — one twin using structured design techniques and the other using the classical approach. In truth, I am not aware of any such experiment, although I would be happy to organize one if any identical twins would like to volunteer!)

4. A number of studies have confirmed that the "90-10" rule applies to programs, too. That is, 10 percent of the code in a typical system will consume 90 percent of the CPU time. Knuth showed in a study published in

Software — Practice and Experience that 5 percent of the code consumed 50 percent of the total CPU time.†
Since only a small portion of the code is significant in terms of efficiency, the strategy should be to get the system working, then isolate the inefficient parts, and optimize it.

5. In general, it is easier to make a working system efficient than it is to make an efficient system correct. Get the system to operate first. *Then* worry about efficiency.

6. Programmers are notoriously poor at anticipating in advance *which* 5 percent of their code will be inefficient. They frequently blame their efficiency problems on the part of the system they found most difficult to design and code, but the problem usually turns out to be an innocent-looking module that is chewing up 75 percent of the CPU time.

5.2.5 *Difficulty defining the proper roles of systems analyst, designer, and programmer*

An unfortunate side effect of using structured design is the identification of an organizational problem in many data processing departments: Systems analysts spend most of their time talking to the user, and only occasionally do a little design. Programmers spend most of their time writing COBOL statements, and occasionally do a little design. As a result, nobody does any serious design and the question of who should learn structured design is unresolved.

Both groups should learn structured design, since it is applicable to systems analysis (more on this in Chapter 15), systems design, and program design.

In addition, organizations should create a new MIS position called the "systems architect." The reasons are that a vacuum exists in the design area of most companies, and a majority of the analysts and programmers I meet are incompetent to fill the design role without serious changes in the way they perform their jobs.

---

† D.E. Knuth, "An Empirical Study of FORTRAN Programs," *Software — Practice and Experience*, Vol. 1, No. 2 (April - June 1971), pp. 105 - 133.

This is particularly true of systems analysts, many of whom have achieved their current positions after years in the user area of the organization. Thus, while they may be competent in describing the user's business and problem (a crucially valuable skill, to be sure), they don't know a computer from a football and it shows in their designs.

Other systems analysts may have worked during the formative years of their career on second-generation machines like the IBM 1401; consequently, they design systems as if they still were working on an IBM 1401. This group, in particular, is guilty of premature packaging, chopping a system into distinct programs at the beginning of the project and dictating that all information will be passed from program to program via magnetic tape files — sometimes in the disguised form of sequential disk files. All of this, naturally, is intended for a sixteen megabyte IBM 3081, capable of holding all of the code in memory at once, and of passing all data from module to module through core memory.

Meanwhile, the programmers in many organizations have never had the opportunity (or perhaps never shown the talent) to carry out any real *design*. They expect to be given a complete design, from which they happily can figure out which assortment of COBOL statements will most befuddle the unfortunate maintenance programmer.

Considering these problems, perhaps we do need a new breed of person in our organization. It is probable that we should distinguish between "business systems design" (talking to the user to find out what he wants), "computer systems design" (determining the structure of modules that will solve a well-specified problem), and "programming" (carrying out the detailed procedural design of each module).

Bibliography

1. Dijkstra, E. *A Discipline of Programming.* Englewood Cliffs: Prentice-Hall, 1976.

2. Jackson, M. *Principles of Program Design.* New York: Academic Press, 1975.

3. Myers, G.J. *Reliable Software Through Composite Design.* New York: Petrocelli/Charter, 1975.

4. Orr, K.T. *Structured Systems Development.* New York: YOURDON Press, 1977.

5. Stevens, W.G., G.J. Myers, and L.L. Constantine. "Structured Design." *IBM Systems Journal,* Vol. 13, No. 2 (May 1974), pp. 115 - 139.

6. Warnier, J.D. *The Logical Construction of Programs.* New York: Van Nostrand Reinhold, 1976.

7. Wirth, N. *Algorithms + Data Structures = Programs.* Englewood Cliffs: Prentice-Hall, 1976.

8. Yourdon, E., and L.L. Constantine. *Structured Design: Fundamentals of a Discipline of Computer Program and Systems Design.* Englewood Cliffs: Prentice-Hall, 1979.

9. Page-Jones, M. *The Practical Guide to Structured Systems Design.* New York: YOURDON Press, 1980.

Chapter Six:

Structured Programming

Having addressed top-down design and structured design in the two preceding chapters, we now turn to programming, specifically, to structured programming, the technique often regarded as the first of the structured techniques.

In keeping with the format of previous chapters, we begin with a brief technical overview of structured programming. Most of this chapter's discussion, however, deals with the problems you are likely to have in implementing structured programming within your organization.

6.1 An overview of structured programming

The term structured programming was coined by Professor Edsger Dijkstra in the mid-1960's, and first came to the attention of a significant number of people at a NATO Software Engineering conference in 1968.* Since then, the topic has been widely studied and discussed in academic circles. Indeed, most of the better university schools of computer science teach structured programming as the data processing students' first exposure to programming.

The concept of structured programming was adopted early by certain sectors of industry as well. IBM, after being exposed to structured programming at that same 1968 NATO conference, introduced the technique on an experimental basis on a project that has come to be known as the New York Times system.* Finding it a tremendously suc-

---

*E. Dijkstra, "Structured Programming," *Software Engineering, Concepts and Techniques,* eds. J.M. Buxton, P. Naur, and B. Randell (New York: Petrocelli/Charter, 1976), pp. 222-26. See also *Classics in Software Engineering,* ed. Edward Yourdon (New York: YOURDON Press, 1979).
*See the reference at the end of this chapter to the article by F.T. Baker.

cessful technique, IBM adopted it throughout its own organization and then introduced it to its many customers. Indeed, IBM's influence may well be one of the major reasons why you are reading this book.

So, what *is* structured programming? From a technical point of view, it could be described as the theoretical basis for all procedural logic, that is, for the kind of logic that we have described traditionally with a flowchart. In the mid-1960's, two Italian computer scientists, Corrado Bohm and Guissepe Jacopini, proved mathematically that any procedural logic, that is, any flowchart, could be derived from combinations of three basic kinds of flowcharts.[†] (See Figure 6.1.)

These three flowcharts form the core of structured programming. They are popularly referred to as *sequence*, IF-THEN-ELSE, and DO-WHILE. Some cynics dub them the holy trinity of structured programming. The discovery that these three are sufficient for any arbitrarily complex logic structure is profoundly important, just as important as was the engineer's discovery that any form of hardware logic can be constructed from combinations of AND, OR, and NOT gates.

Not only are the three flowchart elements in Figure 6.1 simple, but they also have the desirable property of being black-box in nature. That is, they all are characterized by having a single entry point and a single exit point. This feature, too, is profoundly important: It means that we can take any program's flowchart that has been constructed from the three basic forms and examine any part of it as a stand-alone black-box. In contrast, conventional flowcharts wander from page to page to such a degree that neither the development programmer nor the maintenance programmer has the faintest idea of what the logic is supposed to accomplish.

Note that our discussion thus far has been in terms of flowcharts, a documentation tool that, as discussed in Chapter 7, has been abandoned in most organizations. Part of the reason for leading into our discussion of structured programming in this way is that flowcharts are clean and simple: They're language-independent and vendor-independent. In addition, structured programming was developed in this order. The Bohm and Jacopini paper that provided the theoretical basis for structured programming used flowcharts, rather than a specific programming language.

[†]C. Bohm and G. Jacopini, "Flow Diagrams, Turing Machines and Languages with Only Two Formation Rules," *Communications of the ACM,* Vol. 9, No. 5 (May 1966), pp. 366-71. See also *Classics in Structured Programming,* op. cit.

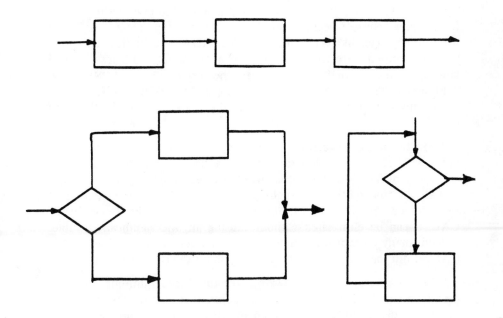

Figure 6.1. Three flowcharts of structured programming.

However, most of our programmers *do* use specific programming languages — COBOL, FORTRAN, PL/I, PASCAL, and a vast number of lesser dialects (ADA, APL, RPG, BASIC, SNOBOL, LISP, and on and on). So, our next question is: What does structured programming mean in terms of specific programming languages?

Quite simply, it means that we should write instructions that are direct implementations of the flowcharts shown in Figure 6.1. Obviously, since all programming languages have a variety of simple instructions which can be arranged in a linear sequence, following that guideline should be no problem.

All programming languages also have some facility for making binary decisions, although not all make it easy to program the kind of decision structure shown in Figure 6.1, in which control returns to a common point. What we need is a language that implements the IF-THEN-ELSE construct. Since we want the ability to build combinations of these structures, we also want a programming language that also allows us to code *nested* IF-THEN-ELSE structures.

Finally, we want our programming language to give us the facility for forming loops, especially simple loops of the type shown in Figure 6.1. In languages like ALGOL, PASCAL, ADA, and PL/I, such a loop is implemented directly with the verb DO-WHILE. In less formal languages like COBOL, we can use the verbs PERFORM-UNTIL and PERFORM-VARYING. In primitive languages like FORTRAN, we are given only the special "iterative" loop, the well-known FORTRAN DO loop.*

In the more powerful programming languages, we find all of the verbs with which to implement the flowcharts of Figure 6.1. As Bohm and Jacopini have demonstrated, we don't need anything else. In particular, the unconditional branching instruction — the GOTO statement — becomes superfluous. In languages like ALGOL, PL/I, and PASCAL, it can be eliminated without causing anyone significant trouble. Indeed, many current introductory university courses in PL/I and PASCAL do not teach the students anything about the GOTO statement.

As you may be well aware, structured programming often is described simply in terms of this last point, that is GOTO-less programming. As discussed later in this chapter, most of the controversy pertaining to the use of structured programming has revolved around the lowly GOTO statement.

To understand why there has been such sentiment against GOTO statements, put yourself in the position of a maintenance programmer for a moment. Imagine that it's 3 A.M., and you're sound asleep in your warm, comfortable bed. Suddenly, the phone rings; it's the computer operator telling you that the WIDGET system has just crashed in the middle of a four-hour production run. The president of the company has insisted that the output from the WIDGET system be on his desk by 9 in the morning, so you've got to come into work to fix the bug.

Let's further imagine that you did not write the WIDGET system; it was written by Charlie, who moved to Afghanistan as soon as the system appeared to be working. You were assigned the job of maintaining the WIDGET system, and your basic philosophy has been to leave well enough alone. As a result, you're unfamiliar with the code.

---

* — unless one is using a "modernized" version of the language based on the FORTRAN 77 standards.

Having staggered to work, you've made it very clear to everyone present that you are interested only in finding and fixing the bug, and then returning to your warm, comfortable bed as quickly as possible. This is not the time to get to know the WIDGET system on an intimate basis, and it surely is not the time to carry on long discussions about structured anything.

Let us assume that the computer operator has given you enough information for you to determine that the system aborted in an area that corresponds to page 123 of the program listing. Turning to page 123, you find the following code before you:

```
SUBROUTINE GLOP
      MOVE A TO B
      X = X + 1
      CALL FOO (A,B)
      GO TO AFGHANISTAN
      .

      .

      .
```

Of course, your first questions are, what does GLOP do? What is its purpose? The ideal situation would be to find that page 123 of the program listing marks the beginning of some recognizable *function*, for example, computing an employee's gross salary, or converting a BCD character string to an ASCII character string, that would have been finished by the time we reached the bottom of page 123. But such is probably not the case with SUBROUTINE GLOP.

Undaunted, you begin reading the code (note that, in order to avoid offending anyone, or perhaps to offend everyone equally, I've included code that is a mixture of COBOL, FORTRAN, and PL/I). The first statement, as you can see, causes the contents of a variable named A to be moved to a variable named B. That seems simple enough, and you might be inclined to shrug your shoulders and move on to consider the next instruction.

However, there are some important things to understand about that MOVE statement: First, you have unconsciously assumed that the MOVE statement will do what it's supposed to do. If you were a paranoid maintenance programmer, you might doublecheck to ensure that the compiler generated the proper object code for that MOVE statement; and if you were very paranoid, you might even check the hardware to ensure that it was executing the assembly language instructions properly.

But chances are, you aren't that paranoid. Besides, it's now 3:30 in the morning, and all you want to do is find the bug and go home. From the evidence that the computer operator gave you, you suspect that the bug is somewhere in the logic on page 123, and there is no reason to descend to the lower levels of assembly or machine language unless you must.

So, once again, you probably are ready to read on past the MOVE statement. But wait. We have two more things to say about that innocent MOVE: Note that after MOVEing, the computer goes on to the next instruction. Trivial as this point may seem, *that* is what we depend on in order to be able to ignore the details of the assembly language code that actually carry out the instructions of the MOVE statement.

Also, note that you could and probably *should* do some investigating of the MOVE statement. It is reasonable to ask: *Why* are we moving A to B? Why are we doing it now? What is the purpose, the rationale, behind using that instruction? Why did Charlie code it?

Assuming that you could answer these questions, you then might examine the next statement. Evidently, the statement increments a variable X by one. Aside from that, it has the same desirable properties as the MOVE statement: Its details can be ignored for the present time. Assume that the instruction can function correctly for the moment, and that, having incremented X by one, the computer will move on to the next instruction.

That instruction, which is a bit more interesting, reads CALL FOO (A,B). Unfortunately, it is not clear what is happening, other than the obvious fact that a subroutine named FOO is being invoked and two parameters, A and B, are being passed to it.

At this point, you might be strongly tempted to search through the program listing to find out what FOO is doing. Wrong. To become involved in the details of the subroutine is to destroy much of what we have wanted to accomplish by applying the concepts of top-down design, structured design, and structured programming.

The point is that FOO probably carries out some kind of *function*, although its exact nature certainly is not clear from its name. Let us assume, though, that Charlie left a minimal amount of documentation behind, and that you, as the maintenance programmer, are able to discover quickly (without finding FOO in the program listing) that the purpose of FOO is to compute the square root of its first argument, and return the answer in the second argument.

That's all we need to know. At this point, we should *assume* that FOO computes square roots correctly, *just as we assumed that the MOVE statement works correctly*. If you ultimately are unable to find the bug on page 123, only then can you justifiably explore the logic of FOO. In the meantime, it's long past 3 in the morning and common sense dictates that you restrict your attention *solely* to the logic on page 123.

Note that, as with the MOVE statement, you should ask some intelligent questions concerning FOO, namely: Why compute a square root at this point? Does it make sense to compute the square root of A? Do I really want to store the answer in B? Indeed, answering these questions might uncover the bug on page 123, and this approach is the kind of top-down debugging that we wish to emphasize.

Having laid the groundwork, you now can see why the GOTO statement is such a disaster. Immediately after the CALL FOO statement, which you *assumed* would return, you see a statement that says

GO TO AFGHANISTAN

Ho! ho! Probably the last statement Charlie wrote before he departed, but at 3 or 4 in the morning, the humor is not amusing. Instead of laughing, you find yourself asking the following pertinent questions:

1. Where is AFGHANISTAN located in the 800-page program listing?

2. Why are we going to AFGHANISTAN?

3. What are we going to do when we get to AFGHANISTAN?

4. Will we ever get back to the code on page 123?

Unfortunately, these questions *cannot* be avoided. It may well be that the instructions at AFGHANISTAN are only minor details, but there is no way to know that, and no way to avoid finding out, as you were able to do with the FOO subroutine.

Thus, you must track down the location of AFGHANISTAN in the program listing, a possibly tedious effort in itself. Chances are, AFGHANISTAN is far away (no pun intended) from page 123. For example, suppose AFGHANISTAN is on page 786, making it necessary for you to do three things:

1. Stick one finger in the program listing at page 123, in the faint hope that you eventually will get back there.

2. Carefully remember what the "state of the world" is at this point; that is, remember what variables A, B, and X contain.

3. Turn to page 786.

Imagine the following code on page 786:

```
AFGHANISTAN.
    X = X+1
    MOVE B TO C
    GO TO MOZAMBIQUE
```

The second statement looks simple enough, just another case of incrementing variable X. Now, what did X contain when you got to AFGHANISTAN? You tried to remember all of that before you turned to page 786; but at this hour, it's hard to remember very much, so you quickly turn to page 123 (thank goodness you left your finger stuck in the listing) to refresh your memory, and then return to page 786.

But wait! How do you know that the only way that the program gets to AFGHANISTAN is from the code on page 123? In other words, how do you *truly* know what variable X contains when you begin executing instructions on page 786? Indeed, there may be a dozen or a hundred devious paths that eventually lead to AFGHANISTAN.

At 3 A.M., your temptation would be to ignore this unpleasant thought, and therein lies the source of many a bug. If you decide to change that first instruction at AFGHANISTAN to something like X = X+2, it may well work for the particular case you were following (that from page 123), but you may have destroyed things for some other, at this point, completely unknown logic path that also ends at AFGHANISTAN.

Indeed, your troubles are just beginning, for, as you can see, AFGHANISTAN executes two relatively simple statements, and then uses a GOTO to disappear to MOZAMBIQUE.

But, where is MOZAMBIQUE? Why are we going there? What is the program going to do when it gets to MOZAMBIQUE? Not knowing the answer to these questions, you have no choice but to stick *another* finger in the program listing at page 786, and turn to yet another part of the listing.

I think you would agree that after finding three or four such GOTO statements, you would be tempted to give up. You've forgotten where you started, you've run out of fingers to stick in the listing to remind you where you've been, you don't know where you're going, and you're becoming very sleepy.

This scenario illustrates what structured programming is all about; or, to be more precise, it is the *antithesis* of structured programming. By eliminating GOTO statements, especially the wild GOTOs that jump hundreds of pages in the program listing, and by restricting ourselves to combinations of the three Bohm and Jacopini forms, the result is code that can be read and understood, literally, from the top down: If we begin reading code at the top of the page and continue reading in a straight-line fashion, by the time we reach the bottom of the page, we have finished doing something.

The result? First, coding in this manner means that the development programmer can understand what he is doing (which our mythical friend, Charlie, probably didn't). Consequently, he can write more code with fewer bugs, thus becoming more productive and more reliable. If the development programmer understands what he is doing, then the code probably will work. As a result, those early morning telephone calls will diminish. If the maintenance programmer *does* get a middle-of-the-night call, it's more likely that he will be able to find the bug in a reasonable amount of time, as well as fix the problem without introducing any new bugs.

So, this is what structured programming is all about. For more details, you and your programmers might want to consult the references at the end of the chapter.

6.2 Management problems with structured programming

By now, you should be prepared for a section on problem areas. We suggested in earlier chapters that programmers, designers, and analysts run into difficulties trying to implement structured analysis, top-down design, top-down testing, and structured design. Why should things be any easier with structured programming?

Actually, things are much better in the mid-1980's: approximately 80 percent of the MIS organizations in the United States now report that their programmers are using structured programming techniques on a consistent basis. Nevertheless, there *are* management problems: you should be prepared for the following difficulties and complaints:

1. Eternal arguments over use of GOTO statements

2. The myth that GOTO-less code is equivalent to good code

3. Weaknesses in the syntax of such high-level programming languages as PL/I, COBOL, and FORTRAN

4. Programmers' ignorance of their programming language

5. Difficulty in applying structured programming to assembly language on most computers

6. Problems with old-timer programmers' attitude

7. Complaints of inefficiency associated with structured programming

8. Conflicts with old programming standards

9. Difficulty in enforcing structured programming standards

10. Difficulty in using structured programming in a maintenance environment

11. Problems with nested IF statements

Let us now discuss each of these problem areas in turn.

6.2.1 Arguments over using GOTO statements

The discussion in the previous section illustrates the major arguments against using GOTO statements. It's not that I — or that Dijkstra, Mills, Wirth, Bohm, or Jacopini — think that the GOTO statement is inherently evil. What concerns us is that the GOTO statement is potentially dangerous and easily can lead to the kind of programming situation described earlier.

Unfortunately, the issue of GOTO statements has become almost a religious one. To say, "I am writing structured programs" is considered equivalent to "I have cleverly managed to avoid writing any GOTO statements in my program."

By itself, that sort of religious mania might not be so bad. Unfortunately, there are times, in the real world, when one desperately feels a need to write a GOTO statement. The major arguments *in favor* of GOTO statements seem to be the following:

- There are times when the programming language makes it difficult, if not impossible, to describe a simple piece of logic without using a GOTO statement. We will have more about this in Section 6.2.3.

- Sometimes a judiciously placed GOTO statement will improve significantly the efficiency of a program, compared to the structured coding of it.

- One occasionally can argue that a GOTO statement is more readable than the equivalent structured code. A good case is the coding for a premature exit from the middle of a loop: Such a case *can* be coded in a structured fashion, but it requires extra switches and some clumsy looking code.

- Similarly, some programmers argue that GOTO statements are a more readable, more comprehensible alternative to nested IF statements. This argument is discussed more in Section 6.2.11.

- Sometimes the programmer simply can't determine how to express a familiar logic in a structured form because he has spent so many years flowcharting and/or coding that logic in an unstructured form.

None of this is worth a major battle. If a programmer considers alternative means of coding some logic and believes that a GOTO statement makes the code more efficient, more maintainable, or easier to understand, then using it probably is legitimate.

If the concepts of top-down design and structured design discussed in Chapters 4 and 5 have been employed, then the issue of GOTO statements is not so critical. If structured design concepts had been enforced, the AFGHANISTAN situation described earlier in this chapter would not have occurred: Charlie would have been required to design his system as a small, independent, highly cohesive, loosely coupled modules that could be coded on one page. Consequently, there would be no GOTO statements jumping from page 123 to page 786, and if there were a few GOTOs jumping around *on* page 123, the objections would be minimal.

Structured programming, no matter how brilliant, cannot compensate for poor design and poor systems analysis. Proper structured analysis and structured design are of paramount importance; they far outweigh the impact of structured programming.

Thus, don't let arguments about GOTO statements go on for more than a few moments. Do make sure that your programmer knows how to express a piece of logic in a structured, GOTO-less fashion before deciding whether to use the GOTO statement. If all else fails, there is the Ashcroft-Manna technique,* described in Chapter 4 of my *Techniques of Program Structure and Design.* This technique is guaranteed to give a programmer a structured means of expressing any logic.

6.2.2 The myth that structured code is good code

Just as there is the belief that GOTO statements are bad, there is the myth that structured, GOTO-less code *must* be good; merely by eliminating the GOTO statements from code, one has readable, understandable, perfectly maintainable, error-free code.

Clearly, this is not so. One *always* can write bad code if one tries hard enough. With or without GOTO statements, a programmer can construct obscure, hopelessly inefficient, perverse code. In fact, if a programmer decides that he doesn't like the idea of structured programming, he may deliberately write bad code in order to demonstrate that structured programming is a bad idea.

Programmers commonly write structured code that is the following:

- *Inefficient* — hopelessly so, as illustrated by

```
DO I = 1 TO 3
    CASE I OF
        CASE 1
            A = 13
        CASE 2
            B = 75
        CASE 3
            C = 86
    END-CASE
END-DO
```

when he could have written

```
A = 13
B = 75
C = 86
```

---

*Briefly stated, the Ashcroft-Manna technique is a deterministic algorithm for converting an arbitrary program into a finite-state automaton.

If that code isn't perfectly clear to you, have one of your programmers to explain it to you. Such gross inefficiencies often occur as a result of a fatal fascination with all of the structured
verbs.

• *Incorrect* — Some programmers write structured code
  that has more bugs than their previous unstructured
  code. This is usually the result of weaknesses in the
  programming language (which we discuss in Section
  6.2.3) or the result of the programmer's ignorance of
  certain features of his programming language, see Section 6.2.4.

• *Obscure* — The coding shown above is a good example
  of obscure code. Obscure code also commonly results
  from the programmer trying to squeeze too many levels of nested loops and decisions onto one page of coding. Perhaps the worst offender, though, is one who
  uses the nested IF statement, which we will discuss in
  Section 6.2.11.

To summarize: Structured programming is not a panacea. Your
programmers still are capable of writing lousy code, especially if they
try!

6.2.3 Weaknesses in high-level programming languages

Perhaps one of the most significant problems in implementing
structured programming is that the most common high-level programming languages interfere with the programmer's natural inclination to
design and code structured logic. That criticism is not really valid with
languages like PASCAL, C, ADA, PL/I or MODULA-2; it is reasonably valid with COBOL; and it is extremely appropriate in the case of
FORTRAN.

Although it is inappropriate in this book to discuss language problems in detail, we can summarize some of the problems as follows:

• *PL/I, ADA, PASCAL, etc..* These languages do have a
  DO-WHILE statement, a nested IF-THEN-ELSE statement,
  formal block structures, and the concept of local variables that are known only within a limited domain.

Some of the lesser-known structured constructs — DO-UNTIL, CASE, and BREAK — recently were added to the language, thus providing the programmer with virtually everything he needs. There still are many complaints that the PL/I language is too verbose or too inefficient, but that problem has to do with the language itself, and not with structured programming.

- *COBOL.* For structured programming, the COBOL language is a mediocre language at best. While it has a PERFORM-UNTIL statement to provide for GOTO-less loops, the body of the loop is required to be out-of-line, in contrast to the in-line DO-WHILE of PL/I. While allowing several statements to be included in one sentence, this kind of block structure is informal and causes trouble when blocks are put inside of other blocks. This informality causes severe problems when combined with the concept of nested IF statements. (These are problems that do not occur in other languages.) In addition, COBOL lacks a CASE structure, a REPEAT-UNTIL loop structure, and, perhaps most important, the concept of local variables.*

- *FORTRAN.* The most primitive of high-level programming languages, FORTRAN lacks any form of nested IF statement and provides no IF-THEN-ELSE statement. It has a loop — the DO loop — but it is of the iterative variety, which covers only a small percentage of the looping applications required by programmers. It has no block structures, and its concept of local variables is primitive — a disaster of a language.

To write perfect structured code, you would be advised to program in a language like ALGOL or PASCAL. But that is roughly equivalent to telling you to carry on human conversations in Latin or Esperanto.

---

* — Improvements to the COBOL language have been proposed and discussed for more than a decade, and a new standard has been published; however, it has not yet been approved by all of the appropriate standards agencies. Some vendors have included appropriate structured programming features in their implementation of COBOL, but not all.

In addition to the technical considerations of structured programming, you must deal with other language considerations, which are addressed in the questions and discussions that follow:

- Can you find a ready supply of programmers who are facile in language X? There is a large supply of COBOL programmers, while far fewer programmers are conversant in ALGOL or PASCAL.

- Can you train your existing programmers to code in language X? Teaching a new programming language to a veteran is much like trying to teach French to an adult American: One has to be prepared for a heavily accented mish-mash of both languages. It's not unusual to find veteran programmers who still are coding FORTRAN or COBOL logic in PL/I.*

- Does your computer vendor support language X? Virtually every vendor has some reasonable implementation of COBOL, FORTRAN, PASCAL, and assembly language. In 1976, when the first edition of this book was being written, only IBM could be depended upon for a decent version of PL/I, although all the other vendors had been talking about it, and a few vendors have implemented. By 1985, when the third edition was being prepared, there were PL/I implementations on many machines, but there was a dearth of ADA compilers. By the early 1990's, ADA compilers presumably will exist on all known computers, but everyone will be complaining about the lack of availability of yet another new language.

So, chances are, you should stick with the language that you currently are using. Take solace from the fact that *all* of the major high-level languages have some weaknesses and clumsy features. Also, keep two other points in mind. The official committees that define FORTRAN and COBOL (for examples, ANSI and CODASYL) are aware of the problems; both committees have developed new versions

---

* — This is a major problem for an organization like the U.S. Defense Department, which desperately wants to begin using ADA as an official programming language: they have two hundred million lines of *old* code to maintain (in COBOL, FORTRAN, assembler, JOVIAL, RP/G, etc.) and some four hundred thousand people to re-train!

of the languages to remedy the weaknesses discussed above. At some point in the next five years, we probably will have much-improved versions of these two most-common languages available from the major computer manufacturers. Second, in the meantime, most of the ugly features of a programming language can be hidden by a *preprocessor*. One of the most popular COBOL preprocessors is ADR's METACOBOL, which provides the appropriate structuring verbs. Dozens of cheap FORTRAN structuring preprocessors are available. The September 1975 issue of ACM *SIGPLAN Notices** contains a survey of approximately twenty preprocessors. One of the best, in my opinion, is called RATFOR; for more information on this preprocessor, see the reference to *Software Tools* at the end of this chapter.

6.2.4 Programmers' ignorance of their programming language

As observed in the previous section, the popular high-level programming languages lack some of the features that would make structured programming convenient. However, there is a much worse problem: Many programmers are ignorant of the language features that must be used to write structured code.

There is a certain irony to this, particularly in regard to PL/I. As we discussed earlier, PL/I probably is one of the more suitable high-level languages, for it has a DO-WHILE, an IF-THEN-ELSE, and various other powerful features. Most people assume that, since PL/I is a powerful language, PL/I programmers must be powerful people. That is, almost everyone assumes that PL/I programmers write good structured code, because, after all, their language makes it so easy.

The trouble is that many PL/I programmers have *never* used a DO-WHILE statement and have no idea how it works. Many of them have never used a nested IF statement and have used a simple IF-THEN-ELSE only on rare occasions. Many of them, you see, still are writing a disguised form of FORTRAN, or COBOL, or RPG, or assembly language in PL/I. A survey of more than one hundred commercial applications in one of my clients' organizations showed that, in one hundred thousand lines of PL/I code, there were only eleven DO-WHILE statements and that in approximately 20 percent of the programs, there were no IF-THEN-ELSE statements.

---

*L.P. Meissner, "On Extending Fortran Control Structures to Facilitate Structured Programming," *SIGPLAN Notices,* Vol. 10, No. 9 (September 1975), pp. 19 - 30.

Things are not much better in the COBOL world. Many COBOL programmers I've encountered never have used a CALL statement, except possibly to CALL a database management function provided by their vendor. Similarly, a majority have never used a nested IF statement and don't understand how a simple IF-THEN-ELSE works. Most of them have never used the PERFORM-UNTIL statement, and are extremely cautious about using the special iterative case, PERFORM-VARYING. Only a very few COBOL programmers have any concept of a block structure, that is, a group of statements that can be treated as if they were a block or an integral unit.

So, what should we do? Shoot all of our existing programmers and get new ones? The idea is tempting, particularly since the better universities are teaching beginners how to use those features of the language that they need to know in order to write structured programs. The real problem is training. The reason most PL/I programmers don't know how to use a DO-WHILE statement is that nobody ever taught them how, and nobody ever suggested that it would be a good idea to use such features of their language.* Similarly, nobody taught the majority of COBOL programmers how to use PERFORM-UNTIL or IF-THEN-ELSE or any of the other structured aspects of their language.

So, if you want your programmers to write good structured code, it may be wise to send them back to school to review the fundamentals of their language. It should take only a day or two of their time, and the effort will be repaid many times over.

6.2.5 Difficulty in applying structured programming to assembly language

The reaction of an assembly language programmer to structured programming is fairly predictable: "What does all of this have to do with me? How can I possibly eliminate GOTO statements in an assembly language program? Everyone knows that assembly language programs have to jump around!"

-----

*My same client's survey, which found that virtually none of the PL/I programmers used a DO-WHILE, also found that 50 percent of the verbs in the PL/I language had essentially *never* been used. PL/I is such a rich language that most programmers learn only the subset that they need to get along, which, of course, is exactly the same phenomenon that one finds in English: Most people use only a few hundred words to carry on their day-to-day conversations.

To answer this, we retreat to the original Bohm and Jacopini work. Any procedural logic can be flowcharted in a structured fashion, as a combination of one-in-one-out blocks of logic. That statement is true regardless of whether we are flowcharting the logic for a payroll system, order entry system, compiler, real-time operating system, or anything else. And it is true whether that logic eventually is coded in COBOL, ALGOL, or assembly language.

The nice thing about COBOL, ALGOL, and the high-level languages is that they accept *directly* the structured flowcharts that we showed in Figure 6.1. In assembly language, we have to hand-compile our structured flowcharts into the primitive instructions that make the machine work.

So, our answer to the assembly language programmer is, "Yes, you have to use branching instructions in your program. But your code should be a direct implementation of well-structured flowcharts; your code should consist of blocks, each with one entry and one exit."

In addition, we offer the following suggestions about writing structured programs in assembly language:

1. If your programmers are working on a large machine (for example, an IBM 308x) or on a small machine with a powerful macro assembler, you may want to consider using macros to implement DO-WHILE, IF-THEN-ELSE, and so on. Several standard packages of such macros are available on IBM computers, and your programmers should be ingenious enough to develop them on other computers if the computer has a decent macro assembler (which many mini-computers don't).

2. You may want to consider a preprocessor that gives you the ability to write IF-THEN-ELSE and DO-WHILE statements intermingled with ordinary assembler statements. This might be useful if your vendor's assembler doesn't have a macro capability.

3. You may want to pester your vendor for a so-called systems implementation language. IBM's PL/S language is a good example of this. Alternatively, you might consider PL/360, which was described in detail by Niklaus Wirth in the *Journal of the ACM.** Almost

---

*N. Wirth, "PL/360, a Programming Language for the 360 Computers," *Journal of the ACM.* Vol. 15, No. 1 (January 1968), pp. 37-74.

all minicomputers and microcomputers have some implementation of a language called $C^\dagger$; Control Data has a language called SWL (Software Writer's Language); and so forth. These languages generally provide the structuring verbs, *plus* powerful means of representing data, *plus* the normal assembly language instructions.

4. You may want to require your programmers to describe their procedural logic in a pseudocode, something that resembles an informal mixture of English, ALGOL, PL/I, and FORTRAN, *but is structured.* This pseudocode expression of their logic can serve as a comment preceding the assembly language implementation. Pseudocode comments also may be placed in the comment field beside each assembly language instruction, but my experience has been that programmers won't maintain these comments as the code is modified in the maintenance phase of the project.

5. Finally, you may decide to ignore structured programming in an assembly language environment. Put your energy into structured analysis and structured design: Make sure that your analysts have defined properly the user's requirements with the graphic techniques discussed in Chapter 3. Make sure that your designers have built their system in terms of small (fewer than fifty statements) modules that are highly cohesive and independent of other modules. If they do their job well in this area, how their code looks won't matter so much — although there is no excuse for disorganized code.

6.2.6 Problems with old-timers' attitudes

We discussed most of the common attitude problems in Chapter 2 of this book. Remember that you *will* encounter some emotional objections, mostly from programmers who have been coding for ten years without ever being told *how* to code.

---

†For two distinct discussions of C, read Kernighan and Ritchie's *The C Programming Language* (Englewood Cliffs: Prentice-Hall, 1978), and Zahn's *C Notes: A Guide to the C Programming Language* (New York: YOURDON Press, 1979).

As a manager, you should be able to respond to the following comments:

- "You're limiting my creativity."

- "My old way works fine."

- "Are you trying to tell me that I've been writing bad programs all these years?"

- "Are you telling me that *you* know how to write programs better than I do — I started programming while you were still in diapers!"

- "It's a great idea, but it'll never work on our system."

- "I don't see what difference structured programming will make."

We also should observe that many of the negative reactions to structured programming have occurred in organizations that enforced GOTO-less programming with a religious fervor. If you're prepared to let your programmers stick an occasional GOTO into their code, particularly to compensate for limitations in their programming language, chances are they won't protest quite so loudly.

6.2.7 Complaints of inefficiency

Most of these complaints are similar to the complaints about the inefficiency of structured design. Most of the answers are the same, too. Rather than repeating the philosophical points made in Section 5.2.5, I'll mention only a few points peculiar to structured programming.

Many programmers do think that structured programming is inefficient. Why? There are a few consistent arguments:

1. The IF-THEN-ELSE statement occasionally generates somewhat less efficient code than the programmer could have written with GOTO statements. Several years ago, the difference in efficiency was significant, often a factor of two or more. Today, the programmer can assume that at worst the IF-THEN-ELSE statement might cost him a microsecond or two and possibly an extra byte of storage.

2. A religious interpretation of structured programming often leads to a few extra flags and switches (mostly so that the programmer can exit from the middle of a loop). That may cost him a microsecond or two.

3. In a few cases, structured programming requires the programmer to duplicate small blocks of code, rather than using a GOTO to jump into the code from several different places. As a result, the program is slightly larger than it otherwise would have been.

In almost all such cases, we are talking about microseconds of inefficiency, whereas the real issue of efficiency involves hours of computer time; and efficiency can be achieved only by intelligent systems design.

6.2.8 Conflicts with old programming standards

Another potential problem you'll face is that the techniques of structured programming may conflict with your programming standards. For example, many traditional programming standards strongly discourage or forbid nested IF statements.

It usually is a simple matter to change the standards manual to conform with structured programming. Indeed, it may require only that you pull out the section that tells the programmer not to use nested IF statements. A more serious problem arises if your standards manual has several examples of supposedly good code, all of which are unstructured.

We discuss the whole question of standards in Chapter 13. In the meantime, you may wish to examine the programming standards developed at YOURDON inc. for COBOL and PL/I, which can be found in Appendices A and B.

6.2.9 Difficulty enforcing structured programming standards

An objection relating to standards enforcement often is raised at this point: "Assuming we develop structured programming standards, how do we enforce them? How do we ensure that a programmer uses a GOTO only when necessary?"

If, as a manager, you wish to enforce dogmatic standards, there is a simple answer: Build a standards-enforcer package and insist that all new programs be run through the package before being put into production. That way, you can ensure that nobody uses any GOTO statements (if that's what you want), that nobody has more than three levels of nested IF statements (if that's what you desire), and that everyone has followed whatever other standards you've decided to enforce.

However, most organizations have soft standards or guidelines which are to be interpreted by the programmer with a certain degree of common sense. Thus, we normally see standards like, "Don't use GOTO statements unless you have to, or unless you honestly think that the code would be more understandable."

How do we ensure that standards of this type are put into practice? Use structured walkthroughs or team programming. If the team thinks that the code is good code, then it probably *is* good code, whether or not it has GOTO statements. Walkthroughs are discussed in considerably more detail in Chapter 10.

6.2.10 *Difficulty in using structured programming in a maintenance environment*

We observed in Chapter 2 that 50 percent or more of the data processing effort in many organizations today is maintenance, patching, correcting, and improving existing programs. Most, if not all, of these programs were written in an unstructured fashion. What relevance does structured programming have in such an environment?

The advantages of structured programming may influence an organization to rewrite an old application sooner than would have been politically possible otherwise. Also, if large chunks of code are to be changed or inserted into an existing program, it should be possible to do such work in a structured fashion.

A few organizations have toyed with the idea of "restructuring:" converting an unstructured program into an equivalent structured program. Such an engine is certainly theoretically possible (indeed, the original Bohm and Jacopini paper suggested the outlines of such an engine), and two organizations have developed commercially available software packages.* However, problems arise with this kind of package:

---

* — One such product is called *Catalyst,* and is available from Peat, Marwick, Mitchell.

- After five or ten years of maintaining a rotten old program, your maintenance programmers finally may *understand* it. A structuring engine would rearrange the code so that they probably wouldn't understand it any more.

- A structuring engine usually is based on the assumption that the program obeys the legal syntax of the language. This is not always true and is particularly invalid for those programs written in COBOL. Programmers have a way of using undocumented, illegal features of the language that shouldn't work, but *do*. A structuring engine would upset this delicate balance.

- A structuring engine cannot transmute lead into gold. It cannot convert a truly bad program into a truly good program. It *can* eliminate the GOTO statements, and it may improve the organization of the procedural logic, but there always is the chance that it will do nothing more than transform a bad unstructured program into an equally bad structured program.

Another problem is that if you teach your maintenance programmers about structured programming, they will become frustrated if they are sent back to their department to continue patching unstructured rat's-nest code. However, failing to teach maintenance programmers anything about structured programming leads to another problem: The first time they are given a *structured* program to maintain, they'll be nervous. "What's this?" they'll ask. "Nested IF statements? And subroutine calls? My God! I can't read any of this!"

Also, the first few structured programs written by your development programmers may be somewhat difficult to maintain. As we suggested earlier, a structured GOTO-less program is not necessarily a good program; and until your programmers fully understand what they're doing, they actually may write some bad structured code. Your maintenance programmers certainly will let you know, and you should listen to them.

6.2.11 Difficulties with nested IF statements

The last problem area that we discuss in this chapter is perhaps the most pervasive one: Programmers seem to have great difficulty writing code of the following form:

```
IF MARITAL-STATUS        = MARRIED
    THEN IF SEX          = MALE
        THEN IF AGE GREATER THAN 30
            BLAH
            BLAH
            BLAH
        ELSE
            BLAH
            BLAH
    ELSE
        IF AGE GREATER THAN 45
            BLAH
            BLAH
        ELSE
            BLAH
            BLAH
    ELSE IF MARITAL-STATUS = SINGLE
        ETC.
```

This kind of code is known as a nested IF. Don't worry if you find it a little difficult to understand; your programmers generally do, too.

Why is the issue of nested IF statements associated with structured programming? Simply because the GOTO statement has been taken away. Previously, your programmers would have written code like the following:

```
IF MARITAL-STATUS = MARRIED AND SEX = MALE AND
    AGE GREATER THAN 30 GO TO X-ROUTINE
ELSE GO TO Y-ROUTINE.
```

Without his GOTO statement, the programmer may find that he is coding more and more IF-THEN-ELSE statements nested inside other IF-THEN-ELSE statements.

Without becoming too deeply into technical issues, I offer the following suggestions.

1. Many of the problems raised above are *training* problems, as we observed in Section 6.2.4. Most of your programmers have never been taught how the IF-THEN-ELSE statement works. Give your programmers a refresher seminar, and most of your problems will disappear.

2. Attitude may be part of the problem: Some program-
    mers just don't like the ELSE statement. This is one
    time when you may decide to back off from a dogmatic
    interpretation of GOTO-less programming, and let them
    do what they want. Make sure, though, that they
    know what they're doing and that they are using the
    GOTO statement because they sincerely believe the
    code is easier to read. Many programmers who use
    this argument don't want to admit that they haven't
    figured out how to eliminate their GOTO statements.

3. Many programmers confuse nested IF statements with
    something quite different: compound Boolean condi-
    tional expressions. Some programmers say, "I don't
    like nested IF statements because I always get into
    trouble with statements like this: IF X NOT EQUAL Y OR
    Z THEN GO TO AFGHANISTAN." True, that statement is
    messy, but it has nothing to do with the problem of
    nested IF statements. While you're giving your pro-
    grammers a refresher course on nested IFs, though,
    you might also give them a short course on Boolean
    logic. Most programmers sorely need it!

4. Many programmers confuse nested IFs with so-called
    CASE structures. There are many situations, for exam-
    ple, in which the programmer wants to write

```
IF MARITAL-STATUS = MARRIED
    BLAH
    BLAH
ELSE
    IF MARITAL-STATUS = SINGLE
        BLAH
        BLAH
    ELSE
        IF MARITAL-STATUS = DIVORCED
            BLAH
            BLAH
        ELSE
            IF MARITAL-STATUS = WIDOWED
                BLAH
                BLAH
            ELSE
                PRINT AN ERROR MESSAGE.
```

The significant point is that the example above is not a nested IF, but instead a simple either-or situation. Either a person is married, *or* single, *or* divorced, *or* widowed. We should write

```
IF MARITAL-STATUS = MARRIED
   BLAH
   BLAH
ELSE IF MARITAL-STATUS = SINGLE
   BLAH
   BLAH
ELSE IF MARITAL-STATUS = DIVORCED
   BLAH
   BLAH
ELSE IF MARITAL-STATUS = WIDOWED
   BLAH
   BLAH
ELSE
   PRINT AN ERROR MESSAGE.
```

When a case is written like this, it becomes obvious that we could string *hundreds* of these ELSE-IFs together without making the code more difficult to understand because we must consider only one IF at a time.

5. Occasionally, there are complaints about the formatting of nested IF statements. Note how the first version of our MARITAL-STATUS example above was indented several spaces for each level; after five or six levels, we run out of room. As we implied, though, this is sometimes a false issue: If the code is written in the ELSE-IF style shown in our second version, we should have no problem.

6. Programmers sometimes complain that it is difficult to understand more than a few levels of nested IFs. Indeed it is. The problem is that of a human trying to comprehend a difficult logical statement, *not* of whether the computer can understand a nested IF. Recognizing that the problem is a human one, we can draw on a wealth of experience and studies of human ability to understand complexity. These studies (conducted by Noam Chomsky in the field of linguistics, and Gerald Weinberg in the programming field, among others) suggest that very few people can understand more than three levels of nested IFs.

7.   If the application requires more than three levels of nested decisions, the programmer should break it into separate pieces, that is, separate modules which can be comprehended separately. Thus, the example at the beginning of this section might have been coded as follows:

```
IF MARITAL-STATUS = MARRIED
      THEN IF SEX = MALE
                 PERFORM MARRIED-MALE-ROUTINE
            ELSE
                 ETC.
```

8.   Finally, many nested IF problems are an indication that the programmer is unfamiliar with decision tables. The code at the beginning of this section, for example, dealt with at least three different variables: marital status, sex, and age. If we wish to recognize five different kinds of marital status, then there are 5 x 2 x 2 different combinations of these three variables; and no matter whether the programmer uses GOTO statements or nested IF statements, he has to make sure that he has considered all twenty different combinations. What leads to bugs is the common tendency to forget a few of those combinations or to confuse them. Thus, a decision table approach is probably the best way to make sure that all combinations are expressed, that redundancies, ambiguities, and contradictions have been eliminated, and that the logic is organized in a way that it can be coded trivially. Ask your programmers to draw a decision table for the MARITAL-STATUS problem. If they give you an uncomprehending look, send them back to school for that lesson before you worry about nested IF statements.

Bibliography

1. Baker, F.T. "Chief Programmer Team Management of Production Programming." *IBM Systems Journal*, Vol. 11, No. 1 (January 1972), pp. 56 - 73.

    An account of IBM's first formal use of structured programming.

2. _____. "System Quality Through Structured Programming." *AFIPS Proceedings of the 1972 Fall Joint Computer Conference,* Vol. 41 (Montvale: AFIPS Press, 1972), pp. 339 - 344.

    A further account of the New York Times system, with statistics on the number of bugs found.

3. Balbine, G. "Better Manpower Utilization Through Automatic Restructuring." *Proceedings of the 1975 National Computer Conference.*

    Contains a discussion of a proprietary package that operates as a "structuring engine," automatically converting unstructured code to structured code.

4. Bohm, C., and G. Jacopini. "Flow Diagrams, Turing Machines, and Languages with Only Two Formation Rules." *Communications of the ACM*, Vol. 9, No. 5 (May 1966), pp. 366 - 371.

    This paper forms much of the theoretical basis for structured programming. Very theoretical and hard to read, the paper is not really necessary for your application programmers. However, you should know that it exists.

5. Dahl, O.J., E.W. Dijkstra, and C.A.R. Hoare. *Structured Programming.* Englewood Cliffs: Prentice-Hall, 1972.

> One of the first, if not *the* first, books on structured programming. Also one of the more academic ones. Probably way over the head of the average COBOL, PL/I, and FORTRAN programmer, but exciting reading nonetheless.

6. Kernighan, B.W., and P.J. Plauger. *The Elements of Programming Style.* New York: McGraw-Hill, 1974.

> An excellent book that emphasizes that the object of the game is not just to write structured programs, but also to write *good* programs.

7. _____. *Software Tools.* Reading: Addison-Wesley, 1976.

> Another excellent book, this gives some five thousand lines of real, working, structured code written in a language called RATFOR. RATFOR is one of the more popular structured preprocessors for FORTRAN.

8. Knuth, D.E. "Structured Programming with GOTO Statements." *ACM Computing Surveys,* December 1974, pp. 261 - 302.

> A slightly different point of view from one of the best programmers in the world, the author of the formidable *The Art of Computer Programming* (Reading: Addison-Wesley, 1968).

9. Lister, T., and E. Yourdon. *Learning to Program in Structured COBOL, Part 2.* New York: YOURDON Press, 1978.

10. McCracken, D. *A Simplified Guide to Structured COBOL Programming.* New York: John Wiley & Sons, 1976.

11. McGowan, C.L., and J.R. Kelly. *Top-Down Structured Programming.* New York: Petrocelli/Charter, 1975.

 > Somewhat more oriented toward PL/I than the other high-level languages. Academic (discussions of proofs of program correctness, etc.) but still very useful for applications programmers.

12. Noll, P. *Structured Programming for the COBOL Programmer.* Fresno: Mike Murach & Assoc., 1977.

13. Plauger, P.J. "New York Times Revisited." *The YOURDON Report.* Vol. 1, No. 3 (April 1976).

 > A follow-up account of the New York Times system after several years of maintenance.

14. Weinberg, G.M. *Structured Programming in PL/C.* New York: John Wiley & Sons, 1972.

15. Yourdon, E. "A Brief Look at Structured Programming and Top-Down Design." *Modern Data,* June 1974, pp. 30 - 35.

 > A very brief overview and not sufficient to get your programmers actually started in writing structured code.

16. _____. *Techniques of Program Structure and Design.* Englewood Cliffs: Prentice-Hall, 1975.

 > Aimed at experienced programmers, one chapter is devoted exclusively to structured programming techniques.

17. _____, C. Gane, and T. Sarson. *Learning to Program in Structured COBOL, Part 1,* 2nd ed. New York: YOURDON Press, 1978.

Chapter Seven:

Documentation for the New Techniques

Up to this point, we have described the most important *technical* aspects of the structured techniques for implementing a set of user requirements: top-down design, top-down implementation, structured design, and structured programming. Now, we are ready to discuss the problems of *documenting* EDP systems produced by these techniques.

You may have noticed that there were few illustrations, particularly technical diagrams, in the previous three chapters. Chapter 5 contained three company organizational charts to illustrate the concept of span of control, and Chapter 6 contained conventional flowcharts to illustrate the basic elements of structured programming. The paucity of illustration is intentional: It is important that the technical concepts of design and programming be understood first, so that the discussion of documentation can build from a solid foundation.

A documentation technique is just what its name implies, and it must not be confused with the concepts of design discussed in previous chapters. A flowchart is only a picture; the act of drawing a flowchart does not ensure a good design. Unfortunately, many people confuse this point: When asked whether they are practicing structured design, they say, "Sure! We *must* be doing structured design; after all, we're drawing HIPO diagrams and a bunch of other funny-looking charts that we never did before!"

HIPO? What's that? Indeed, what *kind* of documentation are we talking about? It is practical to organize into three categories the incredible mass of documentation accompanying the majority of EDP development projects:

- documentation that traditionally is associated with systems analysis
- documentation that describes the *structural* design of a system
- documentation that describes and illustrates the *procedural* design of an individual module of the system, such as that provided by detailed flowcharts

Some of this documentation will not be influenced by the structured techniques, and it is likely that you will continue documenting your systems as you always have to some extent. However, the structured techniques probably will introduce new documentation methods within your organization and may cause you to abandon certain others.

This chapter discusses the impact of structured techniques in each of these areas of documentation and the problems that a manager may have in attempting to implement the techniques. For reasons that will be clear later in the chapter, I begin with the second category.

7.1 Documentation to illustrate a system's structural design

Many organizations have *no* structural documentation techniques. They have narrative specifications, flowcharts, and other bits and pieces of paper. But, in most cases, these classical forms of documentation do little to illustrate the structure or architecture of a system.

For this reason, certain new documentation techniques — introduced in Chapter 5 to illustrate the structured design concepts — have had a profound impact within some organizations. For the first time, designers/programmers have been able to *see* the system architecture that they have been designing blindly for years; and merely seeing what they are specifying often is sufficient for them to make substantial improvements in the quality of their designs.

The three most important techniques for documenting the structural design are the data flow diagram, the HIPO hierarchy chart, and the structure chart. Each technique is discussed separately.

7.1.1 The data flow diagram

The *data flow diagram*, also known as a "program graph" or a "bubble chart," is used to show the flow of data through a large program or system. A typical data flow diagram (DFD) is shown in Figure 7.1.

Although described in Chapter 3 as an analysis tool, in fact it first was used as a design tool. Past experience has demonstrated that one of the best ways to create a good design is to translate a conventional narrative English functional specification into a non-procedural model of the system. Indeed, the data flow diagram basically is identical to the conventional system flowchart, except that it does not indicate whether the processing activities shown inside the bubbles will be implemented as modules, programs, job steps, mini-computers, or some other physical form. Similarly, Figure 7.1 does not show whether the data flowing between the processing steps will be implemented by a tape file, disk pack, telephone communications line, or information transmitted through core memory. In other words, the data flow diagram is a *logical, abstract* system flowchart.

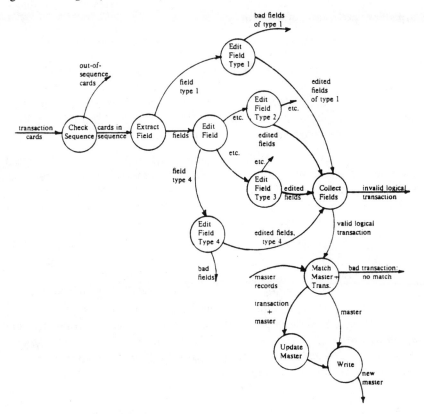

Figure 7.1. Typical data flow diagram.

The data flow diagram is an important tool for the structured design techniques discussed in Chapter 5. In particular, transform-centered design requires the designer to draw a data flow diagram as the first step in what ultimately leads to the systematic development of a good design.

In addition, the system flowchart, a crude, physical form of the DFD, is the most common document that analysts, designers, mainte-nance programmers, and operations people turn to when they want to see an overview of the current system.

The references at the end of this chapter provide additional details on the development of DFDs. Until your technical people have had time to study these details, tell them to pretend that they are drawing a system flowchart, but to eliminate all physical references to tapes, disks, job steps, programs, and so on.

7.1.2 HIPO hierarchy chart

Another documentation concept introduced as a result of the structured techniques is known as HIPO, an acronym for Hierarchy, plus Input, Process, Output. The acronym describes a documentation package developed and popularized by IBM. Figure 7.2 shows a typical HIPO hierarchy chart, or visual table of contents (VTOC).

Another type of HIPO diagram associated with an individual module is discussed in Section 7.2. The diagram shown in Figure 7.2 is intended primarily to illustrate the overall architecture of a system, specifically which modules are subordinate to others, just as in a com-pany organizational chart.

The analogy between a company organizational chart and a HIPO hierarchy chart is a fairly close one. The HIPO diagram in Figure 7.2 does not show the precise sequence in which modules will be executed, nor any detailed decisions or loops, nor any of the detailed processing steps that take place inside any given module. Since it does provide a good overview of a large program, it may be a useful document for dis-cussions between user, analyst, manager, and programmer. However, most MIS organizations have found that it is difficult, if not impossible, for one document to serve the needs of such a disparate group.

7.1.3 Structure chart

A variation on the HIPO hierarchy chart is known as a structure chart, an example of which is given in Figure 7.3. The structure chart conveys much of the same kind of information as the HIPO chart of

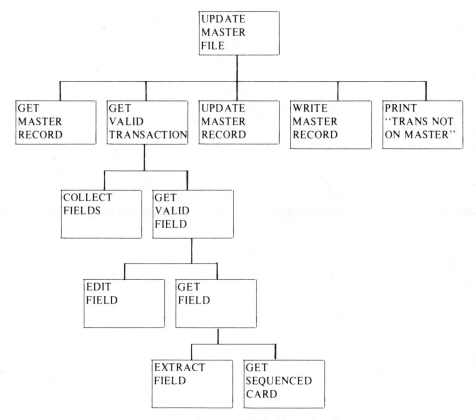

Figure 7.2. Typical HIPO hierarchy chart.

Figure 7.2; many of the differences are cosmetic. Note, for example, that the lines connecting the various modules in Figure 7.3 are drawn in a "tree-structured" fashion, rather than in the horizontal and vertical manner that characterizes Figure 7.2. Note also that connecting lines terminate in an arrowhead, whereas those in a HIPO chart do not.

Significantly, the structure chart shows occasional procedural detail without becoming bogged down in detail. Figure 7.3 shows the presence of some loops and some decisions that the designer believed were sufficiently important to be shown. Such procedural details could be included with HIPO, too, but the official version of HIPO does not include this information.

Perhaps more important, the interfaces between the modules are shown on the structure chart itself. Figure 7.3 shows the inputs and outputs associated with all of the modules.

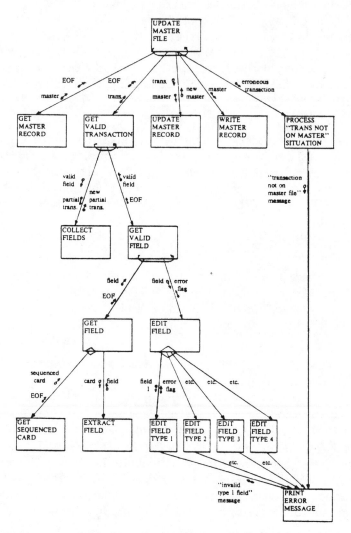

Figure 7.3. Typical structure chart.

In contrast, the HIPO hierarchy chart of Figure 7.2 does not show the interfaces between the modules. Some organizations suggest using an "input-output table," a separate document that lists in a tabular fashion each module's inputs and outputs. Other organizations advise that such details be shown on the document that describes the contents of the individual modules — that is, on the detailed HIPO diagram discussed in Section 7.2.

Many people do not even realize that this is an issue. They draw HIPO hierarchy charts, as in Figure 7.2, and never think about the interfaces until they begin writing the code. Even then, they may not think about the interfaces formally. All of the system's data may be defined in, and available from, the DATA DIVISION of a COBOL program or equivalent forms of global data in other programs, for example blank COMMON in FORTRAN. As a result, the interfaces often are not defined formally, but evolve as the code is written.

To ensure that this critically important interface information is not ignored, designers have found it advantageous to show the intermodule interfaces on the same diagram, on the same sheet of paper, as the hierarchical picture of the system. The danger exists that this extra information will clutter the diagram to the point of unreadability, but not if you follow these rules:

- The designer should record the highest level *aggregate* of data being passed between two modules. If module A passes a master-file record to module B, simply write "master record" on the structure chart; do not write the names of all 178 fields in the master record.

- If the diagram becomes cluttered, usually the design could be improved. One of the signs of a good design is a clean set of interfaces with relatively few distinct forms of data being passed between modules.

- In fact, those designers who draw structure charts of the form shown in Figure 7.3 generally find that the diagram is not cluttered with too much detail.

7.2 Documentation to illustrate a system's procedural design

The documentation techniques discussed in the previous section are useful for illustrating the overall structure of a system, but they provide little or no information about the detailed procedural design of each module. So, what impact have the structured techniques had on detailed documentation?

For a few organizations that use the techniques, nothing has changed. The programmers still write detailed flowcharts and detailed narrative specifications for each module. Serious efforts are made to keep this documentation up-to-date during the maintenance phase of the project, and the maintenance programmer is reasonably confident that the flowcharts resemble the code that he or she is maintaining.

However, not many organizations are continuing to work in this fashion. Although management standards, contractual obligations, and other external pressures may dictate that the detailed flowcharts be produced, they rarely are useful. Programmers will tell you that the reasons are threefold: They never draw the flowchart until *after* the program is working (making it probable that the flowchart shows what the programmer *thinks* his code is doing rather than what his code really *is* doing); flowcharts are not kept up to date during the maintenance effort because it's too much trouble; and, as a result, the maintenance programmers know that they're wasting their time if they look at the flowcharts.

Most organizations that use structured programming have abandoned detailed flowcharts completely. What is substituted in their place? For those organizations that use structured techniques, the answer is nothing. The logic is simple: The structure charts or HIPO hierarchy charts provide an overall picture of the system. If the design has been done according to the principles of structured design, it should be possible for the maintenance programmer to maintain or debug one module without having to know anything about the detailed contents of any other module. If the code has been written according to the principles of structured programming, it should be possible to read the code without any comments. In this context, one could regard a comment as an apology for bad code. In any case, there is no point in maintaining the fiction that detailed flowcharts are accurate. Better to have no documentation than incorrect documentation that breeds a sense of false security.

Even though such an argument may make eminently good sense, it is somewhat radical. Many data processing organizations still require some level of detailed design documentation before the programmer is allowed to write the code and that documentation may well be kept for the benefit of the maintenance programmer.

For those who wish to continue to maintain some degree of detailed documentation, but who are disillusioned with detailed flowcharts, three different types of documentation techniques have gained popularity: pseudocode, detailed HIPO diagrams, and Nassi-Shneiderman charts. Each of these techniques is discussed below.

7.2.1 Pseudocode

Among other terms, pseudocode also is called "computer Esperanto." In Chapter 3, we referred to it as structured English. Pseudocode could be defined as "narrative documentation" constructed from combinations of simple, imperative sentences, written in English, containing a single, transitive verb and a single, non-plural object; IF-THEN-ELSE constructs of the sort discussed in Chapter 6; DO-WHILE constructs of the sort discussed in Chapter 6; and other appropriate extensions to structured programming, such as CASE or REPEAT-UNTIL

An example of pseudocode is shown in Figure 7.4. The example illustrates a general characteristic of pseudocode: It is reasonably well-organized and precise, and yet informal enough to be intelligible to non-programmers. Since it does not require a flowcharting template, pseudocode can be written quickly and easily and even typed into a computer terminal. Thus, it can be kept up to date more readily than a detailed flowchart or HIPO diagram (which means that there is more of a chance that it *will* be kept up-to-date).

MASTER-FILE-UPDATE:
1.   DO WHILE there are more transactions
     or there are more master records.
     a.   IF the master account number is equal
          to the transaction account number:
          1.   Update the master record from the transaction record.
          2.   Write the updated master record.
          3.   Get the next valid transaction record.
          4.   Get the next master record.
     b.   ELSE:
          1.   IF the master account number is less
               than the transaction account number:
               a.   Write the master record.
               b.   Get the next master record.
          2.   ELSE:
               a.   Print an error message.
               b.   Get the next valid transaction.
2.   Close the transaction file.
3.   Close the master file.

Figure 7.4. Example of pseudocode.

Programmers who code in PASCAL, PL/I, or other powerful high-level languages often remark that the pseudocode is so close to the real code that it is a waste of time to bother with it. There is some truth to this. However, remember that a human reader does not require the same degree of precision as a compiler. Pseudocode seems to represent a nice compromise between precision and informality.

Those who program in COBOL have mixed opinions about the usefulness of pseudocode. On the one hand, pseudocode is sufficiently close to COBOL that one wonders whether it provides any useful information. On the other hand, pseudocode does afford the programmer the opportunity to express some structured logic that is *not* natural in COBOL, for example, logic expressed in terms of REPEAT-UNTILS, CASE, and other structured constructs.

For programmers coding in FORTRAN, BASIC, assembly language, and other similar primitive languages, pseudocode definitely is of value. First, it allows the programmer to think in a structured fashion, which his real language does not allow him to do. Second, it provides a convenient basis for hand-compiling the real FORTRAN code, or assembly language code, and so on in an almost mechanical fashion. Third, it provides an easy-to-read overview of the procedural logic for the maintenance programmer.

We must admit, however, that some of the concerns about detailed flowcharts also are valid of pseudocode. For example, how does the maintenance programmer know whether the pseudocode approximates the real code? How can we ensure that the pseudocode is updated whenever the real code is updated? If pseudocode is easier to write, maintain, and update, it is *more likely* to be kept accurate and up-to-date than are equivalent flowcharts. But there are no absolute guarantees that this will occur.

7.2.2 Detailed HIPO diagram

Another form of detailed documentation is known variously as a detailed HIPO diagram, a functional HIPO diagram, or an IPO diagram.'' An example of a detailed HIPO diagram is given in Figure 7.5. Note that it can be cross-referenced to the HIPO hierarchy chart in Figure 7.2.

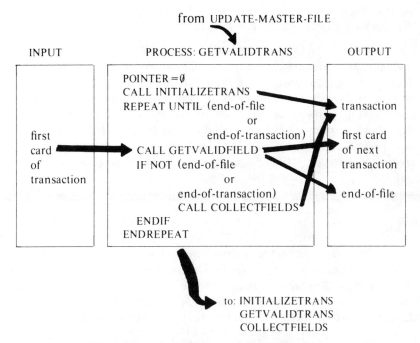

Figure 7.5. Typical detailed HIPO diagram.

Detailed HIPO diagrams show the relationships among inputs, processing logic, and outputs of a module in a highly graphic way. That feature is both a blessing and a curse: The diagram can be used as a means of conveying information to users, management, analysts, and programmers. On the other hand, because it is a graphic technique (as evidenced by IBM's providing HIPO templates, HIPO coding pads, and a detailed manual on how to use HIPO, with specific emphasis on techniques for drawing the fat arrows in Figure 7.5 such that they don't cross), a HIPO diagram requires a non-trivial amount of artwork. What are the chances that a detailed HIPO diagram will be updated if there is a change to the module at three in the morning? Indeed, what are the odds that the real code *ever* bears any resemblance to detailed HIPO diagram? Generally, there is a good chance that after the programmer in each specific case had put considerable time and effort into developing his detailed HIPO diagram, he found, while writing the code, that he had to change some aspect of the procedural design, whereupon he conveniently "forgot" to redraw his detailed HIPO diagram.

Thus, there is a serious concern that detailed HIPO diagrams will degenerate in the same manner as do detailed flowcharts. Several organizations for which I have consulted have abandoned detailed HIPO diagrams for this reason.

Finally, note that the central process portion of the detailed HIPO diagram is essentially the same as the pseudocode discussed earlier. The information shown in the input portion and the output portion of the detailed HIPO diagram *could* be shown on the hierarchy chart or structure chart that was discussed in Section 7.1. Thus, we conclude that there is nothing really essential in the detailed HIPO diagram that could not be obtained with other techniques, and the extra artwork involved in detailed HIPO diagrams poses serious questions of maintenance.

7.2.3 Nassi-Shneiderman diagram

Figure 7.6 illustrates a third method of describing the detailed procedural logic within a module. This technique is known as a Nassi-Shneiderman diagram, in honor of the two men who first published their ideas on the subject. On occasion, Figure 7.6 is referred to as a Chapin chart, a structured flowchart or simply an N-S diagram.

Indeed, structured flowchart is an appropriate term. As we can see, Figure 7.6 is similar to a conventional flowchart, except that it has no arrows. Moreover, the three basic ideographs of Nassi-Shneiderman diagrams correspond to the three basic constructs of structured programming. The simplicity of the N-S diagram is appealing, and several organizations have adopted the technique for this reason alone. However, other people with whom I have spoken recently have observed that an N-S diagram is really just "pseudocode with some boxes around it." If that is the case, why not simply write the pseudocode?

7.3 Documentation associated with systems analysis

A typical EDP project requires a vast amount of additional documentation: cost/benefit analyses, documentation for the operations staff, data dictionaries, and so forth.

Much of this documentation will remain basically unchanged by the introduction of the new structured techniques. However, as seen in Chapter 3, the most significant product of the systems analysis phase

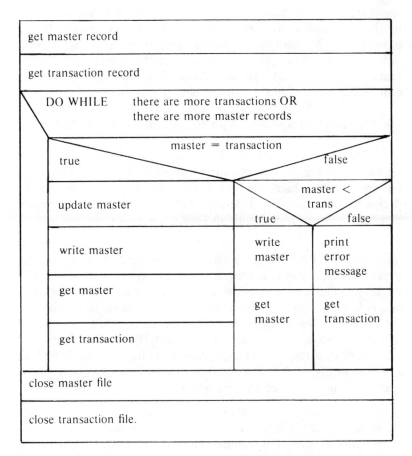

Figure 7.6. Typical Nassi-Shneiderman diagram.

the functional specification, has been altered significantly by the introduction of structured analysis.

Also, the documentation tools used for structured analysis are
similar to those used for structured design and for structured programming. In fact, such techniques as data flow diagrams, state-transition
diagrams, and pseudocode were introduced first in the design and programming, and several years later became tools of structured systems
analysis.

This similarity of documentation techniques has one advantage
which must be emphasized: *consistency*. The documentation produced
by structured analysis can be carried straight into the design and implementation phases with little or no change, which means that we can

minimize the danger that the design will drift away from the specification. In contrast, it used to be common to see a conventional narrative specification translated into a systems design that accomplished slightly more than, slightly less than, or at least something different than, the requirements stated in the specification; and, in the same fashion, the code would accomplish something different than the requirements stated in the original design specification.

7.4 Management problems with the documentation techniques

The primary problem with introducing the new documentation techniques is the danger that they may suffer the same fate as detailed flowcharts. You should be prepared for this problem, particularly if you decide to adopt the use of detailed HIPO diagrams, Nassi-Shneiderman diagrams, or even pseudocode in your organization.

In particular, you should anticipate that your programmers may not keep the HIPO hierarchy charts or structure charts up to date. My experience has been that programmers and systems analysts usually can be browbeaten into redrawing at least the high-level structure charts and data flow diagrams whenever a change is made to the design, since the overall design changes much less frequently than the detailed logic within a module. But I also have heard bitter complaints from programmers who resented being forced to redraw a complicated diagram like that in Figure 7.3, just because one interface has been changed or one new function added to the system.

This "maintenance" problem can be eliminated by using automated tools that are beginning to appear in the marketplace in the mid-1980's and which will be commonplace by the end of the decade.* Such tools are usually implemented on personal computers such as the IBM PC/XT or PC/AT, or on the more powerful 32-bit computers manufacturerd by Apollo or Sun; high resolution graphics are obviously required, and a communications facility between the personal computer and the organization's mainframe is also important.

The other major problems you should be prepared for when introducing the new documentation techniques are religious interpretations of some of the documentation techniques and the myth that the use of the documentation techniques is equivalent to designing.

---

* — Examples of such products are *Case 2000* from Nastec, *Excelerator* from Index Systems, and *The Software Engineering Workbench* from the YOURDON Software Engineering Company.

The problem of religious interpretations seems to be most acute in the case of HIPO. Some organizations have formulated stringent standards about the way HIPO diagrams should be drawn, thereby creating a tendency to draw diagrams to satisfy the standards manual, rather than to illustrate a computer system.

The second problem concerns me more. Occasionally, when programmers are asked if they use structured design, they respond: "Oh, yes, we're using structured design. We're drawing lots of HIPO diagrams!" Implicit in this statement is the assumption that *drawing* a HIPO diagram is the same as *doing* a design.

You should make sure that your programmers and systems analysts understand the distinction between documentation convention and design principles. Many programmers, for example, would argue that the structure chart shown in Figure 7.3 is bad. Imagine the following dialogue, which I actually have had with various programmers from time to time:

Manager:	What do you think of this structure chart in Figure 7.3?
Charlie:	I don't like it . . . . It's bad.
Manager:	Why? What's wrong with it?
Charlie:	Well, the diagram shows a level-two module calling a level-six module, four levels beneath it.
Manager:	What's wrong with that?
Charlie:	That's not the way they do it in HIPO.
Manager:	So what?
Charlie:	I just don't like it. I think it would be a better design — at least it would *look* better — if some additional modules were introduced at levels three, four, and five, so that we could maintain the convention of a module calling only modules that are one level beneath it.

The problem shown in this conversation is that Charlie has a certain belief about the way the diagram should look; apparently, the form and symmetry of HIPO appeal to him. While this response is acceptable, it is bothersome that Charlie's feeling about the preferred form of a *picture* leads him to conclude that the *design* in Figure 7.3 is bad.

Bibliography

1. DeMarco, T. *Structured Analysis and System Specification.*
    New York: YOURDON Press, 1978.

    This book contains a thorough discussion of
    data flow diagrams and should be read by
    analysts and designers.

2. *HIPO: A Design Aid and Documentation Technique,* IBM
    manual, Form GC20-1851-0.

3. Katzan, H. *Systems Analysis and Documentation: An Intro-
    duction to the HIPO Method.* New York: Van Nostrand
    Reinhold, 1976.

    If you've decided to use the HIPO method, this
    book contains a good, thorough coverage with
    plenty of examples.

4. Myers, G.J. *Reliable Software Through Composite Design,* 4th
    ed. New York: Petrocelli/Charter, 1977.

    Myers presents a variation of structure charts —
    a compromise between the official version of
    HIPO, and the kind of structure chart shown in
    Figure 7.3.

5. Yourdon, E., and L.L. Constantine. *Structured Design: Fun-
    damentals of a Discipline of Computer Program and Systems
    Design.* Englewood Cliffs: Prentice-Hall, 1979.

    Chapters 3 and 4 of this book discuss structure
    charts. The appendix contains a detailed set of
    guidelines for drawing structure charts.

6. Page-Jones, M. *The Practical Guide to Structured Systems
    Design.* New York: YOURDON Press, 1980.

    Somewhat easier to read than the
    Yourdon/Constantine book and has a good dis-
    cussion of the interaction between structured
    analysis and structured design.

Chapter Eight:

Chief Programmer Teams

Chapters 8, 9, and 10 discuss some of the organizational concepts that have been introduced into the EDP community along with structured programming, structured design, top-down implementation, and structured analysis.

This chapter treats Chief Programmer Team Organization, or CPTO. It *could* have been a very lengthy chapter, but my experiences during the past ten years suggest that there is not much point: Most organizations in the real world are *not* using the CPTO concept and have no intention of doing so in the foreseeable future. Regarding the specific cases that I have seen, I generally understand and agree with the decisions made within these organizations.

Consequently, this chapter will take on a somewhat less positive approach than the others in the book. As in the previous chapters, I provide a brief overview of the CPTO concept. In addition, I point out the reasons why your organization probably will not even attempt to implement the concept.

8.1 The motivation behind the CPTO concept

Much of the motivation for the chief programmer team has been discussed in previous chapters. We can summarize it in three phrases, as follows:

- a growing awareness of the Peter Principle

- a realization of the vast differences in the abilities of programmers

- a realization of the communication problems that are inherent in large, classical programming organizations

The Peter Principle, as you may recall, suggests that in most organizations, people are promoted until they reach their level of incompetence. There is an important corollary to the Peter Principle, too:

After a certain period of time, all positions in a company are filled by people incompetent to perform them.

Thus, in the computer field, we find that good junior programmers become senior programmers; good senior programmers become systems analysts; good systems analysts become project leaders; and good project leaders are promoted into the upper echelons of DP management, where they may or may not be competent.

This phenomenon is one of the major motivations for the CPTO concept. Programmers have an understandable desire to earn more money and gain more stature in their organization — and these goals usually can be attained only by moving into management. Of course, once they reach the level of project leader, most people consider it beneath their dignity to write code; even if they would *like* to indulge in doing a little coding, they don't have the time.

The chief programmer team concept is seen as a solution to this dilemma. The title chief *programmer* is considered analogous to that of chief scientist or chief engineer in other disciplines — a master of his or her craft with great skill and many years of experience. If such an attitude could be created, the programmer who is dubbed chief programmer would feel honored to be recognized as a master craftsman; moreover, he would have a tangible incentive if his organization accorded an equivalent salary and status as provided to high-level managers.

What kind of salary? How about $75,000 per annum? In some cases, it might be more appropriate to pay $100,000 or even $200,000 a year. You can imagine that such a salary would have quite an impact on programmers' acceptance of the Chief Programmer Team Organization concept.*

---

* — I have difficulty dealing with numbers like these, because my first real programming job paid three dollars per hour, which I considered an enormous increase over the $1.35 per hour salary I was earning washing dishes in the MIT dormitory cafeteria. The first and second editions of this book were published in the 1970's, before salaries were so drastically affected by runaway inflation; this third edition is being written in 1985, during

The second major motivation behind the CPTO concept is the recognition that there is an order-of-magnitude difference in the abilities of programmers. As stated in Chapter 2, Sackman's experiment suggests that talent among *experienced, competent* programmers could differ by as much as a factor of twenty five.

If so, a simple strategy is suggested: Why not fire the majority of mediocre programmers and hire a few hand-picked super-programmers to do all the work? When we consider the number of secretaries, clerks, managers, and other support personnel that also could be eliminated by this wholesale removal of the "Mongolian hordes," it seems quite a bargain to pay our chief programmer a mere $100,000 per year.

Although seemingly rational, the argument has three problems: There are *very* few such talented super-programmers; those few are choosy about where they work and usually will shun the medium-sized commercial organizations; and most organizations won't pay a salary of $100,000 per year to a programmer even if it *is* rational to do so. There are some exceptions, of course: the personal computer hardware/software companies like Apple, Microsoft, Borland, and Lotus, but that doesn't help the potential chief programmer who writes COBOL programs for the Amalgamated Cement Company in Dry Gulch, Montana.

Why does an organization refuse to pay $100,000 to a programmer who can turn out the same amount of work as twenty-five programmers, whose salaries are $25,000 each? The answer is that top management simply cannot understand the concept because their company is not in the computer business. For example, the American Widget Company is in the business of making widgets; their computer department is a necessary evil, existing only to print invoices, paychecks, and other such documents. Top management might be able to understand paying $100,000 a year to their chief widget designer, but the notion of paying such a high salary to someone in their data processing department would be unthinkable.

As a result, top management also is unimpressed with the third motivation of the CPTO approach: the recognition that communication

a period of relatively modest inflation rates of 3 to 5 percent per year. By the time you read this, it may be up to 20 percent per year again, or we may have entered a period of deflation. In any case, the salary figures in this 3rd edition are written (a) based on 1985 economics, and (b) on the assumption that inflation will not increase dramatically in the next few years.

problems between programmers become unmanageable on large projects. Although organizations with projects involving only three or four programmers do not recognize this as a problem, the communication problem becomes apparent in projects involving twenty or thirty programmers, and painfully obvious in projects involving one or two hundred programmers. For these projects, the meetings, memos, interface documents, and standards manuals all are rather futile attempts to maintain some semblance of communication.

The individual programmer's habit of taking initiative whenever he has the opportunity is one reason for the difficulty. In a typical project, each programmer is given a module to design, code, and test. However, the interface between his module and the rest of the system probably has not been defined very precisely. As a result, each programmer takes the initiative to define his interfaces more precisely, or he makes some minute changes to the defined interfaces. With twenty or thirty programmers making such independent design decisions, the project becomes chaotic.

With a chief programmer team, the communication problems are reduced because the chief programmer's talents mean that far fewer people are required on the project. In addition, the chief programmer makes all of the critical design decisions, directing the other programmers on the project, determining the interfaces to their modules, and enforcing these decisions.

With this approach, one person sees the overall picture at all times. In contrast, many conventional projects are characterized by nobody really understanding the whole system. In addition, the chief programmer approach means, at least in theory, that the subordinate members of the team do not have to talk to each other to find out what is happening. Thus, instead of $[.N \times (N-1).] \div 2$ lines of communication between the N programmers in the project, we find that there are only $(N-1)$ lines of communication.

8.2 The history of the CPTO concept

Some organizations believe that they have been using the chief programmer team concept for years. Indeed, I often visit organizations whose managers tell me, "Oh, yes, we've been doing this for quite some time . . . . Charlie, here, is our resident super-programmer." In most cases, Charlie turns out to be a slightly-better-than-average programmer, but no superstar. Also, the *team* characteristic of the CPTO approach (discussed later in this chapter) usually is missing completely.

On the other hand, many of the computer manufacturing organizations and some software consulting firms *truly* have used the chief programmer team concept for a decade or two. The smaller computer firms, for example, have known for quite some time that they could compete with IBM, Honeywell, and Univac only if they could develop their operating systems and compilers with small teams of two or three geniuses.

Using two or three people to develop an operating system would have been an interesting suggestion for IBM during its development of OS/360 in the mid-1960's. IBM frequently has become involved in massive development projects with hundreds, if not thousands, of programmers and has seen firsthand some of the problems discussed in previous chapters. Thus, it is not surprising that IBM took the lead in formalizing and articulating the concepts that other computer vendors had been using unofficially for years.

IBM's first experiments with the CPTO approach involved work on the NASA Manned Spacecraft System in the mid-1960's. The next experiment — more formal and more widely discussed — was the famous New York Times system. Since then, IBM and other organizations have implemented a substantial number of CPTO projects. The stories of the early super-programmer projects are fascinating, but not germane to this book. If you are seriously interested in the CPTO approach, I recommend that you read the papers and books listed in the bibliography at the end of this chapter.

8.3 The nature of the chief programmer team

So far, we have referred rather loosely to such labels as superprogrammer, chief programmer, and chief programmer team. To become more precise, let's define who these people are and identify what functions they perform.

Let's look at the last of these first: Based on the terminology used by Fred Brooks,* we can identify ten different types of people who might comprise a chief programmer team:

---

*Frederick P. Brooks, Jr., *The Mythical Man-Month* (Reading: Addison-Wesley, 1975).

- the chief programmer
- the copilot
- the administrator
- the editor
- the secretary
- the librarian
- the toolsmith
- the tester
- the language lawyer
- the programmer

We will discuss each of these team members individually in the following subsections. All of these tasks involve separate and specific skills, although tasks can be grouped so to be performed by a single person.

8.3.1 The chief programmer

The chief programmer also is called the "surgeon" by Fred Brooks, who describes the role in this way: "He needs great talent, ten years of experience, and considerable systems and application knowledge, whether in applied mathematics, business data processing or whatever."*

From the comments already made, we can assume that the chief programmer is an excellent designer; is familiar with the features of operating systems, database packages, structured programming, and structured design concepts; and is capable of coding ten to twenty times faster than the other programmers in the organization. To put these qualifications into perspective, IBM's Joel Aron reported, "Of the 2,000 programmers on the NASA project, only a handful would qualify as chief programmers."† Other organizations have suggested that only

---

*Ibid. p. 32.
†Joel Aron, "The Super-Programmer Project," *Software Engineering, Concepts and Techniques,* eds. J.M. Buxton, P. Naur, and B. Randell (New York: Petrocelli/Charter, 1976), pp. 188-190. See also Yourdon's *Classics in Software Engineering.*

one out of two hundred programmers is qualified to be a chief programmer. One authority in the field has suggested that there are only a dozen or so chief programmers in the entire world.

In addition to being a superbly gifted technician, the chief programmer personally defines the functional specifications for the system. Not only must he be conversant with the user's application, but he also must be able to express it in a form intelligible to the user. Of course, many managers argue that a super-programmer is unlikely to be able to do both well, which is one reason why Brooks and IBM argue that there are so few people qualified for the job. In other words, merely being a super-programmer is not enough to be considered a chief programmer.

Not only does the chief programmer define the functional specifications, but he also personally designs the entire system: He writes all of the critical code in the system (for example, the top-level modules, and some of the more complex modules in other parts of the system), and he even may write *all* of the code.

In addition, he is responsible for writing all of the documentation for the system — user manuals, data flow diagrams, data dictionaries, structure charts, Nassi-Shneiderman diagrams, narrative descriptions, and anything else that may be required. Clearly, the chief programmer must have a good command of the English language, a capability one finds sorely lacking in many programmers.

Finally, the chief programmer is responsible for supervising the other members of the team. Thus, the chief programmer must have management capabilities, although that part of his job is not assumed to occupy much of his time.

Our chief programmer, then, is a truly marvelous person: a combination of manager, super-programmer, super-designer, technical writer, and analyst. You can appreciate why there are arguments that such people — if there *are* any such people — deserve a salary of $100,000 per year!

8.3.2 The copilot

The term *copilot* appears in Brooks' discussion of chief programmer teams. More common in IBM literature is the phrase "backup programmer."

The copilot generally is an apprentice chief programmer, although he may be (or may have been) a chief programmer on other projects. His purpose is to serve as the chief programmer's alter ego. He shares in performing the design work and knows the code intimately. In addition, the copilot researches alternative design strategies and serves as a sounding board for the chief programmer's more farfetched ideas.

Another important function of the copilot is to act as insurance. If the chief programmer should be forced to leave the project, the copilot probably would be able to take charge. Less dramatically, we could imagine the chief programmer phasing out of a project during the final stages, leaving the copilot to finish the last few detailed modules (note that with a top-down approach, the copilot would not be left with the unpleasant job of system testing at the end of the project).

On the negative side, we can make the following observation: If it is hard to find *one* chief programmer for a project, it will be all that more difficult to find two such highly talented people for a single project.

8.3.3 The administrator

The administrator is the member of the team responsible for worrying about money, budgets, allocation of machine time, and other tasks requiring paperwork. This function is most important in projects in which there are substantial legal, contractual, or financial dealings.

Interestingly, most organizations would refer to such a person as the "project manager;" and, yet, in the Chief Programmer Team Organization approach, this person is *subordinate* to the chief programmer. Such an approach has been used in other fields, but it is considered novel, indeed, radical, in most data processing organizations. The usual reaction is, "What? You're suggesting that the project manager should report to some programmer who makes all the decisions? You've gotta be kidding!"

8.3.4 The editor

As mentioned, the chief programmer is responsible for generating all documentation for a project. Since he actually writes the documentation, the greatest possible technical accuracy and clarity is ensured.

However, an editor can make grammatical corrections to the chief programmer's rough drafts, provide references and bibliographies where appropriate; and, perhaps most important, oversee the mechanical aspects of producing the documentation.

8.3.5 The secretary

Normal clerical duties of typing, filing, and so forth, are carried out by secretaries, just as in any business operation; however, a *formal* chief programmer team is assumed to have two secretaries, one to handle tasks associated with the project administrator and one to assist the editor.

8.3.6 The program librarian

The program librarian maintains the technical records (source programs, listings, and so on). The program librarian's tasks are technical, whereas the secretaries' are clerical. Interestingly, this aspect of the chief programmer team *has* been widely adopted and discussed; Chapter 9 is devoted to the subject.

8.3.7 The toolsmith

The toolsmith provides any specialized program development tools that the chief programmer requires. These might include specialized utility programs (such as tape-to-printer programs of a variety not provided by the vendor); catalogued procedures and JCL; macro libraries; and any text-editing, file-editing, or debugging tools. In many conventional projects, such tools may exist as part of a general-purpose library. On the other hand, the chief programmer may feel that he needs some special utilities. Also, because the tool-building aspect of the project may be only a part-time job, the toolsmith might be able to serve more than one chief programmer team.

8.3.8 The tester

Basically, the tester develops data that can be used for module and system testing. The tester may develop some of his test data from the functional specifications, without regard to the code; other data may be developed *after* the tester has seen the code. In addition, the tester may develop test harnesses, dumps, traces, and other special testing/debugging packages.

Some CPTO projects assign the testing function to the copilot, while others ask the user to develop test data. In a large project, though, generation of test data and test utilities can be a full-time job, requiring certain talents and psychological makeup found only in a full-time tester.

8.3.9 *The language lawyer*

The language lawyer is the expert in various detailed parts of the programming environment: the operating system, database management package, compiler, JCL for the system, and so forth.

The language lawyer exists to answer the following sort of questions: "What really happens — at the assembly language level — when I execute a MOVE CORRESPONDING statement in COBOL?" or, "Does the current version of the operating system *really* implement the XYZ system call correctly?" or, "What's the fastest way of zeroing a table in assembly language on the Widget computer?" These are things that the chief programmer might be expected to know, particularly such static information as the fastest way to zero a table on a specific computer. Much of the information, though, is dynamic: It changes with each new release of the vendor's compiler or operating system. Also, it usually is buried in the small print in the appendix of some manual, if it exists at all.

Thus, while the chief programmer probably is resourceful enough to be able to find the answers to questions of the sort posed above, he prefers to draw upon the knowledge of the language lawyer.

8.3.10 *The programmer*

On small-to-medium sized projects, there may be no need for a programmer because all of the coding may be done by the chief programmer. On medium-to-large sized projects, the programmer writes code that has been specified and possibly designed by the chief programmer.

8.4 Management problems with the chief programmer team

The problems with the chief programmer team can be summarized as follows:

1. Chief programmers are hard to find. Many organizations make the mistake of assuming that their most senior programmers are chief programmers, whereas they probably are not. Other organizations are fooled into believing that their programmers are super-programmers, perhaps because they know more obscure instructions in the programming language than some of the other programmers. Many organizations

find that they have some programmers who can code quickly, but who cannot document, carry on a reasonable conversation with the user, or supervise other people. Such super-coders are not chief programmers.

2. It is difficult to convince organizations to compensate the chief programmer properly. Some organizations claim that they offer dual career paths, but usually such claims are vacuous.

3. Even with appropriate pay and fringe benefits, it is difficult to convince a chief programmer to work for an ordinary company. Why should he waste his time writing another payroll system on IBM System/3 in RPG-II, when he could be working on state-of-the-art applications for a more glamorous firm with an on-line, real-time, multi-processor system?

4. Organizing a chief programmer team so that it fits into the organizational structure of most companies is awkward. Theoretically, the chief programmer is in charge of the chief programmer team. But where does that leave you, the project manager? Are you willing to be replaced by a twenty-two-year-old super-programmer?

5. The chief programmer team concept is hard to reconcile with the classical view of the systems analyst. Theoretically, the systems analyst would be subordinate to the chief programmer, the opposite of the political structure in most organizations. Indeed, the purist CPTO approach suggests no need for systems analysts at all, since the chief programmer can carry out that function. So what do we do with our systems analysts?

6. Finally, it is difficult to introduce the CPTO concept into an organization that currently employs hordes of less-than-super programmers. What does one do with them? Fire them? Let them die of old age?

These questions are not easy to answer, and ironically the people who must provide the answers often are those whose empires, political stature, and jobs are threatened by the CPTO approach. As a result, the majority of MIS organizations I have visited have abandoned the concept. A few others have given their senior (and possibly mediocre) programmer the new title of Chief Programmer, thus deluding themselves into thinking that they successfully have adopted the CPTO concept.

Several organizations have adopted those aspects that can fit into their current method of doing business, particularly the program librarian concept, and the structured walkthrough or egoless programming concept. Each concept is discussed in Chapters 9 and 10, respectively.

So, if you meet someone who says that his organization is practicing the chief programmer team approach, chances are that the organization has introduced walkthroughs and program librarians and labeled the result a chief programmer team.

An alternative to the chief programmer team concept is the "egoless team;" see Chapter 10 for more details.

Bibliography

1. Aron, J. "The Super-Programmer Project." *Software Engineering, Concepts and Techniques.* eds. J.M. Buxton, P. Naur, and B. Randell. New York: Petrocelli/Charter, 1976, pp. 188 - 190.

2. Baker, F.T. "Chief Programmer Team Management of Production Programming." *IBM Systems Journal,* Vol. 11, No. 1 (January 1972), pp. 56 - 73.

3. Brooks, F.P., Jr. *The Mythical Man-Month.* Reading: Addison-Wesley, 1975.

4. Mills, H.D., and F.T. Baker. "Chief Programmer Teams." *Datamation,* Vol. 19, No. 12 (December 1973), pp. 58 - 61.

Chapter Nine:

Program Librarian

As we pointed out in the previous chapter, most MIS organizations have *not* adopted the concept of a team of specialists built around a super-programmer. However, one aspect of the chief programmer team concept has begun to gain wide acceptance: the program librarian.

This chapter, written on the assumption that you may wish to use program librarians independent of the CPTO concept, begins with an overview of the librarian concept and includes a discussion of the qualifications for librarians, the duties of the librarian, and the concept of a development support library. We conclude with a discussion of the problems that you are likely to encounter in introducing the librarian concept within your organization.

The concept of a program librarian has evolved considerably during the past ten years as MIS organizations have begun to use computers to automate the clerical functions of source code control, document control, and configuration management in large projects. Today, the program librarian is more an administrator than a clerk: with the support of automated documentation tools, he can spend his time coordinating the documentation-oriented activities of the project team members, rather than spending his time making copies of documents and manually filing them in file cabinets.

9.1 The objectives of the librarian concept

The concept of a formal librarian usually is associated with IBM's early experiments with the chief programmer team in the mid-1960's. From the beginning, there have been two major objectives in using the librarian: to make programmers more productive by eliminating the clerical part of their work; and to organize and control all technical information generated by the programming team, thus eliminating much of the chaos currently found in MIS development projects.

You may recall from Chapter 2 the statistics supporting that first objective: Weinwurm's study indicates that the average programmer spends only 27 percent of his day actually programming. Your programmers may spend more of their time coding, but it should be obvious to you as a manager that a substantial part of your programmers' activities are clerical in nature.

The significance of this point has been confirmed in a number of recent structured projects. IBM, for example, reports the following: Two programmers supported by a librarian generally are as productive as three programmers working alone. Some of my clients have gone even further: They report that one programmer supported by a librarian is equivalent in productivity to two programmers without clerical support.

The other motivation for the librarian concept is more difficult to quantify. Nevertheless, it is clear to professionals in the field at least that most MIS development projects need much more clerical organization than they currently have. Now, every programmer tends to keep his own private file of source programs, his own listings, his own special patches to the system, and so forth.

To appreciate the significance of this problem, put yourself in the position of the development programmer. Imagine that you have been told that the only reason a new system doesn't work is because of a bug in *your* module. Since you can't get any machine time during the day, you decide to work at night to fix the bug. In the midst of debugging — at about 3 o'clock in the morning — you discover that the bug is *not* in your module, but instead is in Fred's module.

Being a civilized person, you decide not to wake Fred from a peaceful sleep. Instead, you walk into his office to retrieve a copy of his program listing to see if you can discover the nature of the problem. Unfortunately, in his office you find not just one program listing, but some ten or twenty, all of which are marked "new," or "current," or "experimental." Which version of Fred's module is the latest, "official" version? Have you been using the right version in your debugging activities? Or, have you wasted an entire night debugging with an obsolete or experimental version of dear Fred's module?

Because Fred is paranoid, he has locked all of his listings in his desk before leaving for a three-week fishing trip in the wilds of Lower Slobovia where he can't be reached by telephone.

With scenes like these all too common in the data processing industry, you can see why there has been such a strong argument in favor of the librarian concept. Another way of looking at it is this: The development programming groups should have the same degree of control over source programs, listings, and object modules as the maintenance department has had for years. Maintenance groups could not survive for long if they permitted the chaos currently found in most systems development groups, and development groups are beginning to find that they can't survive either.

9.2 Qualifications for librarians

Having introduced the general idea of a librarian, we should address the kind of person best suited to be a librarian. There are a number of very different opinions about this subject, *all* of which are right.

The librarian can be whatever you want him or her to be. Your selection of that person should depend on the duties you want the librarian to perform. While there may be differing points of view concerning the qualifications needed, generally they fall into three categories:

- *clerical* — having competency in typing, keypunching, filing, organizing, and acting as a gofer.

- *programming* — being capable of interacting with a time-sharing system, talking to operators, understanding what programmers are doing

- *managerial* — having sufficient personal presence and strength of personality to effectively control access to source programs, listings, and so on, and being capable of reporting on a project's status to the manager

The most common type of librarian is one who performs primarily clerical duties. A great deal of a librarian's usefulness involves handling such simple clerical burdens as redrawing a data flow diagram; taking a program downstairs to the computer room to be compiled; and transcribing a legible, but handwritten, page of coding onto coding sheets so that the keypunch department will accept it. These tasks require nothing more than an intelligent, well-organized clerk.

Some organizations find that a secretary who already has worked in a programming department makes an excellent librarian if the librarian's job is defined strictly as a clerical function. Other companies have recruited people from the keypunch department or from other departments that are involved peripherally with data processing.

Other organizations stress the idea of a librarian as a junior apprentice programmer. Such a librarian is *not* a programmer, but, on the other hand, he or she does not find the computer programming environment totally alien. Thus, a librarian might be any one of the following: a student in a computer science curriculum from a local university (especially a co-op student who works on the job for six months at a time); a junior computer operator (senior operators may feel that becoming a librarian constitutes a loss of status); an RJE terminal operator; a senior, intelligent keypunch operator (who has been correcting programmers' COBOL coding errors for years); or one of the various types of programmers who dislike the intellectual, physical, and psychological rigors of being a real programmer.

Finally, some organizations have suggested that the librarian may be a person with management talents. If the librarian is responsible for controlling access to the vital documents of a project, it would be helpful for him or her to have the strength, intelligence, and force of personality expected of a future manager. In addition, the librarian is in the unique position of knowing the current status of the development project (which modules have been compiled, which modules have been tested, and so forth), which is precisely the kind of information the project manager needs to know. Thus, some organizations regard their librarians as the project managers of the future.

Hence, you have to decide whether your librarian should be a clerk, an apprentice programmer, or a fledgling project manager. One other suggestion: The word librarian may not be the most diplomatic job title in some cases. You might decide that it would be more appropriate — diplomatically and politically — to call such a person a "junior computer systems officer, grade 1," a "systems administrator," a "systems maintenance technician," a "programmer's assistant," or a "programming technician."

9.3 Duties of the librarian

The librarian's duties obviously depend on the qualities of the person you select and on your view of the librarian as either a clerk, junior programmer, or junior manager.

Most organizations, however, define the librarian's duties as some combination of those described below:

1. *Accept raw source programs.* The librarian usually is expected to accept code written by the programmer on a coding sheet or in longhand on ordinary paper. One or two experiments have been tried with the programmer dictating his code into a tape recorder.

2. *Prepare a machine-readable source program.* The librarian may type or keypunch the program into a time-sharing terminal.

3. *Arrange for compilations/assemblies.* This task may require the librarian to add some standard control cards (JCL) to the beginning of the program. The librarian may not understand the details of those control cards, but may be aware simply that that is part of the process known as "compile." The librarian also may be required to take the source program to the computer room to be compiled, or he may be required to direct the compilation from a time-sharing terminal or an RJE terminal. Presumably, the librarian also would be required to give a copy of the compiler output to the programmer. If the librarian's job is defined to be junior apprentice programmer, then he may need to correct trivial keypunch and syntax errors and carry out appropriate recompilations of the program before returning it to the programmer.

4. *File copies of appropriate documents in a library.* As mentioned earlier, one of the more important functions of the librarian is to control access to source programs, listings, and so on. Usually, the critical documents are filed in a library, the nature of which is discussed in Section 9.4.

5. *Carry out editing, recompiling, and other maintenance activities.* In most cases, the programmer will want to correct bugs, make changes, and add new code to the initial version of his program. These tasks usually are accomplished by allowing the programmer to submit a marked-up program listing to the librarian, who then repeats many of the steps described above. The marked-up listing also should be filed in the library.

6. *Perform executions and test runs of programs.* The librarian may use standard control cards or JCL for this function, or the programmer may provide special instructions. In both cases, the librarian's responsibility remains the same: to assume the clerical burden of such tasks, and to maintain control over the associated documents. One of the most common and important examples of this task is something we might call "system building:" From time to time, the librarian will gather together all of the official versions of individual modules and "build" (or "link" or "link edit") a new official version of the entire system.

9.4 The development support library

In most cases, each project and each company develop slightly different standards and procedures for the librarian and for the library maintained by the librarian. However, normally the librarian maintains the following categories of information.

1. *Handwritten documents.* This part of the library presumably would be maintained in ordinary file cabinets, and would contain such things as original data flow diagrams, structure charts, source programs (on coding sheets), marked-up program listings, original handwritten test data, and programmers' instructions for test runs.

2. *Machine-readable documents.* These would be maintained on the computer system itself, perhaps with the assistance of such packages as PANVALET and LIBRARIAN, among others. Such a library would consist of source programs, object modules, load modules, test files, and so on; in an environment that has sophisticated analyst workbench tools, the librarian would also maintain machine-readable versions of data flow diagrams, structure charts, entity-relationship diagrams, state-transition diagrams, data dictionaries, and minispecs. Note that prior versions of such files also would be maintained in addition to the current version.

3. *Program listings.* It is possible, of course, to maintain the program listings on a computer file along with the source programs and object modules; however, the

volume of the listings usually makes this prohibitive. Thus, the library would include, as one of its major elements, an official copy of the program listing of all of the modules of the system, plus appropriate back-up listings.

4.   *Operating instructions.* This part of the library consists of run-books and standard JCL for editing, compiling, executing, and testing programs. In most large development environments, the instructions probably would consist of catalogued procedures; on other systems, they might consist of specially prepared control cards.

5.   *Library maintenance information.* This is an index, indicating where everything is stored, how to access it, what procedures are used to update information, and so on. Its primary purpose is to provide insurance in case the librarian is absent temporarily or withdraws entirely from the project.

9.5 Management problems with the librarian concept

As with the other structured techniques, you should be prepared for problems when introducing the librarian concept into your organization. The problems emanate from three different areas of the organization: from upper echelons of management, from the programmers, and from the librarians themselves.

9.5.1 Problems with management

One of the problems you probably will find is a classical one when introducing a new *type* of job into the organization: The personnel department might resist your action, for example, telling you that there is no job description for librarians. What civil service grade should he get? How much should he be paid? Unfortunately, there is no immediate, simple answer to any of these questions. It depends on precisely how the job is defined, and whether one selects a clerk, a junior trainee programmer, or a junior manager for the job. Also, it can take from six months to a year to provide the appropriate data to the personnel department. If you are working for a large, conservative organization, be prepared for some delays.

A more immediate problem faced by some organizations is the lack of money in the budget. As many data processing managers have told me, they are allowed to hire a certain number of bodies each year. It doesn't matter to upper management whether those bodies are librarians or Ph.D. computer scientists. In other companies, things are even more simple: A hiring freeze may prevent the manager from hiring either programmers or librarians.

A different kind of problem occurs in organizations in which the top-level DP management came from the programming ranks. In this case, you should be prepared for the following reaction from your boss: "What's the matter with today's young whipper-snappers? Why, when *I* was a programmer, we used to keypunch our own programs, and operate the computers ourselves! Today's programmers are too lazy to do their own work!"

Some of the problems with management are understandable, albeit frustrating. You can understand why the personnel department will insist on formal job descriptions before allowing you to hire a librarian. Also, you certainly can appreciate that an economic slump can lead to a general hiring freeze throughout the company.

Nevertheless, it is less understandable to hear from management that programmers don't deserve librarians and that they should do their own dirty work. If you get this reaction from your management, try pointing out that your programmers are too highly paid to waste their time doing a job that could be done by a clerk. If your management demurs, they may be telling you that they view your programmers as nothing more than highly paid (if not *overpaid)* clerks and that they don't understand why clerks should require subordinate clerks to help them do their job. Such an attitude may be fashionable in certain circles and is compatible with the belief that "someday we won't need programmers. The users simply will talk to the computers, and the computers will program themselves." But, it is contrary to the idea that programming is a *profession.* Indeed, such an attitude from your management might be a signal that the time has come to begin circulating your resume to other, more progressive, organizations.

9.5.2 Problems with programmers

You might not have realized that *programmers* may object to the introduction of librarians. Sometimes, the programmers are just being ornery, but they occasionally have valid objections.

For example, some programmers complain that the librarian simply will be one more middleman between them and the machine. According to this view, life was wonderful in the "good old days" when the programmer keypunched and operated his own programs. Things started degenerating when computer operators were introduced and worsened when the programmer was told to submit all of his keypunching to a separate department (which tended to lose his keypunching, or confuse his oh's and zeros); and *now*, the programmer complains, you want to introduce a librarian!

Obviously, the librarian is not supposed to decrease the programmer's efficiency, indeed, quite the opposite. On the other hand, the programmer's complaint provides good warning: It tells us that we may well be defeating our cause if we set up a pool of librarians for the entire MIS organization. A librarian department may cause the same problems as the keypunch department, simply because it is a separate political organization with its own loyalties. To illustrate, as a manager, would you rather have your memos and letters typed by your own secretary, whose habits and idiosyncrasies you have come to know or by an anonymous member of the hundred-person typing pool in your company?

Also, in more and more organizations, programmers have access to on-line program development facilities and computerized librarian software packages, and thus they don't see the need for a *human* librarian. This point may be valid *if* there are sufficient terminals, *if* the programmers can type more than two or three characters a minute, and *if* the time-sharing system contains sufficient software to organize the various source programs and object modules in a controllable fashion.

You also should be prepared for the programmer who asks, "Gee, if I give all this work to the librarian, what's left for me to do?" This often is an indication that the programmer has a poor view of himself. If he thinks that he is *supposed* to be doing work that is primarily clerical, and if he can't think of anything better to do, something is terribly wrong.

Finally, anticipate the programmer who thinks, "If I give all this work to the librarian, I won't have any excuse to get up from my desk and wander around. I'll have to program eight hours a day!" To some extent, this complaint is valid. Serious design and coding can be a mentally fatiguing activity, and an occasional break is needed. Since taking a formal break is rather difficult to do in some companies, many programmers have found that one of the safe ways to relax for a few moments is walking to the computer room to pick up output from a test run, and then walking to the keypunch room to pick up the keypunching, in other words, to deliberately take on some of the duties of the librarian.

Unfortunately, the above complaints give the impression that the programmer really doesn't want to program eight hours a day, that programming is unpleasant and difficult. If you sense that your programmer would like to do as little programming as possible, I would suggest either of two options: fire him, or make him a librarian.

9.5.3 Problems with librarians

Finally, you can have problems with the librarians themselves, whose complaints seem to fall into three categories:

- "I don't understand the job. The terminology and the technology are alien to me."

- "I don't like working with programmers. I would rather be working with human beings."

- "I'm bored with the job. I want to be a programmer."

The first two objections are likely to come from librarians recruited from clerical ranks. To avoid this problem, recruit your librarian from areas already associated with the MIS department. Thus, a person currently working as a secretary in the programming department can become a librarian without feeling such an acute sense of being in an alien environment.

The third complaint — boredom — is most likely to come from librarians who have the training, experience, and/or aptitude for programming. If you hire someone with a bachelor's degree in computer science, and put him to work as a librarian, you can expect to hear this complaint after a week or two. If you recruit someone from the computer operations department, you can expect such a complaint after a few months. Indeed, no matter *who* the librarian is, if he is bright and has absorbed some of the rudiments of programming, be prepared to deal with this problem.

Assuming that the librarian is clever enough to become a programmer, you should let him make the jump. Thus, your discussions with the personnel department (recall Section 9.5.1) should include a possible career path into programming.

Bibliography

1.   Brooks, F.P., Jr. *The Mythical Man-Month.* Reading: Addison-Wesley, 1975.

> Brooks' discussion of chief programming teams touches on the subject of librarians. In addition, Chapter 12 of his book emphasizes the importance of controlling program libraries in a development project.

Chapter Ten:

Structured Walkthroughs

In Chapters 8 and 9, we addressed two concepts that could have a major impact on the organization of programmers in your company. This chapter discusses another such organizational concept: structured walkthroughs. One of the more important activities of a programming team, structured walkthroughs can be an extremely important activity for *any* group of programmers, whether or not they work in teams.

What is a walkthrough? Why are walkthroughs usually associated with programming teams? Where did the term originate? These questions are discussed in this chapter, which begins with an overview of the technical concepts and proceeds to a discussion of the problems you as managers are likely to encounter when implementing the techniques in your organization.

10.1 Egoless teams

Before discussing the notion of "walking through a program," we need some background. The original application began with G.M. Weinberg's *Psychology of Computer Programming.**

Weinberg's work introduced into the computer field such phrases as egoless programming, programming teams, democratic teams, egoless teams, adaptive teams, and even programming families. One can draw analogies with efforts in other industries (for example, such automobile companies as General Motors, Volvo, and Saab) to establish teams responsible for well-defined areas of production. The idea also

---

*G.M. Weinberg, *The Psychology of Computer Programming* (New York: Van Nostrand Reinhold, 1971).

has been greatly influenced by such psychological theories as transactional analysis (for example, "I'm OK, you're OK").

The purpose of teams in the programming field is primarily to change programming from "private art to public practice,"* as Baker and Mills put it. Or, to slightly paraphrase Weinberg, the intention is to change programs from private masterpieces to corporate assets. There is a growing recognition that many programmers have been working *alone* throughout their careers and that they have been more interested in the personal, intellectual pleasure of writing programs than in seeing the programs work for the user.

A programming team, if it is successful, creates an environment in which everyone feels free to discuss and critique everyone else's programs. This environment is necessarily *egoless* and discussion is formalized in a walkthrough.

Many other aspects of egoless teams are sufficiently radical that the concept has not yet gained wide acceptance. For example, experience with egoless teams indicates that different people will emerge as the natural leader at different stages of the project. One team member may dominate during the design phase of the project, others may dominate during the coding, while still others may take control during the debugging and testing phases.

Another characteristic of the egoless team is that nobody is really in charge — nobody is the boss, in the traditional sense. This feature generally makes outside management somewhat nervous ("Whose rear end are we going to kick if the project comes in behind schedule?"), although that problem sometimes can be circumvented by nominating one team member as the spokesperson for the group. The absence of a formal boss also may be difficult for certain team members to handle, for they may be accustomed to and prefer an authoritarian manager who tells them what to do.

Note, also, that the egoless team may not have any superprogrammers. If it did, we probably would call it a chief programmer team. However, as we observed in Chapter 8, most companies don't have a super-programmer anyway, so the egoless team perhaps is the best way to effectively use the large number of average programmers a company may employ.

---

*F.T. Baker and H.D. Mills, "Chief Programmer Teams," *Datamation,* Vol. 19, No. 12 (December 1973), p. 58. See also *Classics in Software Engineering.*

Obviously, the mere act of putting three or four people into a project does not make them function as a *team*. Implicit in the concept of a team is the notion of working closely together, reading each other's code, sharing responsibilities, knowing each other's idiosyncrasies (both on a technical and a personal level), and accepting a group responsibility for the product. If this attitude can be instilled, the effect is synergistic: Five people working together on a team may produce twice as much as they would working individually.

We should make one other comparison between the chief programmer team and the egoless team. If you have a super-programmer in your organization, the chances are that he's not egoless: He's very good, and he's happy to tell everyone just how good he is, destroying the democratic flavor of the team, especially when it comes to walkthroughs. You may find that the chief programmer wants to review all of the code by himself, rather than making it a group activity. This sort of one-on-one confrontation between an individual programmer and the chief programmer is hardly likely to be egoless.

Many feel that egoless teams will predominate in the future. In organizations in which such a concept has been implemented successfully, the results have been impressive, and the programmers will tell you that they would never revert to their old way of doing things. On the other hand, other organizations have found that they simply cannot implement the concept: There are too many psychological problems, too many personality clashes, and too many political problems.

In summary, then, it seems that the concept of true programming teams, or families, probably will suffer the same fate as the chief programmer team concept. We do not discuss it further in this book, but I recommend that you read Weinberg's book, as well as related books by Semprevivo and Thomsett, if you find the idea interesting.

If egoless teams are a failure, why are we addressing them, especially in this chapter? The reason is simple: About the only aspect of the team concept likely to be implemented in the typical organization is that of a walkthrough. Walkthroughs approximate team programming and are one of the first steps toward establishing programming teams.

10.2 Types of walkthroughs

Most discussions about walkthroughs concentrate on code: That is, people sometimes think that the only purpose of a walkthrough is to examine a program listing. In fact, there are a number of different types of walkthroughs:

1. *Specification walkthroughs.* As the name implies, the primary purpose of this type of walkthrough is to look for problems, inaccuracies, ambiguities, and omissions in the system *specification.* Such a walkthrough presumably would consist of the user, systems analyst, and one or more programmers on the project, and would involve examining the data flow diagrams and other documents produced by structured analysis.

2. *Design walkthroughs.* The purpose of this walkthrough is to look for flaws, weaknesses, errors, and omissions in the architecture of the design before code is written. This walkthrough might involve the user, certainly the systems analyst, and the senior programmer (chief programmer); and probably all of the other programmers as well. The documents used for this walkthrough would be HIPO diagrams and structure charts (see Chapter 7).

3. *Code walkthroughs.* A code review includes the programmer who wrote the code, the other programmers on the team, and, possibly, a few programmers from outside the team.

4. *Test walkthroughs.* This walkthrough's purpose is to ensure the adequacy of the test data for the system. It is *not* intended to be a forum for examining the output from the test run. Attendees would include the programmers on the project; the tester, if such a person exists (recall the discussion in Chapter 8); the systems analyst; and perhaps the user, if he can be enticed to join in the fun.

Specification, design, and test walkthroughs are not new; they usually are called reviews in most organizations. Unfortunately, the very phrase *design review* terrorizes analysts and designers, evoking images of a formal political ritual, in which users, analysts, and programmers spend an entire day yelling and insulting each other's ancestry while the big bosses from the user and programming departments sit in the back of the room smoking cigars and taking notes. Or, the phrase may connote a political ritual of another kind: a dull meeting convened to rubber-stamp a design that nobody understands.

The point is that design and specification reviews tend to be formal and somewhat political. Of necessity, they tend to be global in their examination of a design. Because of the number of people involved, they can be convened only occasionally, and since it is such a hassle getting the design review committee together, one feels obliged to make a formal presentation, complete with flip charts, foils, and 35mm slides, of the entire design.

By contrast, walkthroughs tend to be informal and local in nature. The people who participate in the walkthrough may meet three times a week, or even three times a day, discussing small parts of the design, specifications, or code quietly. As a result, a great deal more usually is accomplished.

It is important that walkthroughs take place in the order presented herein. It is extremely unpleasant to discover in a *code* walkthrough that there was an error in the specifications or that the design is unacceptable to the rest of the team. By the time design begins, the team should have uncovered the major weaknesses in the specification; by the time coding starts, the team should have discovered the major problems in the design.

10.3 Objectives of a walkthrough

The objectives of a walkthrough should be explicit. The major objective, of course, is to find errors: an omission, a contradiction, or a logical error of any kind. Happily for all of us, walkthroughs are quite successful in this respect: The number of errors in production systems decreases by a factor of five in organizations that use walkthroughs diligently.

Another major objective is to look for errors of style. The walkthrough usually will point out major efficiency and readability problems in the code (for example, cryptic data names), modularity problems in the design, and poorly stated requirements in the specifications. Arguments will arise in this area of style. What appears reasonable to one person will not necessarily seem reasonable to another.

There are other less tangible objectives of a walkthrough. For example, the mere threat of a walkthrough tends to improve the quality of the code, design, specifications, or test data. Clearly, one does not want to look foolish in front of one's peers. At the coding level, this phenomenon sometimes translates into something more obvious: The other members of the team may be unwilling to walk through anything other than structured code developed in a top-down fashion.

Also, team reviews or walkthroughs, serve as a consciousness-raising session for everyone. Not only do the junior people learn techniques from the senior people, but the senior people often get new ideas and insights from the junior people. Weinberg has made a further observation: He claims that for a junior programmer, one year working as part of a team that practices walkthroughs is equivalent to two years of working alone.

Frequent walkthroughs minimize the chance of having to throw work away if someone is forced to leave the project. In conventional projects, we usually find that a half-finished program is worthless if the author leaves because a new programmer or systems analyst finds it impossible to figure out what the original programmer was doing; hence, he throws the half-finished code away, and starts over.

10.4 When should a walkthrough be conducted?

The guidelines for scheduling walkthroughs are simple: A walkthrough should be conducted as frequently as possible, so that *small* pieces of work (code, or design, or specifications, or test data) are reviewed. However, a walkthrough should be scheduled only when the programmer or systems analyst is ready. One of the worst things you as a manager can do is to legislate walkthroughs every Friday afternoon, or after every one hundred lines of coding, or after every seven bubbles in a data flow diagram.

The scheduling of specification walkthroughs and design walkthroughs is fairly well determined by the stages of document development. When a unit of documentation is available for review, a walkthrough should be scheduled. However, a code walkthrough could be held at any of the following stages:

- before the code is entered into the computer

- after the code is entered into the computer, but before it is compiled

- after the first compilation

- after the first clean compilation

- after the first test case has been executed successfully

- after the programmer thinks that *all* test cases have been executed successfully

There are both advantages and disadvantages to scheduling walk-throughs at each of these stages. Conducting a walkthrough can be relatively unpleasant, for example, when the source document consists only of an illegible, handwritten coding sheet: Each sheet of paper probably contains only ten or twenty lines of code, requiring the reviewer to turn the pages constantly to see what the program is doing. Furthermore, the reviewer sorely misses symbol tables, cross-reference listings, and other helpful aids that the compiler or assembler normally produces.

On the other hand, a walkthrough scheduled for this same time-frame takes advantage of the earliest opportunity for code review. Delays sometimes occur in the keypunching and compiling of a program, and the team may wish to ensure that the code is correct before wasting a day, or as much as a week, waiting for it to be keypunched. Thus, some organizations conduct their walkthroughs after the code has been keypunched, but before it has been compiled. The source document is usually a simple 80-80 listing produced by an EAM machine.

It is much more common, though, to conduct a walkthrough *after* the program has been compiled. At that point, the reviewers are working with a more legible document, with more information on each page, and with the symbol tables, cross-reference listings, and other helpful information that the compiler provides as a matter of course. Some people argue that the walkthrough should not take place until the programmer has produced a clean compilation without syntax errors. In most cases, this makes sense *if* your organization has reasonably good turnaround time for compilations. Obviously, you must strike a balance here: While you don't want to waste the entire team's time looking for syntax errors when they can be found easily by a compiler, neither do you want the author of the program to spend several days compiling his program repeatedly to rid it of difficult syntax errors.

It usually is a bad idea to delay the walkthrough until the programmer has begun testing his program, and it definitely is a bad idea to wait until the programmer thinks he has finished all of his testing. First, much time probably already has been wasted with the programmer looking for his own program bugs. The *team* could have spotted the bug more quickly.

In addition, ego problems may arise if you wait too long before having a walkthrough. For example, if one of the team members suggests that the code be revised to make it more readable, the author of the program is likely to become defensive. He's invested time and energy, psychic as well as physical, and he is not strongly interested in listening to someone else's suggestions about rewriting the program.

Another reason to hold a walkthrough early in the project is that finding bugs in a program has a positive psychological effect on the team. Many organizations contend that the more bugs found in a walkthrough, the more successful the walkthrough has been.

On a personal level, a programmer generally doesn't mind spending an hour or two reviewing someone else's code if he finds a bug or two. He feels that his time has been well invested. However, if he spends an hour reading through the code and does *not* find a bug, he could think that he's wasting his time. He may become sloppy, thinking that there won't be any bugs in *any* code that he walks through.

10.5 Conducting the walkthrough

In many cases, walkthroughs are so informal that one cannot really say they are "conducted." The programmer takes someone else's code home in the evening, curls up in front of a roaring fire with a bottle of wine, and spends a pleasant evening looking for bugs.

In more formal circumstances, there usually is a prescribed pattern to the walkthroughs; that is, they tend to be structured. What follows is a set of guidelines to be modified as you see fit. For more details, consult the references at the end of this chapter.

- A coordinator, who may be the chief programmer, chairs the meeting and sees that order is maintained. This implies, of course, that the meeting is sufficiently large and formal and that the personalities are disparate enough that order does have to be maintained. The coordinator also schedules the walkthrough, reserves a conference room, distributes materials, and so on.

- The author generally makes a presentation of his product (the specification, the design, or the code) to the reviewers.* During this overview or presentation phase, general comments and questions may be entertained, but specific questions ("How does your system handle an XYZ transaction?") should be deferred.

---

*There are varying opinions regarding the author's presentation: Some people feel that if the product requires an overview presentation, something must be wrong with it. It should be possible for the reviewing audience to understand it without any help. Others give a different argument: An overview presented by the author is likely to brainwash the reviewers into making the same logical errors as the author, and they will overlook bugs in the product. Thus, some people feel that the author should *not* make a presentation, but should be present only to answer questions from the rest of the group.

- Following the general discussion, the author walks through the product in minute detail, reviewing each piece. This walkthrough is not usually done with specific test cases. Instead, it is based on a logical argument of what the code or design will do at various stages.

- After the general walkthrough, members of the reviewing audience may ask to walk through specific test cases. This process continues as long as anyone can think of situations in which the behavior of the product is suspect.

- The coordinator normally resolves disagreements if the team is unable to reach a consensus. Such disagreements might include questions of style, efficiency, or interpretations of the specifications. These can continue interminably if they are not stopped by the coordinator.

- Additional walkthroughs may be necessary to review corrections and changes to the code. It usually will be evident whether a second walkthrough is required, and the team should be able to reach an agreement in this area relatively quickly. Many organizations require that the team take a formal vote to determine the need for a second walkthrough.

The above comments may give you the impression that at more formal walkthroughs no one is allowed to speak unless he has raised his hand and received recognition from the chair. Such is usually not the case: Walkthroughs tend to be rather informal, give-and-take sessions among peers who need little outside supervision to maintain order.

10.6 Other aspects of walkthroughs

Every organization conducts its walkthroughs somewhat differently. How your programmers and analysts conduct their walkthroughs will depend on their personalities and their surroundings. However, the following suggestions are useful in most organizations:

1. Have your people schedule their walkthroughs in advance — a day ahead usually is sufficient. If possible, have them distribute appropriate materials (data flow diagrams, data dictionaries, coding sheets, listings, HIPO diagrams) to the participants a day in advance as well and encourage private reviews prior to the public walkthrough. Many of the bugs and problems are trivial and need not take up the time of the entire group.

2. Make sure that you as the manager stay out of the walkthrough and keep out any other big bosses, too. You may be curious about the walkthrough mechanism, and you may wish to sit through one after your programmers and analysts have had an opportunity to become used to the technique. However, you should be aware that your presence, especially during the first few walkthroughs, probably will be extremely inhibiting.

3. See that proper notes are kept during the walkthroughs, not only of bugs but also of suggested changes and improvements to the product. Such suggestions tend to be forgotten, and if the author was not enthusiastic about the suggested improvements, he is *very* likely to forget about them.

4. Create a proper attitude for the programmers and analysts: Make them see that it is good to find bugs. Impress upon them that *everyone* in the team is responsible for bugs: the author who put the bug into the product *and* the people who failed to find it in the walkthrough. Make them all sign their initials on the product when they are convinced it is correct. Then, when the system has been implemented, call *all* of them into the computer room in the middle of the night when an undiscovered bug blows up the program during a production run!

5. Make sure that your people understand that the major purpose of the walkthrough is error *detection*, not error *correction*. If the solution to a bug can be demonstrated easily to the author, no harm is done, but it is a disaster to see half a dozen programmers and analysts dash to the blackboard and begin arguing about the

correctness of a fix they each have just invented for a bug. It is sufficient to let the author know that the bug exists. Let *him* decide how to fix it.

6. Keep the walkthroughs short and sweet. An hour is long enough, and ninety minutes is probably the absolute limit. Studying someone else's code, design, or specification is mentally fatiguing, and one's attention begins to wander after an hour or so. Also, don't schedule walkthroughs one right after the other.

10.7 Management problems with walkthroughs

As you may anticipate, there can be problems with the walkthrough concept. Perhaps the first problem occurs in the management area: Many MIS managers are not convinced that walkthroughs are a good idea.

Some managers, for example, argue that it's a waste of time to tie up so many people to examine code. "Six technicians sitting in a room for an hour!" a manager will exclaim. "How can that possibly be cost-effective? Chances are they spend most of their time talking about football or sex!" If you hear this complaint from other managers in your organization, you should have these four answers:

1. It probably would take the author considerably longer to find the same number of bugs. After all, if the author put bugs into his program or specifications, then he undoubtedly will create test data that repeat the same logical errors.

2. Some bugs would *never* be found by the author. It's worth a few hours' effort by a team to find such bugs. Otherwise, they'll be discovered at a later stage in the development of the system (for example, analysis errors detected during the coding phase) or, even worse, after the system has been put into production, at which time, the bugs are *much* more expensive.

3. There is no other reasonable way of ensuring that the style of the product is acceptable, reflecting a proper implementation of the principles of structured analysis, structured design, and structured programming.

4.   Case studies such as those discussed in Chapter 2
     confirm that walkthroughs are productive.

You also should be prepared to answer the managers in your organization who are convinced that all testing and debugging should be
done by the computer. Again, there are some fairly standard arguments that you can give:

1.   Machine time is cheap compared to the cost of people,
     but the machine turnaround time is terrible. It is like-
     ly that your programmers will have to wait a day or
     two to get a program compiled, and chances are, your
     people aren't as productive as you may think while
     they're waiting for that output.

2.   The machine only will find bugs that the programmer
     exposes through his test data. Again, the author of the
     program unconsciously tends to select test cases that
     will demonstrate that his program *works*, not that it has
     a bug.

In some cases, it may be preferable to let the computer find the
bugs. If the turnaround time is acceptable, it usually makes sense to let
the author of the program find his own syntax errors with the assistance
of the compiler. It also may make sense to let the programmer eliminate the more trivial logic errors in his program, but be careful not to
wait too long for a walkthrough, or the author will become too egotisti-
cal about his code.

Still another common viewpoint is that junior programmers and
analysts should not be allowed to participate in walkthroughs. Many
managers feel that reviews should be done only by the chief programmer or the project manager. Your response to this suggestion should
be one or all of the following:

1.   The possibility of ego confrontations increases with a
     one-on-one situation, particularly between the pro-
     grammer and his or her superior. The team environ-
     ment has a mitigating effect on the clash of egos.

2.   The chief programmer or project manager is too busy
     to give the product a thorough walkthrough and prob-
     ably will skim the code, looking only for obvious er-
     rors.

3. Even if the chief programmer spends a significant amount of time, he's only human and can make mistakes. Subjecting the product to a team walkthrough increases the chances that *someone* will find the bug.

4. To paraphrase the old proverb, "Out of the mouths of babes (and junior programmers) come pearls of wisdom." Junior programmers often have refreshingly different approaches to design and systems analysis. Analysts as well can contribute equally refreshing ideas in the areas of coding and design.

Finally, management is likely to be concerned about the possibility of ego problems. The programmers in their group may have very strong personalities, and the concept of a walkthrough may be viewed as an open invitation to fisticuffs. The comments we can make in this regard include the following:

●   Arguments of this sort are healthy. Since personality conflicts exist anyway, why not get them out into the open?

●   A strong coordinator should be able to mediate most ego conflicts, and prevent arguments from dominating.

●   Many conflicts can be avoided by establishing standards at the beginning of the project. This point is discussed more fully in Chapter 13.

●   Almost all arguments can be avoided by disallowing discussions of style and restricting the walkthrough to an exercise in finding bugs. This limitation is unfortunate, but it is better than having no walkthrough at all.

●   Ego problems are easier to cope with if the review comes after a small investment of time has been made, not after the author has spent six months developing what he considers to be a perfect product.

As you might expect, not all of the objections to walkthroughs come from the management community; the programmers and analysts create a few problems of their own. You should anticipate the following problems when implementing walkthroughs:

- *Attitude problems.* Some of your programmers and systems analysts will be unwilling to cooperate. If they can't be convinced to participate in the walkthrough approach after a few months of practice, you have two alternatives: Fire them, or put them in a corner to work by themselves. If you choose the latter approach, I strongly recommend that they be forced to maintain their own work.

- *Inexperience at giving or taking criticism.* Many programmers and some systems analysts seem to have had little exposure to the group dynamics involved in walkthroughs. Indeed, one often finds that certain people are attracted to the data processing field because they find it easier to deal with machines than with people. If you find this to be a problem, you should consider giving your technicians some training in transactional analysis, the I'm-OK-You're-OK approach.

- *Unenthusiastic reviewers who don't try hard enough to find bugs.* Everyone knows about the programmer or systems analyst who is overly critical in a walkthrough; he makes his presence known. But, we sometimes overlook the person who sits quietly in a corner and never says a word. It is worth repeating a point made earlier: Make *everyone* feel responsible for the bug. It may help to give the quiet programmer a call at 3 A.M., asking him to come into the office to help track down a bug that he didn't bother trying to find in the walkthrough.

- *Walking through too much at one time.* Watch out for this one: Your programmers and systems analysts sometimes will try to spend an entire day walking through several thousand lines of code or several dozen data flow diagrams. As stated, anything tried after the first ninety minutes probably will be a waste of time.

- *Fear that walkthroughs will be used to judge performance.* This problem can be serious, particularly in programming. It's a paradoxical issue, since everyone knows that programmers are not paid solely on the basis of their performance (as pointed out in Chapter 8, nobody is willing to pay $100,000 for a super-programmer). So why should a programmer care if a few bugs are found in his program? On the other hand, you can appreciate his fear. In response, you should do two things: First, stay out of the walk-through, especially if the programmers view you as an ogre rather than a friend. Second, impress upon everyone that the *code,* not the person, is being reviewed.

- *Arguments over style.* There is no magical way to prevent programmers and analysts from arguing over such things as the merits of nested IF statements in COBOL, or from debating the advantages and disadvantages of a particular machine language instruction. However, you should recognize that arguments over style sometimes are interminable. The best thing to do is to leave the team alone. Although team members may waste a considerable amount of time at first, sooner or later they tire of such arguments and will learn to discipline themselves. An alternative is to establish standards to which everyone can adhere, but self-imposed discipline is much more effective than standards imposed without.

Bibliography

1. Weinberg, G.M. *The Psychology of Computer Programming.* New York: Van Nostrand Reinhold, 1971.

    This book first introduced the concept of walk-throughs. I consider it "must" reading for both programmers and managers.

2. Yourdon, E. *Structured Walkthroughs,* 3rd ed. New York: YOURDON inc., 1985.

    A more thorough discussion of walkthroughs than was possible in this chapter.

3. Semprevivo, P. *Teams in Information Systems Development.* New York: YOURDON Press, 1980.

    An alternative viewpoint to the formation and motivation of teams in an MIS organization.

4. Thomsett, R. *People and Project Management.* New York: YOURDON Press, 1980.

    A delightful book about the politics of programming teams, written in the same cheerful, readable style as Weinberg's book.

5. Block, R. *The Politics of Projects.* New York: YOURDON Press, 1983.

    Not about teams *per se,* but about the political climate and pressures which a project manager must deal with on a day-to-day basis. Recommended as a "survival manual" for project managers, and good reading for managers thinking of implementing walkthroughs.

Chapter Eleven:

Which Techniques
to Implement First

We have discussed structured analysis, top-down implementation, structured design, structured programming, chief programmer teams, program librarians, and structured walkthroughs. In this chapter, we address ourselves to questions frequently asked by organizations exposed to all of the structured techniques for the first time: Which techniques should we implement first? Should we start with structured programming? Or would it make more sense to begin with structured design? Or should we jump in with both feet and try all of the new techniques?

There is no single right answer to these questions. What's right for one organization may not be right for another. From what you've seen thus far in this book and from what you know of your own organization, *you* have to decide what would be best. Nevertheless, there are about a half-dozen things to consider when deciding which structured technique to implement first.

11.1 Implementing all of the structured techniques at once

Some organizations can execute such a feat: After reading about the techniques or getting a presentation from their hardware vendor, they decide to use all of the new techniques at once. As you might expect, this plunge is more likely to happen in the smaller MIS organizations with only a half-dozen or so programmers and not very likely to occur in the larger organizations.

Sometimes, an organization will decide to try all of the structured techniques on a single pilot project, discussed in the next chapter. Even in such a limited situation, however, experimenting with several new techniques at once usually leads to chaos.

The reasons are obvious. Structured programming, structured design, and structured analysis are not simple concepts, and a lot of concentration is needed to make them work correctly. If the programmers and systems analysts are trying to implement walkthroughs *and* chief programmer teams, as well as adjusting to having a librarian to relieve them of particular tasks, it will be difficult for them to succeed with any of these techniques.

11.2 Techniques involving organizational changes

As suggested in Chapters 8, 9, and 10, some organizations will find it difficult ever to implement chief programmer teams, librarians, and walkthroughs. Even if you can, you'll probably find it more difficult to introduce one of these as the first structured technique. Usually, it is easier to introduce first a relatively innocuous *technical* concept, like structured programming, which neither threatens anyone's empire, nor conflicts with current organizational philosophies.

Similarly, you may have trouble introducing structured analysis as the first structured technique in your organization, especially if your department engages solely in programming and implementation, while an entirely different department carries out systems analysis. In addition, while most users react favorably to data flow diagrams and other documentation tools described in Chapter 3, a hostile user organization may reject these new tools for political reasons. Some users may not be willing or able to conceptualize their requirements by looking at the abstract, pictorial models that structured analysis generate; for such users, the concept of prototyping discussed in Chapter 18 may be appropriate.

Once you've demonstrated that structured programming, top-down implementation, and structured design are good ideas, then you probably will be in a strong enough political position to say to the boss, "The last three structured techniques that I introduced to the company have turned out to be winners. Why not gamble a little now, and let me try something like structured analysis?"

Again, I'm not suggesting that you *must* follow this tack. Your top management may be more intrigued with the organizational aspects of the structured techniques and uninterested in such seemingly trivial technical concepts as structured programming.

11.3 Using structured code alone

Earlier in the book, we discussed that structured coding is a solid idea and probably a significant improvement over your current approach, but alone it's not enough to solve all your problems. If your design techniques are poor — if your designers still are creating large, sloppy modules that are strongly "coupled" to other equally sloppy modules — then the best coding won't help. In fact, even if you're using structured design, you may be in trouble: You may be creating brilliant solutions to the wrong problems. Structured design *and* structured analysis are crucial for structured coding to have any value. To clarify this point, examine the references at the end of Chapters 3, 5, and 6.

Grasping this point is important because if you introduce the structured techniques with great fanfare and promises of spectacular improvements, then your first structured technique needs to demonstrate spectacular improvements. But, if you try structured programming alone, you might not achieve such overwhelming improvements. My recent experience with a few projects involving only structured coding has been that the initial gains in productivity and reliability of the code will seem quite impressive, but the long-term maintainability of a system may not be very impressive at all. For a good example of this, see P.J. Plauger's article, "New York Times Revisited," in *The YOURDON Report.**

Consequently, it may make sense to begin with structured design or structured analysis; and when either is working properly, *then* introduce structured coding. Once you've overcome the objections, battles, and problems associated with structured analysis or design, introducing structured programming will be almost trivial.

11.4 Using top-down design and implementation first

As we discussed in Chapter 4, many of the advantages of the top-down approach are political. Compared to classical approaches, the method allows you to demonstrate something to the user at an earlier

---

*P.J. Plauger, "New York Times Revisited," *The YOURDON Report,* Vol. 1, No. 3 (April 1976), pp. 4 - 5.

stage, to survive deadline crises more gracefully, and to manage machine test time better.

These benefits are very noticeable to the user community, to higher levels of management, and to the computer operations manager. For this reason alone, many MIS managers have decided that using the top-down approach is a good way to introduce the structured techniques within their organizations.

However, this strategy can backfire. As mentioned in Chapter 4, many programmers view top-down implementation as an invitation to start coding *before* they've done any real design. Especially on your crucial first few projects, beware of this danger.

11.5 Conducting informal walkthroughs

Informal walkthroughs are a good way to start implementing the structured techniques because you can't expect an individual programmer or systems analyst to understand and implement any of the other structured techniques by himself. By forcing everyone to talk about their designs and their code in a low-key, non-threatening fashion, you can maintain quality control when you most need it.

This point needs emphasizing. If you send all thirty of your programmers to a class about structured programming, they will grasp thirty different versions. They will write thirty different kinds of structured programs, some good, some mediocre, some downright bad. If nobody looks at the code, you'll never know who truly understands structured programming.

If you begin by establishing an environment in which everyone's code, design, and specifications are exposed to public discussion, then you'll ensure that a relatively uniform version of top-down implementation, structured design, and structured programming can be implemented later.

You may conclude that walkthroughs by themselves are not significant enough to deserve being the only technique introduced within your organization; you may decide to introduce walkthroughs together with structured programming, structured design, or structured analysis. Once again, *you* have to make the decision.

Chapter Twelve:

Choosing a
Pilot Project

Most organizations consider a pilot project to be a formal experiment in the use of one or more of the structured techniques. Indeed, being an experiment is its primary virtue. If structured programming is a bad idea, it is preferable to discover this fact in a low-cost, low-risk experimental project. If the pilot project confirms that structured programming is a good idea, then the success of the project provides the political leverage for introducing structured programming throughout the organization.

There are other benefits, too. A pilot project is a good way for people to learn the structured techniques, and learning by doing almost always is preferable to learning from a textbook, seminar, or videotaped training course. In addition, the programmers who work on the pilot project can be used to "seed" subsequent projects as the structured techniques begin to be implemented on a larger scale.

Not every organization feels that it needs a pilot project. A small MIS organization whose members all have been exposed to the structured techniques in depth may decide to formally adopt the techniques without any experimentation. However, most large organizations are unable to change this swiftly, and a pilot project may be politically necessary to convince programmers and project managers to try something new.

Hence, the idea of pilot projects is good, although there are good pilot projects and bad pilot projects and a bad pilot project is sometimes worse than none at all. This chapter offers advice on the characteristics of a good pilot project.

12.1 A good pilot project should be of a reasonable size

Some organizations make the mistake of trying the structured techniques on too small a project, such as a two-hundred statement program. In most cases, such a tiny pilot project won't be very convincing. First, some overhead is involved in the new techniques, especially if the organization adheres to the guidelines of structured design and structured programming in a formal, "religious" fashion. Also, by the time a programmer figures out how to use structured design and structured programming on his two-hundred statement problem, another programmer could have finished designing, coding, and testing using classical methods.

However, a more fundamental objection to the use of the new techniques on a small pilot project exists. Most of the techniques of structured analysis, structured design, structured programming, top-down design, and structured walkthroughs are intended as a means of dealing with *complex* data processing systems. They're not needed on small problems, for we can use conventional techniques on small problems as we have since the 1950's. Bluntly, anyone can write two hundred lines of code and eventually get them to work, and if he has had a lot of practice doing such jobs, anyone can write a two hundred statement unstructured program faster than a programmer can finish *his first attempt* at writing those two hundred statements in a structured fashion.

So, choose a medium-sized system as your pilot project. A project involving three to six person-months is reasonable, but interpret medium-sized within the context of your organization.

12.2 The pilot project should be useful, visible, and low-risk

Implementing an on-line chess-playing program as your pilot project will not be effective because nobody will use it, and nobody will care whether it is better or worse than a classical on-line chess-playing program. It's preferable to choose a project whose output will be visible to the organization and whose success will be appreciated by the organization. Ideally, the pilot project should be one that your organization was planning to implement anyway.

In addition, your pilot project should *not* be critical to the success or the solvency of your organization. The project might fail, and using the structured techniques for the first time on a risky, highly critical project may destroy both the project *and* the reputation of the new techniques. The structured techniques might turn out to be too much for the programmers to cope with, especially if they already are coping with unreliable hardware, difficult customers, tight schedules, and internal politics. If the project does fail, the failure may be blamed on the structured techniques, even if the real reason for the failure were the schedule or the computer vendor.

However, sometimes you might not have an alternative: If you are in charge of a project that appears doomed, you may decide to gamble on the structured techniques with the hope that they will produce a miracle. I know of one or two organizations that have been forced into this position, and, luckily, they have succeeded. But it's a risk that you should avoid if you can.

The ideal pilot project might be a redesign of an existing system that is so old, patched, and difficult to maintain that everyone agrees that it should be scrapped and redeveloped. Your new structured version probably will be a success, giving you the added advantage of having something with which to compare it. Selecting an existing system to redesign using the structured approach also provides you with a safety valve; even if the structured version fails, you probably can survive by continuing to use the old system.

12.3 The pilot project should be measurable

One of the purposes of the pilot project is to demonstrate the virtues of the structured techniques to the rest of your organization. This objective strongly implies that you should measure various aspects of the pilot project, such as the following:

- the number of lines of debugged code generated per programmer per day in the pilot project

- The number of bugs found after the system was put into production

- The efficiency of the structured product compared to an equivalent unstructured version

- The amount of time spent in walkthroughs

- The number of bugs found in a typical walkthrough

- The amount of time spent in the analysis phase using structured analysis compared to

the amount of time traditionally spent in
the analysis phase

These few categories may prove sufficient, or you may decide to turn the pilot project into a full-scale research project. The point is, hard numbers usually will convince the rest of your organization to believe the success of the pilot project.

One potential problem in measuring the pilot project is that you may not have any other figures in your organization for comparison. Many MIS organizations today have no idea how productive their programmers are, how many bugs exist in their production systems, or how much effort they are spending on maintenance. As a result, it becomes difficult to determine whether the pilot project is substantially better or worse than the classical method. One solution might be to compare the results of your pilot project with the figures that are reported in the literature, for example, case studies that are reported regularly in *Datamation*, *Infosystems*, *Computerworld*, and other journals. Unfortunately, true comparison is difficult because every organization measures these factors differently.

For this very reason, however, many organizations feel that the ideal pilot project is a redesign of an existing system. With some investigation, one usually can accumulate relevant statistics about the current version of the system pertaining, for example, to development time; number of bugs discovered during the past N years of maintenance; number of maintenance programmers assigned to the system; and, of course, the amount of CPU time and memory consumed by the current system. Hard statistics can be collected regarding CPU time and memory, and these help convince skeptics about the merits of the structured techniques.

Chapter Thirteen:

Developing Standards for the Structured Techniques

The subject of standards eventually arises in any discussion of the new structured techniques. The purpose of this book is not to provide you with all the standards you'll need in your organization. However, I will offer some brief advice on when and how such standards should be developed.

First, many of your standards won't be affected by the introduction of the new techniques. Many large organizations have an immense collection of standards, much of which is unrelated or only peripherally related to the issues of structured programming, walkthroughs, and the other techniques. One of my clients, for example, even has a standard that determines the colors of the standards manuals: Systems standards manuals are green, programming standards manuals are blue, operations standards manuals are yellow, personnel standards manuals are red, and so forth. Presumably, the structured techniques would not upset this scheme!

Even in the areas of systems analysis, systems design, and program design, many of the conventional standards can remain unchanged. Your organization probably has standards that dictate the use of disk packs and of file names, and the paperwork to be completed before a job is given to the computer operator. I would estimate that 90 to 95 percent of this can be left intact, much to the relief of your standards organization!

Probably only a few aspects of your standards manual should be scrapped:

1. Scrap dogmatic rules outlawing isolated programming statements, particularly COBOL standards that outlaw PERFORMS and nested IFS, and PL/I standards that outlaw procedure calls.

2. Scrap any emphasis on the microsecond-level of efficiency. Large portions of some organizations' standards manuals are concerned with the relative merits of COMP-2 versus COMP-3 data representation in COBOL, and the relative efficiencies of obscure string-handling statements in PL/I. As we emphasized in previous chapters, concern about efficiency at this level usually is irrelevant.

3. Scrap most of the sections concerning "packaging." If your standards dictate that systems *must* be broken into job steps in a certain way and that data *must* be passed between job steps on a certain kind of tape file, you probably should rewrite the standards in light of the packaging concepts of structured design, or eliminate the standards altogether.

A few other suggestions can be made about standards for the new techniques. These are discussed in the sections that follow.

13.1 When standards should be developed

A few organizations make the mistake of trying to develop a whole new standards manual before they have any experience with the structured techniques. Indeed, the members of the pilot project may wish to develop a few informal standards, mostly so that they won't waste time quibbling over details in their structured walkthroughs, but these would be quite different from a formal set of standards issued by a standards department.

The cardinal rule to follow is don't develop standards until a pilot project has been completed. The reasoning here should be obvious, since you can't really tell what kind of standards will be appropriate until after you have tried the structured techniques. For example, how can you tell whether nested IF statements are bad until you or your programmers have tried writing a few of them?

13.2 Hard standards probably will be ignored

As suggested in earlier chapters, some organizations interpret the guidelines of structured programming, structured design, structured analysis, structured walkthroughs, and other techniques as religious rules. These rules have a nasty habit of appearing in standards manuals.

Thus, some standards manuals contain the following kinds of statements:

- *All* walkthroughs must be between thirty and sixty minutes in duration.

- *Every* programmer must have a walkthrough of his code on a weekly basis.

- GOTO statements will not be allowed under *any* circumstances.

- The span of control of a module must *never* exceed seven.

- The specification of the new logical system may not commence until the old logical system has been *completely* and *totally* specified.

It may be possible to force programmers and analysts to follow these dictatorial standards for a while; but sooner or later, they'll fall into disuse, just as all previous sets of hard standards did.

13.3 Summary

From the preceding comments, you can anticipate the approach that I favor: a modest set of style guidelines, combined with frequent walkthroughs.

It is intriguing that many of the organizations that have developed structured programming standards have been able to express all of their guidelines in ten or twelve pages. Further, many of the managers indicated that a deliberate effort was made to keep the standards to a restricted length to ensure that the programmers actually would read them. By way of example, I have included the structured COBOL and structured PL/I programming standards used in my company. You'll find them in Appendices A and B.

The factor that will determine the success or failure of your standards is the *walkthrough* concept discussed in Chapter 10 and treated at greater length in my walkthroughs text.* Indeed, one could argue that if the walkthrough concept is successfully implemented, no programming standards are needed, certainly not any hard standards.

This point has to be emphasized, particularly in the organizations that have fallen in love with their standards manuals. What is the purpose of standards in the area of program design and coding? Presumably, they ensure that the programmers will turn out *good* programs. But goodness ultimately must be judged by a human being, typically, the maintenance programmer who is called upon to make such judgments at 3 A.M., when he is looking for a bug. Similarly, what is the purpose of standards for functional specifications? It's not to keep the members of the standards department gainfully employed. On the contrary, their purpose is to ensure that analysts and users can communicate effectively.

My point is simple: If a team of programmers reads through the design and code for a system and honestly thinks that it is good, then it probably *is* good, regardless of what the six-volume standards manual may state. If the team thinks that the program is bad, then it probably *is* bad, even if the programmer scrupulously has obeyed all the rules, all the do's and don't's of the standards manual. Similarly, if a team of analysts and users decides that a set of functional specifications is understandable and correct, then, in my opinion, strict adherence to standards, especially those pertaining to the format and style of the specification, is secondary.

---

*E. Yourdon, *Structured Walkthroughs* (New York: YOURDON Press, 3rd edition, 1985).

Chapter Fourteen:

Impact on Scheduling, Budgeting, and Project Control

One of the issues raised frequently about the structured techniques is their effect upon classical project management: classical estimating, scheduling, budgeting, resource allocation, and project control. Implicit in this concern is the assumption that everything that the project manager has learned about managing MIS projects now is useless because the new structured techniques will change everything.

The primary purpose of this chapter is to reassure you that most of the knowledge and experience you've gained in this area still is valid. Specifically, the chapter addresses the effect of the new techniques on estimating and scheduling activities, and on milestones as they are classically understood, and on the kind of milestones that are used in structured projects.

14.1 The effect on estimating and scheduling

I am cynical about this area because I honestly don't know how people estimate projects or how they determine when a project can be finished. I am aware that there are complex formulas for estimating how long a project will take and how many people will be required to complete it in the allotted time.* Also, I am aware that there is a body of knowledge on scheduling manpower for large projects.[†]

---

*See for example, the discussion in Barry Boehm's *Software Engineering Economics*, (Englewood Cliffs: Prentice-Hall, 1982), or De Marco's *Controlling Software Projects* (New York: YOURDON Press, 1982).
[†]See Philip Metzger's *Programming Project Management* (Englewood Cliffs: Prentice-Hall, 1975).

Nevertheless, I remain a cynic. In my experience as a consultant, I have seen too often that people cannot devise reasonable estimates because they are working on a programming project of a type never before experienced.

For example, Charlie, the programming manager, has just been placed in charge of developing a new on-line order entry system to be run on a Brand X computer with a Brand Y database management system and a Brand Z telecommunications monitor. The only kind of order entry system that Charlie has worked on before was a smaller, simpler batch system that ran on a Brand W computer, using a different programming language and different programmers. How is Charlie going to develop an accurate estimate?

In many cases, Charlie doesn't have to devise a schedule because the schedule is determined for him. Part of the assignment is "Get this system up and running by the first of January!" Charlie then does the obvious interpolation between where he is now and where he must be by January 1: This is April 1, and I have four programmers, and I've got to be finished by January 1. That means that I'd better have the design finished by June 1, and I better start coding by July 1 . . . and . . . and . . . ."[‡]

You may not agree with this assessment. You may have your own method of estimating and scheduling systems, in which case I congratulate you and suggest that you keep your method secret, guarding it as carefully as you would a winning technique for betting on the stock market or the horse races.

But *I* don't know how to estimate projects in a scientific, rational, error-free manner, and I suspect that you probably don't either.

I do know that however you've been estimating and scheduling your projects, you should continue in the same way with the new structured techniques, with the possible exception of applying the same fudge factor. For example, your present scheme might involve asking programmer Fred for an estimate of the time required to program module x. If Fred estimates that the job will take him thirteen days, you normally might double that estimate because you know Fred is outrageously optimistic. Then you might add a fudge factor of 50 percent to cover unforeseen circumstances. With the structured techniques,

---

[‡]Tom DeMarco, in his delightful *Structured Analysis and System Specification* (New York: YOURDON Press, 1978), refers to this phenomenon as backwards Wishful Thinking.

there's a good possibility that you will be able to eliminate the fudge factor after the first few projects, although you'll want to continue compensating for Fred's optimism.

The effect of the structured techniques on your actions should be fairly minor, but the efect on your results will be dramatic: The chances are good that you'll be able to meet the schedule and the estimates that you make. With your current projects, you are doubling Fred's estimates, adding 50 percent just to be safe, and yet probably finding the project still is three months late. With the new structured techniques, your scheme should be to double Fred's estimate, add 50 percent to be safe, *and then meet that schedule as estimated.*

Consider this idea for a minute: *Why* are your current projects three months late? Aside from totally unforeseen catastrophes, what is the cause of the schedule slippage? It's usually not the time required to design the system, nor the time required to write the code. Most of the slippage occurs during that nebulous time called system test and integration. That category, which you probably never scheduled in a properly conservative fashion, is the one that will be decreased significantly with use of the new techniques.

Lest you think that I am being unnecessarily cynical, let me reassure you that I, too, make an honest attempt at scheduling and estimating the computer systems with which I become involved. How? Probably the same way you do by breaking the system into small pieces (modules), each of which is assigned to an individual programmer or to a small group of programmers. Then I ask each programmer or group for an estimate, and I adjust the estimate up or down based on my knowledge of past performance. I then add all of the estimates from all of the programmers, throw in another fudge factor or two, and *voilà*! I have the overall estimate for the project.

With the structured techniques, particularly structured analysis and structured design, this process will be more accurate. Both structured analysis and design favor the development of smaller modules. Also, the techniques favor highly *independent* modules so that the overall effort required for the project can be more nearly approximated by the sum of the individual parts. In the past, the estimates tended to be based on larger modules whose completion was more difficult to estimate accurately and on modules that tended to be more *dependent* on one another (a fact that often wasn't discovered until systems integration).

14.2 The effect of structured techniques on classical milestones

In the past, data processing projects have been characterized by these recognizable milestones:

- request for system received

- approval to begin system study received

- system study completed

- specification for new system completed

- specification for new system accepted

- computer systems design for new system completed

- detailed module design completed

- coding completed

- unit test completed

- system test completed

- acceptance test completed

- system in production

Each milestone served as an opportunity for various members of the organization to gather and review the status of the project. If the milestone had been achieved on schedule and within the budget constraints, everyone assumed that the project was proceeding according to plan.

With the new structured techniques, many of these classical milestones will disappear. How *many* will disappear depends upon whether you elect the conservative top-down approach or the radical top-down approach (recall the discussion in Chapter 4). If you elect to follow a conservative approach, all of the milestones up to and including "detailed module design completed" will remain the same.

If you elect to follow the radical approach, only the first two milestones listed above will remain the same, up to and including "approval to begin system study received."

Sooner or later (sooner if you follow the radical approach, later if you follow the conservative approach), you should expect to see the influence of the structured techniques on your milestones: an integrated pattern of specification and design and coding and testing.

With the new techniques, therefore, you may expect that some analysis and design will be occurring all the way up to the day before the deadline. You even can expect your programmers to write code till the day before the deadline. These events would have caused ulcers had you been following the classical approach because you would have expected such coding efforts to be followed by several months of that ill-defined activity known as system test and integration.

14.3 Milestones and the structured techniques

If many of the classical milestones will be eliminated with the structured techniques, what new milestones will take their place? If you recall the discussion of Chapter 4, the answer should be obvious: The milestones correspond to the delivery of various *versions* of the system. The first few milestones will be the same as they are in the classical approach: We usually are required to produce a systems study and detailed statement of requirements; and, in a conservative approach, we also may need to produce a detailed design of a proposed new system. Then milestones can be expressed as versions. What gives the structured approach such a tremendous advantage over the classical approach is that each version can be defined by a definite date of implementation and by its features and capabilities.

For example, the simple payroll system in Chapter 4 could have the following set of milestones, if we assume a slightly conservative approach:

January 1	--	request for new payroll system received
February 1	--	approval to begin system study received
March 1	--	system study completed
April 1	--	specification for new system completed
May 1	--	version 1 payroll system in operation
June 1	--	version 2 payroll system in operation
July 1	--	version 3 payroll system in operation
August 1	--	version 4 the final version in operation

The advantage of the version milestones is that they are tangible. For instance, from Chapter 4, we recall that Version 1 would not hire or fire anyone, could not give anyone a salary increase or decrease, paid everyone one hundred dollars per week, withheld fifteen dollars per week in taxes, and paid everyone with a paycheck printed in octal. Since Version 1 thus can be defined in terms of such tangible characteristics, it should be obvious by the specified deadline whether or not Version 1 works.

This last point is crucial. With the classical method of project management, a typical milestone would be described as "detailed module design completed." But what does this mean? How do we know exactly what has been accomplished? How do we know that some design problems have not been postponed, to be discovered at some later milestone?

It is interesting to observe what happens at each milestone of a structured project. When the deadline arrives for Version 1, for example, the system may not be working. In the case of our simple payroll system, that means that the programmers still will be unable to produce an octal paycheck for one hundred dollars.

"But that's not fair," the programmers will complain. "Actually, we're done — it's just that there's this one little bug that's preventing us from getting the right output."

To which the project manager will reply, "Too bad! You're not done. You didn't meet the deadline."

The programmers will cry, "We're 99.7 percent done. All we have is one last bug. And we think the bug is in the compiler."

The manager will respond, "Too bad! As far as I'm concerned, Version 1 either works, or it doesn't work. Evidently, your system is incapable of producing octal paychecks for one hundred dollars, so it doesn't work!"

At which point, one of the programmers might say, "But that's not fair! *My* module works just fine! It's Fred's module that's causing all the trouble!"

To which the manager might state, "I don't care whose fault it is. Version 1 does not work. Therefore, the entire project is behind schedule."

The version approach to milestones is *extremely* powerful. If you carefully define your versions, particularly in terms of completed modules on a structure chart, the rate of progress is much more evident at a much earlier stage in the project than it used to be.

14.4 Summary

To summarize the effects of structured techniques on estimating and milestones:

1.   Prepare your estimates as you always have;

2.   Expect that the first few milestones — perhaps through the end of systems analysis — will be much like they always have been; and

3.   Eliminate the rest of your milestones, and replace them with *versions* of a top-down systems implementation.

Chapter Fifteen:

What Will Go Wrong?

This chapter is intended as a brief summary. So far, this book has addressed the myriad little problems that you'll encounter when you begin to implement structured programming, structured design, structured analysis, and the other structured techniques. But on a larger scale, what disasters should you expect? What major failures await you? On a philosophical level, what will go wrong?

None of the structured techniques are magical. Structured programming will not produce miracles. Structured design will not improve your sex life. Structured walkthroughs will not reduce the number of cavities in your children's teeth. Top-down implementation will not make it significantly easier to get along with your boyfriend/girlfriend/husband/wife/mistress/lover/dog/cat.

Having said that, we still are left with the question: *What* will go wrong? I think you should be prepared for four major problem areas, each of which is discussed below.

15.1 Political problems

Virtually all of this book has been written with the assumptions that you are a manager working in a rational environment, that you supervise rational programmers and analysts, and that you work with rational users. A further assumption is that everyone in MIS management agrees that it would be desirable to develop maintainable, reliable software in a reasonably economical fashion.

Unfortunately, these assumptions are not valid in some organizations. You may encounter an irrational user who refuses to discuss his requirements with you. More likely, you'll work in an environment in which deadlines, schedules, and budgets are dictated from higher levels, and the opportunity for estimating, or even negotiating, is absent entirely.

If your organization has had a history of failures and overruns, you may not be able to invest the substantial time required to carry out proper structured analysis and structured design before you're rushed into the coding phase.

It may be possible in such cases for you to introduce a "quiet revolution:" begin using walkthroughs, structured programming, structured design, and structured analysis without a fuss, and possibly without even telling anyone that you're doing it. Then, when people eventually ask you why your project was so successful, you can tell them. Ideally, the MIS function will become increasingly visible in the organization, and top management will make the investments that are necessary to perform the job properly.

15.2 Personnel problems

Almost everyone who has been in the computer field for ten or more years has fond memories of "the good old days." Those were the days, the old-timer will tell you, when everyone knew how the compiler, the operating system, and even the hardware worked. This knowledge was necessary because one had to patch all three on a day-to-day basis to get any work done. Those were the days when people worked throughout the night, slept in the computer room, operated their own programs.

Naturally, these stories are exaggerated, but they have some truth, too. In particular, the memories suggest that people lived to program, whereas today, people program to live. For a majority of computer programmers and analysts now, their jobs simply occupy them from nine to five and enable them to pay the rent and buy two color televisions.

Something happened to the personality and mentality of the data processing profession as a whole as we moved to the ultra-sophisticated on-line, real-time, fourth-generation and fifth-generation machines of the 1980's and 1990's. The profession began to attract people who, regardless of their race, creed, color, or university degrees, are *clerks*. They think like clerks, they talk like clerks, and they approach computer programming and systems analysis with all the enthusiasm of a sleepy civil service clerk who knows that he's just one year away from retirement.

Having met some twenty-five thousand analysts, designers, and programmers throughout the world, I found a surprising number of them have *never* read any computer articles or even opened a copy of *Datamation* or *Computerworld;* have never heard of ACM, DPMA, IEEE, ASM, or any other professional organizations; can't spell Dijkstra's name and probably have never heard of him; aren't aware of the structured techniques and wouldn't be interested if somebody showed them.

When such programmers and systems analysts are *forced* to learn structured programming, structured design, top-down implementation, and structured analysis, a frighteningly large number of them are unable to learn them. In addition to being uninterested in their profession, they are incompetent at their profession. It's literally all they can manage to write programs in the helter-skelter fashion to which they have become accustomed. To suggest that they should introduce some organization, some common sense, some *structure* into their work is beyond their ken.

If it appears that I'm taking potshots at *your* organization, I apologize; yours may be one of the organizations with good programmers and good systems analysts. My experience has been that small organizations — especially those that *must* make a profit on a year-to-year basis to survive — usually have good systems analysts who still are sufficiently competent technically to write their own programs. Conversely, large, stagnant, conservative organizations that survive by inertia, by *being*, without necessarily making a profit, tend to attract incompetent programmers and somnolent systems analysts; unfortunately, that description fits a lot of big banks, insurance companies, government agencies, and even some of the major manufacturing organizations.

If it seems as though I'm damning the entire programming profession from a lofty perch, I apologize again. However, it discourages me to meet programmers who have been programming in COBOL for ten years and who have no idea how a PERFORM statement works, but are considered among the brightest in their organization!

15.3 Time delay problems

Even if your programmers and analysts are of average intelligence, you may run into another problem. It easily can take two or three years for the effect of the structured techniques to be felt in your organization. On a global scale, structured programming was introduced in the 1965 — 1968 era, discussed widely in the literature during the 1969 — 1973 period, and hailed formally in 1973 by *Datamation** as the greatest invention since the advent of the subroutine. Yet, many organizations still have not used the structured techniques.

The reasons for this lapse vary from organization to organization, but a familiar pattern exists. First, nobody in company X heard about structured programming for a long time because they all were too busy working on current projects. Nobody had read any issue of *Datamation*, attended any computer conferences, or talked to anyone in any other companies.

When they did hear about structured programming, they weren't quite sure how to react. Probably the hardware vendor brought it to their attention, and everyone suspected that structured programming really was a subtle plot by the vendor to sell more memory or another disk pack. After a while, perhaps someone decided to set up a committee to study the relevance of the structured techniques to their organization; and the committee studied the matter for six months before producing its report.

Once the committee had decided that structured programming is a good idea, someone else made a copy of a technical article on the subject for each of the programmers, attaching a memo that read, "The boss thinks this is a good idea." The programmers ignored it for several months. Another memo circulated, which dictated, "The boss wants everyone to use structured programming from now on."

At that point, the programmers began writing their own interpretation of structured code. It didn't work; they didn't like it; the COBOL compiler wouldn't compile it. So they ignored structured programming again, knowing that the boss never read their code anyway.

Having seen that the effort was getting nowhere, someone then decided to take a more organized approach. The brighter programmers were sent to a training course, or given a book to read, or put in front of a videotape machine. A pilot project was attempted; and when it achieved only mediocre results, a second pilot project was attempted.

Because a pilot project eventually was successful, standards were developed, meetings were held among all the project managers, and structured programming was declared officially to be a good thing. Everyone was told to organize and train his staff, so that structured programming could begin in earnest.

Datamation, Vol. 19, No. 12 (December 1973).

Some project managers demurred: They were in the middle of a critical project, and they couldn't afford to rock the boat with newfangled ideas. "*Next* project," they promised, "we'll start using structured programming." Other project managers objected to using the structured techniques for the various political reasons outlined throughout this book.

Meanwhile, *some* managers actually did begin using the new techniques on a large-scale three-year project. But no results were immediately forthcoming. Besides, the unconvinced managers didn't want to believe the possibly favorable results until the *end* of the project.

How long does implementing the techniques take? I've seen a few organizations switch to the structured techniques overnight, but most of the larger ones take anywhere from one to five years to begin seeing *measurable* results. Meanwhile, during that transitional period, you somehow have to keep suffering with bugs, low productivity, and maintenance headaches.

15.4 Maintenance problems

The final problem has been mentioned several times in the book: Even with all the new structured techniques, you still have to maintain the programming garbage accumulated over ten or twenty years.

I don't have to tell you how difficult it is to maintain an IBM 1401 AUTOCODER program on an IBM 308x, especially when the listing and the source program for the 1401 program were lost long ago, and only a patched object module exists. Some organizations have hundreds of such rotten, old programs.

If you're one of those unlucky managers who is stuck with the maintenance of one thousand man-years of unstructured code, there's not much I can do for you, other than offer you a lot of sympathy, and one last little bit of advice: If you don't start *now* to write your new systems in a structured fashion, you'll be in the same position ten years from now.

Chapter Sixteen:

The Impact of
Personal Computers

16.1 Introduction

During the mid-1980's, personal computers began predominating the corporate environment. At the time this edition was prepared, approximately 10 percent of all "knowledge workers" in the United States had access to a PC (though not necessarily one on their own desk); by the end of the decade, it is estimated that more than 50 percent of the knowledge workers will be so equipped.

The arguments about whether or not personal computers are beneficial and whether or not users are making productive use of them are beyond the scope of this book. However, the subject is moot since users are getting the machines regardless of what anyone in the MIS organization thinks.

Many MIS professionals and managers will argue that the end-user can accomplish useful tasks with a personal computer, but also that they can get themselves into terrible trouble. I share that opinion so emphatically that I recently authored a book entitled *The Perils of Personal Computing* (New York: YOURDON Press, 1985).

The purpose of this chapter is not to explore in great detail all of the ways that users can wreak havoc with personal computers, but rather to explore the subject in the context of software engineering and structured techniques. Is structured analysis irrelevant in an organization where the end-users have their own personal computers? Should users learn structured analysis on their own?

16.2 Classification of users

Before proceeding, we should remember that not all end-users are alike. Members of the MIS community, myself included, often forget this point, and it is a crucially important one when we begin discussing the things that the user will do with (or to) his computer.

One way of differentiating among users is by level of experience. Roughly speaking, there are three important categories: the rank amateur, the cocky novice, and the veteran. The rank amateur has never seen or touched a personal computer and may be frightened of it. He will need help simply learning which end of a floppy disk should be inserted into the disk drive. The cocky novice is someone who successfully created a small spreadsheet using Lotus 1-2-3, or who managed to put his Christmas shopping list on a computer using dBaseII. From these successful experiences, he has concluded that he can tackle the accounting application in his organization, which involves functions and data elements one thousand times more numerous and complex than his "toy" problems.

There are also a few veterans, although professional programmers and systems analysts may not like to admit that they exist. End-users who have been project team members on large systems development projects in the 1970's and early 1980's may be in a good position to learn the workings of an IBM PC/XT. Also, there are people who majored in computer science in college, but who wound up working in the marketing department ten years ago. Finally, there is a generation of children beginning to enter the job market with an increasing amount of computer literacy: it is estimated, for example, that a child born in 1980 will have written ten thousand lines of code by the time he or she graduates from high school.

Generalizations also are possible about the reaction of end-users to personal computers based on their age and job category, even though a generalization may be wrong in any individual case. Indeed, because generalizations may be dangerously wrong, it is important to realize that users are different. It is clearly wrong to assume that all users are illiterate about computers; it is also wrong to assume that all managers will be opposed to personal computers (because, according to the generalization, male managers don't know how to type, and female managers don't want to type because it is demeaning).

So, the first question that should be asked when anyone in the MIS organization wants to know how the quality of systems will be affected by widespread distribution of PC's is what kind of users are we talking about? What do they know? What are their attitudes towards personal computers? What are they willing to learn? Are they willing to learn lessons that the MIS organization has learned slowly and painfully over the past twenty years, or do they want to start all over again?

16.3 The dangers of personal computing

In most cases, personal computing has brought tremendous benefits to the user community. MIS personnel occasionally remark that the typical personal computer is only used for one hour a day (so what?), or that it is used only to maintain the end-user's calendar and diary, but there are far more stories of users accomplishing important and useful tasks with their own computer. Users have a strong sense of power when they discover that they can build their own applications quickly, and that they can control the way the systems are run, rather than having to depend on a centralized MIS empire that they often regard as dictatorial and unresponsive.

However, things don't always work as well as the personal computer advertisements on television would have you believe. Though many users have not yet discovered them, the following problems typically occur when *real* systems are developed by amateur or cocky novice users on a personal computer:

- *Lack of testing.* Most users don't write their own BASIC programs, but they do create complex applications using spreadsheet programs and such fourth generation languages as dBaseIII. In many cases, they don't spot-check the results of the spreadsheet calculations to ensure that the spreadsheet are correct; nor do they do testing to ensure that their request for a report of "all customers in Wyoming except those over sixty-five and those who are left-handed, but not the ones who have brown eyes in Montana" produced what it was supposed to produce.

- *Proliferation of local databases.* The MIS community has spent the past twenty years dealing with the problem of fragmented "local" files. Many would argue that we now understand the problem and know how to solve it, but that it will take another five to ten years to implement the solution. Now we have users creating their own databases without any supervision from the MIS organization. A user with a 10-megabyte hard disk (which is becoming obsolete as I write this in 1985) or a 20-megabyte disk (which will be out of vogue by 1987) can store an incredible amount of data; if every user in every department starts using this potential, the problems of redundancy, synchronization, and data integrity can be staggering.

- *Backup and security.* The majority of end-user databases are not backed up on a regular basis, nor are there backup copies of many critical application programs. Confidential information is stored on floppy disks or hard disks that are easily accessible to anyone who wanders through the office while the user is away from his desk. Again, the MIS organization has only begun to deal with this expensive problem on the large mainframe computers, and it is not at all clear that most users have any awareness of the problem.

- *The lack of documentation.* Since most users don't write "real" programs in BASIC or PASCAL, we don't have to worry about program documentation. But they *do* build systems by creating their own databases and writing programs in fourth generation languages, or by purchasing commercial packages which have to be customized to deal with the user's special needs. In many cases, none of this information is documented; nor are the operating procedures documented; nor are the interactions between the new personal computer and the existing user organization documented. When the user is transferred to another department, retires, quits, or is fired, all of this "informal" information will be lost, a problem which, once again, the MIS organization also has dealt with.

- *The difference between a program and a system.* Many users believe that they are using a personal computer to improve the productivity of some *local* activity within their own microscopic area of work, such as by automating a calculation that would otherwise be done manually. However, inevitably they will begin to use their new computer power to add new functions, or change their interfaces with other departments, or cause other departments to change their way of operating simply because of the *speed* with which they can now do their work. Hence, what begins as a local activity (which could be thought of as a program) inevitably ends up as a modification, or perturbation, of a system. But users don't usually think in terms of systems; nor do they have modeling tools naturally available to them to study the impact that their changes will have upon an existing system.

16.4 Structured techniques and personal computers

Thus, users with personal computers *do* need to learn about the structured techniques discussed in this book. Some of the users need to learn about all of the techniques, and all users need to learn about some of the techniques.

All users, in my opinion, should learn about the system life cycle discussed in Chapter 2 and Chapter 3 of this book. They should learn that there are two distinct activities, called *analysis*, and *design*, even if the programming part of their work is trivial. They should learn the importance of testing and should hear dozens of stories to impress upon them how easy it is for their organization to lose millions of dollars because of a misplaced semicolon or a sloppy piece of Boolean logic.

When the user is building a system with a database, (for instance, a customer database, a personnel file, or a product file), he should be given an introduction to the data modeling portion of structured analysis; he should learn how to think of his "database" in terms of *entities* and *relationships*. He should also learn about the "messy" operational issues of backup, security, recovery, audit trails, and redundancy of data.

For example, many personal computer users find that organizing a customer list is one of the first things they do with their new machine. A customer is an entity, something about which we store data. One attribute of a customer is his name; another is his address. But many first-time users unconsciously develop a model in which "customer name" is a single, indivisible unit of information consisting of the person's title, first name, and last name. If the customer list is implemented in this fashion, then all the components of the customer's name will be stored, retrieved, and manipulated as a single, atomic chunk of information. Similarly, we might imagine the user defining the city, state, and zip code portion of the address as if this material were one indivisible unit. This method may be acceptable for the user's initial applications, and one can imagine the user laboriously entering thousands of customer names and addresses. With such database packages as PFS:File and dBASEII, the data entry probably would take place by responding to a series of prompts from the computer; thus, a typical dialogue between the user and the database program might look like this: CUSTOMER NAME: Mr. John Q. Smith ADDRESS: 123 Main Street, Snarkville, New York 10297.

Six months later, it may become painfully obvious that the customer's zip code has to be treated as an individual unit so that the mailing list can be produced in zip code sequence for bulk mailing at the post office. Also, the customer's first name has to be accessed by itself so that one can write a form letter that begins, "Dear X," with X being the customer's first name. Because of the original conceptual model of the data, and because of the implementation of that conceptual model, it is now virtually impossible to use the thousands of customer names that have been typed into the computer.

When the user is going to be developing a system, he should learn the concepts of structured analysis presented in Chapter 3 of this book, regardless of whether the system is going to be implemented in COBOL, BASIC or some higher-level fourth-generation language. Normally, the user needs between sixteen hours and thirty hours of classroom lectures and workshops to absorb the details of the modeling techniques presented in Chapter 3 and to become adept at developing models.

Chapter Seventeen:

Fourth Generation Languages

17.1 Introduction

Just as we speak of generations of computer hardware that have been developed during the past thirty years, it is now fashionable to speak of generations of programming languages. Fourth generation languages have attracted considerable attention, and many MIS systems developers wonder how the structured techniques are affected by the use of these languages.

For perspective, we should characterize the first three generations of popular computer programming languages:

- *First generation* — machine language programming, in which the programmer had to be familiar with the binary one's and zero's that formed individual machine instructions. This most primitive form of programming was used primarily in the 1950's, when most of us had never heard of computers.

- *Second generation* — assembly language programming, in which the programmer could use symbolic codes to describe machine instructions (for example, LOAD, ADD, and SHIFT) as well as symbolic codes to refer to machine addresses. This generation began in the early 1960's and continues to be used in some MIS organizations even today. However, it had begun to be replaced in most organizations by the early 1970's.

- *Third generation* — the conventional compiler-oriented procedural languages such as COBOL, FORTRAN, and PASCAL. These languages are significant because they allow programmers to deal with abstractions: programs can be organized with DO-WHILE and IF-THEN-ELSE constructs, even if there is no single machine instruction available for carrying them out. Complex data elements could be manipulated without much regard for how those elements will be stored and manipulated within the computer hardware. Third generation languages still predominate most organizations.

17.2 Characteristics of a fourth generation language

In the late 1970's and early 1980's, a new kind of programming language began to emerge; examples are FOCUS, NOMAD, MAPPER, ADR/IDEAL, MARK V, RAMIS, and such languages as MICRO-FOCUS and dBASEIII for personal computers.

These fourth generation languages, or 4GL's, usually have the following features:

- *Convenient facilities for defining and creating a database.* The database may be a simple file structure, or, with some of the more sophisticated 4GL's, the user may have the ability to create a relational database. The user normally has a facility for defining the data contents of each record; for example, he can indicate that his new customer file should consist of records that contain a customer's "last name," "first name," and "street address." In most cases, the user specifies the maximum size of each field, and in some cases, he may be able to indicate the field type — alphabetic or numeric — and perhaps even a range of permissible values. Similar facilities allow the user to add new records to his database.

- *The languages usually are implemented as interpreters rather than compilers.* With third generation languages, the user/programmer writes a program, perhaps consisting of several hundred statements, then compiles it (that is, arranges for it to be translated into appropriate machine instructions). If an error is detected, he must correct it before the program is executed. Once he begins executing the program, he may discover errors, and then the process of revising, compiling, and executing the program must be repeated. However, with an interpretive language, each statement can be examined as soon as it is entered into the computer. Thus, trivial syntax errors can be corrected while the information is still recent in the programmer's mind; runtime errors also can be corrected more easily, often with the ability to continue the execution of the program from the point where the error was detected. The problem with interpretive languages is that they are typically between ten and one hundred times slower than compiled languages. This problem was major in the 1960's and 1970's, but whether it remains a problem in the 1980's is a subject that will be discussed below.

• *"User-friendly" features.* Even though COBOL originally was intended as a language for "ordinary" people, it quickly became evident that its syntax is so complicated that only a professional programmer would be able to use it; the same is true of FORTRAN and even BASIC if one wants to write more than two or three lines of code. In contrast, the fourth generation languages typically make a more serious effort to use English-like words rather than cryptic abbreviations for commands. The user-friendliness also is augmented by the 4GL's tendency to assume default values for tedious details that the non-technical user often doesn't want to worry about. A common example is report formats. Many users don't want to bother specifying such details as the placement of page numbers, and column headings. The 4GL's also provide extensive "help" facilities (which is possible partly because of the interpretive nature of the language) so that a befuddled user can ask for guidance on his CRT screen, rather than having to grope through a manual that may not be easily accessible.

• *Most details of report generation are handled automatically.* As mentioned above, this feature contributes significantly to the user-friendliness of the 4GL's. However, most of the 4GL's also have provisions for customizing reports, so that a finicky user can place page numbers and headings and arrange the format and layout of the report in whatever manner he wants. For customizing, the user usually has a menu of choices that he or she can select and change at will, a method considerably simpler and more appealing than programming the same information in COBOL.

- *Ad hoc inquiry facilities.* One reason for building a database is to permit *ad hoc* inquiries: the user wants to inspect a single record in the database or perhaps all records that match certain criteria. Again, this facility is provided in a format that is command-driven with English-like commands, or menu-driven, in which the user makes his choices in a simple, convenient format. The same task can be done in COBOL, but requires the user to (a) find a programmer, (b) describe what records he wants to retrieve, (c) wait for the programmer to write the program in COBOL, (d) wait for the program to be compiled, and then perhaps revised and compiled again, and (e) wait for the programmer or the operations department to run the program and produce results, which may show the user that he really wanted slightly different selection criteria for his retrieval (for example, "all customers over sixty-five living in Montana" rather than "all customers over sixty-five").

17.3 Advantages of fourth generation languages

There is no shortage of information about the benefits of fourth generation languages. Language vendors and industry gurus praise the 4GLs in all of the popular computer magazines and journals. The primary advantages seem to be the following:

1. *The productivity of the programming phase of a project can be increased by a factor of ten.* Obviously, this increase can be significant: it may mean that a six-month project can be done in two weeks, and that a two-week project can be done in a day. Because of this fast turn-around, all of details about the project are still fresh in everyone's mind so that problems and misunderstandings can be resolved more quickly — in contrast to the typical three-year project that the MIS organization carries out in which everyone involved at the beginning of the project has disappeared by the time the program testing is finished.

2. *4GL's avoid reinventing the wheel on trivial programming matters.* In a typical third generation programming environment, a substantial amount of time is spent coding the details of file definitions, record layouts, report formats, and so forth. Inevitably, each programmer duplicates much of the work that another programmer has done the day before. With the 4GL's, all of this specifying is either done au-

tomatically or with simple commands that require little duplication.

3.   *4GL's can vastly improve the productivity of program maintenance.* Many maintenance changes to an existing computer program require little or no systems analysis or design. Such changes merely reflect the user's need to make a small change to the format of a report or one of the calculations in the program ("Hey, we just heard that the sales tax was increased to 4 percent yesterday. We better change the program!"). If such programming details can be accomplished ten times more quickly than would be possible in a COBOL environment, then the user can do it himself, rather than waiting for the MIS organization.

17.4 Disadvantages of fourth generation languages

Companies that develop fourth generation languages don't like to talk about the disadvantages of their products, nor do consultants who make their living by preaching to top management that an "instant solution" to the applications backlog problem now exists. But there are some important disadvantages:

1.   *4GL's improve the programming process, but not the systems analysis process.* The programmming phase occupies only about 15 percent of the time and resources of a typical project. Hence, improving that activity by a factor ten may not accomplish much, unless the user's requirements are known and no systems analysis is necessary (which is often the case for maintenance programming). But for a complex system involving many different users or different groups of users in different geographical locations, the systems analysis activity is still the most difficult and time-consuming.

2.   *Incompatibility with existing databases.* For a new system, the user/programmer sometimes has the ability to create a new database that is compatible with or even created by the fourth generation language. Often, though, the new system must use an existing file or database which may not be accessible by the 4GL. There may be a facility for translating the current database format into the format required by the 4GL, but even this step may be awkward: if the new system updates the database, then it will have to be translated back into its original form (and meanwhile, other users may have been updating the original copy of the database).

3.   *Efficiency problems.* As mentioned, the fourth generation languages are interpretive, which makes them approximately ten times more costly in terms of CPU usage. In addition, some of the newer 4GL's use artificial intelligence technology to permit "natural English" interactions with the user, placing a heavy burden upon the computer. In some environments, efficiency is not a concern, such as in many personal computer environments where the user has full access to the machine. In some mainframe environments, though, the centralized computer facility may not be able to handle the processing requirements of several hundred users simultaneously running 4GL programs. Also, a 4GL program that was easy to develop may not be suitable for a high-volume application, like on-line order entry or airline reservations, when fast response time is critical.

4.   *Inadequacies in the language itself.* As mentioned in the previous section, fourth generation languages attempt to be user friendly and to relieve the user of many of the details of programming, such as the format of report layouts. Not all are successful. What the language developer thinks of as user friendly may not appear very friendly at all to the users in your organization, especially when the user does something wrong: the 4GL's still have a tendency to produce unintelligible messages — verbose, with lots of detail, but unintelligible nonetheless — that leave the user shaking his head in bewilderment.

17.5 Conclusion

The above discussion is not intended to discourage you from using a fourth generation programming language because, in the proper environment, they can be a powerful tool. Indeed, their greatest application is in the maintenance area where so many of the programming activities are trivial and could be accomplished directly by the user.

On the other hand, 4GLs are not going to provide an instant solution to the problem of building large, complex systems. We must still invest a considerable time and energy modeling the user requirements and then use structured design to model the architecture of the system. *Then* we can use a fourth generation language to implement the system, if that language is appropriate for the machine, the database, and the operating environment.

Chapter Eighteen:

Application Prototyping

18.1 Introduction

In the past few years, there has been strong interest in the concept of prototyping of information systems, that is, using a combination
of high-level languages, "screen painters," database facilities, and report generators to enable the systems analyst to build a mockup of a
proposed system as an alternative to the "paper" models described in
the earlier chapters of this book. Some consultants and writers even
have argued that the growing availability of such prototyping tools may
have rendered the structured techniques obsolete. The conclusion that
my colleagues and I at YOURDON inc. have reached is that prototyping
tools are a useful adjunct to the structured techniques and *occasionally* a
useful, even necessary, alternative to structured analysis; but it is
dangerous and wrong to suggest that the structured techniques have
been rendered useless by the introduction of prototyping tools. The
rest of this chapter discusses the reasons for this conclusion.

18.2 The motivation for prototyping

There are three major motivations for using prototyping tools.
The first has to do with communication between users and systems
analysts. While it is almost universally agreed now that the classical
functional specification fails to facilitate communication between user
and analyst, some organizations have found that data flow diagrams and
the other related tools of structured analysis have failed, too. The
latter communication problem sometimes has been caused by a failure
to introduce the diagrams to the users properly and to train the user
community in their use. Nevertheless, sometimes despite the best

efforts of the systems analyst, the user refuses to look at such abstract, paper models. In other cases, the user willingly looks at the diagrams, but is unable to comprehend them. If this is the case, the prototyping approach offers an alternative: a working model of the system that uses real terminals and supposedly real inputs and outputs.

Another reason for the popularity of prototyping tools is the ease and quickness with which a prototype can be constructed and revised. A prototype of a small to medium-sized system might be constructed in days, while the equivalent paper model created by the structured analysis approach could require months. If the user wishes to change the prototype either because the prototype reflected the analyst's misunderstanding of the user's requirements, or because the user wanted to explore some different scenarios, the change can be accomplished within hours or even minutes. With the paper model approach, the change could require days, and, as discussed earlier, the user might have difficulty visualizing the consequences of the change while viewing an abstract model.

Part of the problem is that the paper model approach of structured analysis and structured design almost universally has been conducted manually, using nothing more sophisticated than paper and pencil. In Chapter 20, we discuss the concept of an analysts's workbench, which allows models to be composed on a personal computer workstation and modified at will. Early results from the use of such automated tools show that the productivity of the systems analysis process can be improved by approximately 30 percent just by automating the drawing and revising of diagrams. Automation could significantly reduce the frustration that users feel while waiting for the model to be developed.

Such user frustrations also have been the result of early versions of project management methodologies that first embraced the use of structured analysis. Specifically, several methodologies (including that described in the first edition of my *Managing the Systems Life Cycle* and the previous edition of this book) emphasized the importance of developing current physical models of the system that the user intends to automate. Unfortunately, this process can be time-consuming and wasteful and does not provide the user community and management tangible evidence of progress. In the worst case, a nervous systems analyst can spend forever modeling the user's current physical system because it is non-threatening and easy to accomplish without any creativity. In such an environment, prototyping obviously can be an attractive alternative. However, most current project methodologies (including that described in the second edition of *Managing the System Life Cycle)* de-emphasize the need to model the user's current system and suggest that whenever possible, the analyst begin modeling the essential characteristics of the user's new system.

A final reason for the popularity of prototyping is that it highlights the man-machine dialogue, by letting the user play with alternative screen formats and report layouts. While not necessarily illuminating important functions and data elements of the system, this ability makes prototyping an attractive approach for many users, especially those who actually will be performing data entry operations with the terminal.

18.3 The premises in a prototyping environment

For a prototyping approach to work successfully, one has to assume that the following conditions are true:

- *There is only a single user or at most a small group of users who are "localized" in the sense that they work in the same organizational group and within the same physical location.* It is far less likely that prototyping will be used on a project with diverse users in different organizational groups and different physical locations.

- *The data model exists or can be easily created.* This assumption is safe in an environment where (a) the user wants a new system that will interact with an existing database, and (b) the MIS organization has already developed an information model of that database, complete with data dictionary definitions, entity-relationship diagrams, and so forth. For a completely new system with a completely new database, it may still be possible to derive the information model fairly quickly and create a data dictionary that can serve as the foundation for the prototype.

- *The application is small to medium.* With the power of some prototyping tools and with the power of fourth generation languages that may eventually be used to implement the "production" version of the system, the term *medium-sized* may have to be redefined in many MIS organizations. A system consisting of fifty thousand lines of COBOL may be considered large in a classical environment, but only medium-sized in a prototyping and/or fourth generation language environment. Nevertheless, most MIS organizations would not use prototyping tools to develop a complete prototype of a system that will eventually consist of 5 million lines of COBOL. Similarly, nor would prototyping be used in a system requiring only fifty lines of COBOL.

- *Everyone agrees that the prototype is only a "toy" system and that it is intended as nothing more than a model of the production system.* As Bernard Boar points out so eloquently in *Application Prototyping* (New York: Wiley & Sons, 1984), a system developed with prototyping tools almost always lacks some features that are essential for a "production" system: backup, recovery, extensive error-checking, audit trails, and performance engineering, that is, appropriate "tuning" to make the system operate with sufficient efficiency for high volumes of input transactions.

18.4 The dangers of prototyping

From this discussion, it should be evident that there is an intrinsic difficulty with the prototyping approach: the users and the systems analyst may not agree on the basic premises discussed above, or, even worse, they may not even discuss the premises. Obviously an opportunity exists for frustration, disappointment, and disillusionment ("so prototyping turned out to be just one more panacea that didn't work out," mused one discouraged MIS director to me recently) for both users and systems analysts.

Specifically, the problems that MIS organizations have encountered with the prototyping approach are as follows:

- *The prototype is put into full-scale operation.* During World War II, several "temporary" buildings were constructed, often at great haste with flimsy wooden materials and thin tin roofs; one of the more common examples is the ubiquitous Quonset hut. I lived in a Quonset hut six years after the end of World War II; nearly twenty years after the war, I observed that some of the administrative offices in my college were located in similar "temporary" buildings; no doubt there are parts of the world where such buildings continue to be occupied today, more than forty years after everyone put down arms. I fear that the same phenomenon will occur with MIS systems built with prototyping tools, especially when the prototype is deceptively "real" and is being built for a user desperate to automate some portion of his business. The problems may not be apparent in the short term, but the long-term consequences of a "toy" system without backup, recovery, and audit trail facilities could be devastating.

- *The prototype may be thrown away.* In order to avoid the problem described above, the prototype *should* be thrown away and replaced with a properly designed and implemented production system. But if the prototype is thrown away, then there will be no model of the requirements of the system, a disastrous state that is characteristic of most, if not all, MIS systems in existence today.

- *The prototyping approach eliminates the idea of essential or logical models.* By definition, a set of prototyping tools provides a specific implementation environment for building a "toy" system; we assume that the prototyping environment is compatible with the implementation environment that will be used for the production version of the system *from the user's point of view*, for example, that the production system will use the same kind of terminal, with the same man-machine dialogue, and so on. But, the analyst and user are brainwashed into exploring system requirements within the constraints of the hardware/software technology provided by the prototyping tools. Thus, it is likely that with the prototyping approach, no one will develop an essential model of the system, nor will anyone seriously consider alternative implementation technologies, such as different man-machine boundaries or using a distributed system consisting of personal computers and a mainframe computer.

- *The prototype may be regarded as wasted time.* If the prototype is thrown away and replaced with a separately developed production system, someone in the user community may complain, "Why did we waste so much time building the prototype if it was going to be thrown away?" The problem is usually that the users did not understand at the beginning of the project that the prototype was never intended as anything but a model. This problem often is exacerbated by the fact that the production version of the system takes much longer to build than the prototype.

18.5 Conclusions and comments

Though the previous section dwelled on the problems and dangers of prototyping, you should not conclude that prototyping is a bad idea, or that I or my colleagues at YOURDON inc. are opposed to prototyping.

Prototyping should be regarded as a tool that can be used well, used poorly, or used in circumstances where they were never intended to be used. A superbly crafted tool in the hands of a mediocre technician will not accompish much, and, in fact, could do much harm. Conversely, a brilliant technician can accomplish miracles even if the available tools are mediocre or primitive.

Two other points should considered about the concept of prototyping:

- For a large system, it often makes sense to develop two or three levels of high-level data flow diagrams, together with appropriate data dictionary entries, entity-relationship diagrams, and so on, to get a feeling for the major subsystems that eventually will be built. Then, any one of those subsystems could be implemented with the prototyping tools available to the organization.

- The top-down implementation techniques discussed in Chapter 4 could be regarded as an alternative form of prototyping; the difference is that the early prototypes, that is, the early versions of the system, are constructed from real code that should continue to be used in the production system. As we saw in Chapter 4, there are several factors that influence the project manager's decision to follow a radical top-down approach or a conservative top-down approach; thus, it is possible that the project team could begin coding their first version of the system on the first day of the project. In such an environment, the only difference between the top-down approach and the prototyping approach discussed is likely to be the sophistication of the programming tools: the top-down approach in most current MIS organizations will probably involve classical third generation programming languages like COBOL, whereas the prototyping approach is more likely to involve high-level, fourth-generation languages supported by sophisticated on-line terminal facilities. Nevertheless, it is important to remember that the prototyping concept and the structured techniques are not mutually exclusive.

Chapter Nineteen:

Data Modeling

19.1 Introduction

The purpose of this brief chapter is to put to rest a debate that raged through some parts of the computer industry in the late 1970's and early 1980's: the debate between advocates of information modeling (or data modeling, or "those database fanatics") and advocates of structured analysis (or function modeling, or "those guys who draw bubbles").

The fundamental problem was that neither group understood the other or acknowledged the possible importance of a different viewpoint on the subject of systems modeling. The database group argued, "Model the essential *information* within an enterprise — the functions are simple and will fall into place naturally." The structured analysis group seemed to be arguing, "Model the functions and the flow of data between the functions — the database is straightforward and will fall into place naturally." Meanwhile, a third group, largely ignored by both groups, consisted of the people building real-time systems, for whom the time-dependent behavior of the system was the most important aspect of systems modeling.

To a large extent, the arguments of each camp reflected the kind of systems they dealt with in their organizations. All systems have some functional and some data and some time-dependent behavior. However, it is often true that one dimension of the system dominates the other two. Thus, we could imagine a three-dimensional space in which the X-axis represents increasingly complex functions within a system, and the Y-axis represents increasingly complex information (objects and relationships), and the Z-axis represents increasingly complex time-dependent behavior. Figure 19.1 illustrates.

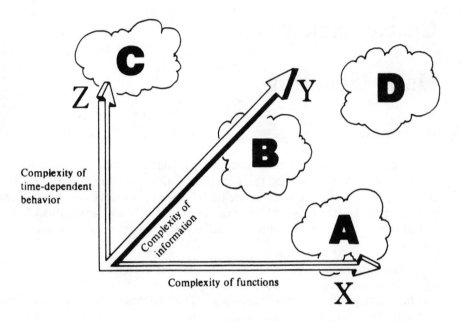

Figure 19.1 Three dimensions of system characteristics

From this perspective, it is fair to say that the structured analysis advocates of the late 1970's made their arguments with the assumption that all important systems (namely, the ones they worked on) fell into the area marked A on Figure 19.1. Similarly, the database advocates made their arguments on the assumption that all important systems fell into the area marked B, and the real-time fanatics made the assumption that all important systems fell into the area marked C.

19.2 The current situation

During the past few years, each camp finally has begun to understand the other two; more importantly, we all have begun to realize that there are systems that are complex in all three dimensions. Thus, we now find ourselves dealing increasingly with systems that fall into the area marked D on Figure 19.1. Banking systems now exhibit real-time behavior; real-time process control systems now have complex databases; and on-line database inquiry systems have increasingly complex functions to ensure that the data is entered correctly and retrieved in a meaningful fashion.

The result is a recognition on the part of each camp for the other two. People who build operating systems and process control systems will sometimes acknowledge that a system built with COBOL could have some real-time characteristics. People who are long-time database fanatics grant that dataflow diagrams are sometimes useful, and structured analysis fanatics acknowledge that information modeling is an important aspect of most complex systems.

Equally important, most professionals now realize that the function modeling viewpoint, the data modeling viewpoint, and the state-transition viewpoint are not mutually exclusive. Rather, they provide three complementary views of a system. A formal relationship among the various views sadly has been lacking until recently. It is now clearly understood, as discussed in Chapter 4, that there are formal one-to-one relationships among the data flow diagram, the entity-relationship diagram, and the state-transition diagram, and that the data dictionary is the linchpin that holds all three models together.

Naturally, there are still many systems that fall into the category shown as A or B or C in Figure 19.1. For such systems, one type of model may be the primary one. But for more and more systems in the 1980's and 1990's, all three models will be important and to favor one and ignore another is a great mistake.

19.3 Current issues

Most MIS professionals agree that all three models are important. However, there are still some unresolved questions, particularly two concerning structured analysis and information modeling: Which model should be developed first? At what level in the user organization should the models be developed?

The question of which comes first is best answered by the classic phrase, "It all depends . . . ." Some typical scenarios are the following:

- If there is a strong, centralized database administration group within the organization, then it is likely that the data models will have been developed before your project commences. In that case, the function modeling presumably will take place with an initial data model, though modifications to the data model may be required as a result of the new project.

- If no data analysis has been done, then it is likely that the function model (the data flow diagram) and the data model will be developed concurrently. In practice, it often happens that the data model is derived from some of the questions raised in the function modeling process (for example, "Where does the data come from? What happens to the data? Where does it go after it has been processed?")

- In an organization where there has been no corporate-wide data modeling and where the data itself is not complex or intrinsically interesting, function modeling may take place without any data modeling.

This last scenario leads us into the second common question: At what level in the organization does all of this modeling take place? There are three common levels: the project level, the departmental level, and the corporate level. When the modeling activities occur strictly within the context of an individual project, function modeling tends to dominate; when done at the level of an entire organization, data modeling tends to dominate; and at the department level, both types of modeling are equally important. Of course, the third type of modeling, time-dependent behavior, is a third dimension that is extremely important at the project level, less important at the departmental level, and generally unimportant at the corporate level.

This perspective reflects the political realities that exist at different levels in the organization: if one is working on an individual project to serve the needs of an individual user, then functions are all-important and the global aspects of data often are irrelevant. Conversely, the systems analyst attempting to model an entire organization is uninterested in the functions carried out by any individual group, but is extremely interested in the information common to all groups. At the departmental level, both functions and data are important.

Chapter Twenty:

The Future of
Structured Techniques

20.1 Introduction

When the first edition of this book was written in 1976, the structured techniques were so new and radical that there was no need for a chapter on the future: the theme of the book was that all of the structured techniques represented the future.

Nearly ten years later, as the third edition of this book is being prepared, the concept of structured techniques is well known in many organizations (which has little or nothing to do with the degree of use in those same organizations); the techniques are widely taught in universities; and several hundred thousand copies of textbooks on structured analysis, structured design, and structured programming have been sold. So now, in a sense, the structured techniques are "old stuff," and people are beginning to ask: "What's next?"

The last four chapters have addressed some of the "What's next?" questions that are being debated in the mid-1980's. By the end of this decade, the debate will have ended as current hot topics, such as personal computing, prototyping, fourth generation languages, and data modeling, will have (a) replaced the structured techniques, or (b) been incorporated into the structured techniques, or (c) been rejected as unworkable.

However, several other interesting concepts are appearing that are compatible with the structured techniques and that have not become hotly debated topics yet in most average MIS organizations. This last chapter addresses several of these future trends.

20.2 Automated tools

Throughout this book, we have seen that the structured techniques rely heavily on the concept of modeling. In particular, graphical modeling techniques have been emphasized: data flow diagrams, entity-relationship diagrams, state transition diagrams, and structure charts have been presented as useful tools for illuminating various aspects of a system. Unfortunately, the graphical models have been hand-drawn in virtually every MIS organization in the world for the past ten years. While this is easy in a textbook where small examples are used and where the author has access to a professional artist, it is not easy in a real-world environment, where (a) large systems involve dozens or even hundreds of diagrams, and (b) the diagrams have to be re-drawn many times as the user requirements change, and (c) the diagrams are drawn by professional MIS people who don't think of themselves as artists or draftspeople. But there was no practical alternative; though CAD/CAM technology already had been developed within the aerospace and automobile industries, nobody in the MIS world could imagine justifying hardware/software packages that typically cost one hundred thousand dollars or more.

However, these problems began to diminish during 1983 to 1984, when powerful personal workstations began to appear on the market at a cost less than ten thousand dollars. In fact, the original version of the IBM PC was below this critical price threshold, but it did not have adequate graphics. Similarly, machines like the Apple II were not adequate. But by 1983, the Apple Lisa computer made it obvious that it was possible to produce a hardware/software combination of high-resolution graphics and low cost. Also, by then a large number of add-on peripheral products and software packages for the IBM PC made it possible to develop IBM-based hardware/software configurations that would provide appropriate tools for the programmer and systems analyst. Others began developing products on the assumption that more powerful and more expensive 32-bit machines such as the Apollo or Convergent Technologies computers would soon fall below the critical threshold of ten thousand dollars.

As a result, there has been a veritable explosion of automated tool products from 1984 to 1985, and it is evident that the dozen or so products already announced are only the first generation of a family of products that will begin to appear in the marketplace throughout the next ten years. A small and incomplete list of such products includes the following:

- PROMOD, from GEI Systems, Inc.

- Excelerator, from Index Systems

- Case 2000, from Nastec Systems

- PSL/PSA, from ISDOS, Inc.

- The Software Engineering Workbench, from YOURDON Software Engineering Company

- SA Tools, from Tektronix

- STRADIS-Draw, from McAuto

All of these products provide some form of the following critical features:

- *Graphics support.* Using a hand-held mouse or some other appropriate device, the workbench allows the technician to create a diagram on the screen, revise it, and produce a hard-copy on a standard dot-matrix printer and/or a high-resolution plotting device. Experience has shown us that the technician spends almost as much time on the workbench to compose the initial version of the diagram as he would have by hand; however, revisions can be done in minutes instead of hours.

- *Data dictionary support.* In addition to the graphical models, the workbench products provide some form of data dictionary so that the data elements, process names, and other items named in the graphical models are properly defined.

- *Consistency checking.* This feature is the most important of the workbench products, and it is an area that will undergo various levels of improvement during the next several years. The workbench can ensure that all items named on the graphical models *do* exist in the data dictionary, that items are not defined more than once in the dictionary, and that net inputs and outputs at one level of a data flow diagram correspond exactly to the net inputs and outputs of the parent bubble in the next higher level diagram.

Since more and more programmers and systems analysts are likely to have personal workstations on their desks in the coming years, the incremental cost of the software and high-resolution graphics facility for analyst workbench products will be relatively modest. Early indications from some users of such products suggest that an improvement of 20 to 30 percent in productivity is achieved easily, more than enough to justify the cost of the products. The long-term economics should be even more impressive as we anticipate a factor-of-ten improvement in software reliability and maintainability using such tools.

During the next five to ten years, we can expect to see several more generations of software engineering support tools that will provide the following capabilities, several of which are discussed in more detail in subsequent sections of this chapter.

- Networking of workstations so that several systems analysts can work together on different components of a large project. Networking could be accomplished with a local area network, or by using a more powerful minicomputer to control and coordinate the activities of the stand-alone workstations.

- Global error-checking. If several systems analysts are working on different portions of the same system, there must be a project-wide data dictionary and global consistency checking to ensure that analyst A's work is consistent with analyst B's work.

- Code generation and reusable code

- Complexity models

- Proofs of correctness

- Project management and change control

- Simulation and prototyping

- "Expert" assistance in the development of the requirements model

20.3 Reusable code

Observers of the computer field repeatedly have pointed out that programmers have a tendency to write programs that have already been written. At a higher level, systems analysts and project managers have a tendency to build systems that have already been built. For at least twenty years, some MIS organizations have tried to remedy this problem by creating libraries of reusable modules, subroutines, programs, and whole systems.

The effort, though well-intentioned, usually has been a failure as programmers continue to write programs that have been written dozens of times before — indeed, even programs that they themselves wrote before. The reasons for the failure of the reusable code library have been threefold:

- The "modules" that were put into the library were often too large and ambitious in scope. A program that tries to do all things for all people often fails because it doesn't satisfy anyone for any specific application.

- The "modules" often were built in a way that they could not be used in combination with other modules. Someone writing a logarithm subroutine or a date-conversion subroutine is usually clever enough to realize that the subroutine cannot make any assumptions about the environment in which it operates. On the other hand, the person who develops an on-line text editor almost invariably makes the assumption that the environment consists of a human being providing commands through a keyboard. Consequently, the text editor typically can't be used in any other environment, even though it contains pattern-matching and string-searching functions that would be useful in many different applications.

- Though it was usually trivial to insert a new module into the library, it was often difficult to retrieve a module from the library to find out what modules were in the library, what their properties were, and how thoroughly they had been tested.

During the late 1970's and early 1980's, it became apparent that one could create an environment conducive to the development of reusable modules. The paradigm of such an environment, in my opinion, is the well-known UNIX® operating system, which my colleagues and I have had the pleasure of using since 1976. Aside from its other advantages and disadvantages which continue to be debated throughout the industry, the UNIX® operating system environment effectively solves two of the three problems discussed above: by providing a library of some seventy-five utility routines as a role model, it encourages system developers to create new modules which are small, capable of carrying out only one, small, well-defined task elegantly, and make no assumptions about the source of its input or the destination of its output.

Hence, the UNIX® command language (roughly equivalent to catalogued procedures on some mainframes or batch command files on some personal computers) allows the systems developer to create new, unique systems by creating a unique combination of existing library modules, with perhaps one or two new, unique modules of his own.

Since this system-building process is so easy in the UNIX® environment, it is an attractive option for systems analysts, programmers, and users. Even in such an environment, there always will be some evidence of the "Not Invented Here" syndrome that encourages MIS personnel to re-invent the wheel. Only a vigorous management campaign can correct this habit by encouraging, and rewarding the use of library modules. It is certainly possible to gradually create an MIS culture that looks upon the creation of unique code and custom-built systems as something to be done only in dire emergencies.*

The one ingredient that still is lacking in most MIS organizations is the librarian function that will control the introduction of new modules into the library, ensuring that new candidates don't duplicate old ones, ensuring adequate levels of quality, and assisting the MIS technician who wants to know if there is an existing module that fits his needs.

Some of this innovation requires managerial involvement, for example, the creation of a software tools group if the MIS organization is large enough; some of it always will involve some human talent, for instance, the concept of a toolsmith that was discussed as a component of the Chief Programmer Team in Chapter 8. But a larger and larger component of the reusable code concept can be accomplished with the assistance of the workbench tool discussed in the previous section. An on-line library of reusable code, designs, and specifications should carry with it appropriate mechanisms for browsing, searching, indexing, and cross-referencing. An appropriate place for this kind of automated support might be the project-level minicomputer discussed in the previous section. In the next ten years, we should expect to see some expert

---

* — advocates of fourth generation languages may violently disagree with this approach, since it is apparently so easy to create new, unique, customized applications. What is important here, though, is not the duplication of lines of code, but the duplication of intellectual activity. If someone has spent a day of his time developing an elegant implementation of some well-defined task in any language, then that effort should not be needlessly repeated simply because another programmer wants to experience the intellectual satisfaction of solving the same problem again.

system features that will provide automated assistance for the MIS technician who is looking for a module that can't quite be described precisely.

20.4 Complexity models

Since the mid-1970's, there has been considerable interest in the concept of modeling the complexity of computer programs, and thus, ultimately, the complexity of entire systems. When we use the term *complexity*, we mean complexity as a human observer perceives it. Hence, it may be possible for someone to write a program in BASIC or PASCAL that is easy for another person to comprehend, but difficult for a computer to handle (for example, expensive in terms of CPU resources, or disk accesses). More importantly, it is easy for a human to write a program that is easy for a computer to handle, but difficult for another human to comprehend. Since the program must be debugged by the original programmer and maintained by as many as ten generations of maintenance programmers before its ultimate demise, this issue of complexity is an important one.

The subject of program complexity is still a controversial one in the mid-1980's; however, it is evident that some progress has been made. Throughout the 1960's and much of the 1970's, the only metric of complexity was the length of a program: it generally was assumed that a longer computer program would be more difficult to understand than a shorter program. While this assumption often is valid, many times it is not, and it has led to a number of silly programming standards in MIS organizations. History eventually will record the number of programmers who were shot at dawn for writing a fifty-one statement subroutine when the company's programming standards insisted that no subroutine be longer than fifty statements.

In the late 1970's, Maurice Halstead first introduced the view of program complexity as a function of something more than lines of code. His measure of volume, documented in *Elements of Software Science* (New York: American Elsevier, 1977), is a landmark; since then, there have been many other models of program complexity, including McCabe's measure of cyclomatic complexity. For further information on this area, see Tom DeMarco's *Controlling Software Projects,* (New York: YOURDON Press, 1982).

As mentioned above, considerable debate still exists about many of these metrics, and available statistics can be used to either prove or disprove most of the theoretical complexity models in existence. However, most evidence tends to support the notion of a "Pareto Principle" for components of a system: 80 percent of the complexity of a system (and thus, 80 percent of the bugs and 80 percent of the maintenance costs) can be associated with 20 percent of the code. The trick is to find out *which* 20 percent of the code is critical. The mathematical complexity models are beginning to give us some insights in this area; by the end of this decade, we should be able to pinpoint complex, and thus intrinsically troublesome, modules by the end of the systems analysis phase of a project.

20.5 Proof of correctness

It has long been known that testing of conventional computer systems is, at best, a defensive measure. "Testing," as Edsger Dijkstra has said, "demonstrates the presence of errors, not the absence of errors." Exhaustive testing is impractical for almost all MIS projects and is impossible for many; consequently, we must live with the reality that many of today's critical systems may have bugs lurking within them that nobody has yet been able to find.

One solution to this problem has been discussed for nearly two decades: developing a formal, rigorous, mathematical proof of correctness of a computer program. Efforts in this area have been conducted within academic circles for the past two decades, but were largely ignored within the MIS community because (a) the academic community was attempting to develop correctness proofs for small programs (less than one hundred lines of code) while industry was trying to deal with systems of one million lines of code, and (b) the examples used by academia were of no interest to industry, that is, the mathematical proofs of correctness involved programs that dealt with chess problems or other similar game-playing situations.

Academia and industry are still far apart, but the U.S. Department of Defense (DOD) has formed an important bridge between the two. As one can imagine, DOD currently is involved in building systems for which a proof of correctness has enormous value. Hence, much of the practical work in this area for the remainder of the 1980's will probably be in the DOD realm, and the economics are interesting: to provide a machine-assisted proof of correctness of a system involving five to ten thousand lines of code, DOD must be willing to spend approximately half a million dollars (as of 1985). This amount may sound expensive until one contemplates the cost of a failure in such a system. Military systems are an obvious example of the usefulness of proofs of correctness; however, electronic funds transfer systems and other high-volume consumer-oriented systems might also be viable candidates.

In the mid-1980's, virtually no commercial, business-oriented MIS organization in the U.S. invested money to provide mathematical proofs of correctness for their systems. I predict that this malaise will change drastically in the next ten years and that the *standard* for large, complex systems will involve such proofs. While most MIS organizations have neither the talent nor the time to pursue this area today, it is an important area to be aware of because most of the practical developments (for instance, software packages that will provide computer-assisted proofs of any application program) eventually will be made available free through the courtesy of the U.S. Department of Defense. (It's not usually so blatant, but much of the important R & D work in the computer industry has been done by, or sponsored by, such DOD organizations as DARPA, and the results eventually trickle down to private industry).

20.6 Project management

Project management for MIS systems is better than it was twenty years ago; however, it is still commonly true than MIS projects are substantially behind schedule and over budget. The average project in 1985, according to Capers Jones, is one year behind schedule and 100 percent over budget. As the MIS function becomes increasingly important in both large and small organizations, management gradually will insist on better and more accurate methods of managing MIS projects. In the extreme case, they may abolish MIS projects through the simple expedient of commercial packages and facilities management services if the MIS organization cannot manage itself.

It is widely assumed that software engineering techniques will improve the ability of the project manager to control the events that occur in the development of a large, complex system. By introducing activities and products that show tangible evidence of progress, the project manager is able to avoid the "95 percent done" syndrome that is often evident on the second or third day of a typical project. By improving the process of systems analysis, together with the introduction of top-down implementation, the testing phase of a project, which was previously the most time-consuming and unpredictable part of a large MIS project, becomes simple and straightforward.

However, we should not fool ourselves: software engineering will not eliminate all project management problems. In particular, we still are left with the difficult job of estimating the size and cost of a project at a sufficiently early stage that top management can make an intelligent decision to approve or cancel the project. Also, we still need better quantitative measurements so that the project manager can evaluate progress during the project. These issues are discussed at length in two excellent books: *Software Engineering Economics,* by Barry Boehm (Englewood Cliffs: Prentice-Hall, 1982), and *Controlling Software Projects,* by Tom DeMarco (New York: YOURDON Press, 1982).

In addition to the difficulty of making good estimates and deciding what metrics are most appropriate, the project manager has another major problem: much of the data that he uses is provided by the programmers and analysts working on the project. Thus, when he asks Gwendolyn, "How are you doing on the XYZ subroutine?" she is likely to meditate for a moment or two and then respond, "It's 95 percent done, boss!" When he asks Ferdinand, "How many lines of code have you written today?" Ferdinand might open his program listing and scan it for a few seconds before responding, "Oh, about a hundred and ten lines, I guess!"

The problem with this information is that (a) it is subject to misinterpretation because the data is being provided by the workers themselves, often in an atmosphere where it appears that the data will be used to evaluate their work; and (b) it requires additional work and thus will not be done unless the manager insists upon it. The long-term salvation for project managers is a mechanism that provides project metrics *automatically* and as a natural by-product of the work itself. The analyst/programmer workbench discussed earlier in this chapter is a natural tool for capturing this data, and the better-managed MIS organizations will begin taking advantage of such tools during the latter half of the 1980's.

An added benefit to the use of such data-gathering tools is that they help create a database of metrics over many projects within the MIS organization. Thus, it eventually will be practical to look at the last ten programs that Ferdinand wrote to see if there are any obvious patterns. It also will be possible to look at the last ten payroll projects within the organization (at which point someone might well ask why it was necessary to write ten different payroll systems!) to see if there are any obvious patterns.

20.7 Artificial intelligence

Since the early 1980's, artificial intelligence has been an important and exciting topic in the computer industry. Practical applications, ranging from robotics to medical diagnosis, are beginning to appear as commercial products, and we can look forward to a continuing stream of developments in the decade ahead.

Artificial intelligence can be important in developing computer systems and thus, artificial intelligence or, more specifically, expert systems soon will be an important adjunct to software engineering.

Consider the analogy of medical diagnosis. A patient describes his symptoms to the doctor — or to an expert system that has been given the rules of judgment that an expert human doctor would use. Based on the symptoms described by the patient, the expert may ask more questions or prescribe certain tests. Eventually, the expert produces a diagnosis, as well as a prescription for medication to cure the problem. In most cases, there is not a 100 percent certainty that the diagnosis is correct; the degree of certainty is both a function of the degree of expertise of the doctor as well as the nature of the illness.

Now consider the same situation in the field of systems analysis. The patient is the user who has some fuzzy ideas about his needs for automating some portion of his business. He can describe some of his "symptoms," and that initial description usually prompts more questions from the "doctor." At the end of one or more such discussions, the expert (systems analyst) diagnoses the problem and prescribes a cure (inevitably it's a new computer system!).

The significant point is this: There is a world of difference between expert (human) systems analysts and amateur systems analysts. Over a period of years, the expert has accumulated a number of rules of judgment. He knows what questions to ask and what answers to believe. He has seen enough similar cases (and users) to have a good idea of the problems affecting this user. The amateur, on the other hand, is lost. He doesn't know what questions to ask, nor does he know when to stop asking questions. He doesn't know whether the user is describing a problem, or merely symptoms of a problem, or perhaps symptoms of someone else's problem.

Thus, it would seem highly likely that the expertise of several veteran systems analysts could be captured by an expert system, so that the user-analyst dialogue eventually could occur between a human user and an automated systems analyst. Most probably, this dialogue would be restricted to specific, narrowly defined applications, such as accounting or inventory control or some other specific topic. Twenty to twenty-five years from now, though, it is conceivable that we could have general-purpose automated systems analysts.

Finally, we human systems analysts and programmers would be forced out of the computer business and would find it necessary to get an "honest" job. I expect that day to coincide with my sixty-fifth birthday, and I look forward to my retirement with great excitement!

APPENDIX A

Suggested Standards for Structured Coding
in COBOL

Introduction

The objective of this style guide is to produce readable structured code from a structured design of independent function modules. The standards are not intended for rigid enforcement, but are meant to serve as a springboard for each software development group in deciding what will be acceptable in code reviews.

Topic: PROCEDURE UNITS

Standard:

The basic procedure unit is a paragraph; several paragraphs may be packaged into a section, especially if their functions are temporally bound, as, for example, initialization functions.

Rejected Alternatives:

1) Basic unit is a section.
2) Basic unit is a separately compilable entity.

Discussion:

A module is defined as one or more code statements together fulfilling a single function, with one and only one label by which the function may be invoked.

The COBOL construct that most nearly satisfies this definition is the paragraph. Using the section as the basic unit with no paragraph names has been recommended because some compilers then would enforce the discipline of an EXIT statement. This is not the case in ANS 74 COBOL. An EXIT statement should be provided only if required as the target of a GOTO within the procedure.

Having a separately compilable entity as the basic unit, with no labels inside each entity, is possible and gives excellent interface clarity; but the repetition of Data Divisions makes for less readable source code.

We envisage micromodules (paragraphs) being packaged into macromodules (compilable entities) by the program designer after completion of the structured design. Where segmentation is important, or in certain forms of case structure, paragraphs may be packaged into sections.

Implicit in the definition of a module is that no matter what level in the hierarchy, it should have only one entrance (the label) and one exit. Control never should be allowed to pass implicitly across any procedure name; that is, control should not be possible to "fall through" from one procedure to the procedure that happens to be physically next in the code.

Micromodules should be marked off visually from each other by a blank line before and after.

The size of a macromodule or program is not critical for readability. However, it may be desirable to have separately compilable entities for changeability, and there may be constraints on main storage size.

Topic: PROCEDURE NAMES WITHIN A MACROMODULE

Standard:

> Each procedure name should express the function of the procedure and should have a prefix, consisting of a letter plus a digit, which gives its relative location within the Procedure Division.
>
> This prefix may be omitted from Procedure Divisions covering less than two pages.

Rejected Alternative:

> Use of a suffix.

Discussion:

> When micromodules form a hierarchy, they should be numbered A1 - A9 for the first level, B1 - B9 for the second level, and so on; for example,

```
        PERFORM A1-INITIALIZATION.
        PERFORM A2-PROCESS-RECORDS.
        PERFORM A3-WRAPUP.

    A1-INITIALIZATION.
                .
                .
                .

    A2-PROCESS-RECORDS.
                .
                .
                .

        PERFORM B1-READ-RECORD
            UNTIL ALL-DONE.
```

Topic: DATA NAMING AND DEFINITION

Standard:

1) Data names should be as meaningful as possible while not being overlong, and should be given a suffix if they are used in the macromodule interface: -IN for input, -OUT for output.

2) Working storage (suffix, -WS) will consist of a level Ø1 for each micromodule. Working storage used by that micromodule will be defined under this Ø1. Shared working storage will be defined as:
   Ø1   COMMON-WS.

3) No micromodule may modify another module's private working storage.

4) The VALUE clause is used to establish only parameters and tables that never change. Variables should be initialized in the Procedure Division, near where they are used. The need for initialization should be kept to a minimum.

5) Hyphenation should be used to add meaning, for example, CD-MF-AC-NO, rather than CDMFACNO.

6) Only counters and binary flags may be coded as literals. All numbers other than Ø and 1 should be coded as initialized variables with meaningful names. Values Ø and 1 should be given names whenever they represent true or false or similar condition values.

7) The use of level-88 names should be avoided because their use obscures the relationship between the setting and testing of flag values. Instead, make free use of numeric parameters for such values; for example,

```
IF RECORDS-LEFT = NO
MOVE YES TO DONE
```

Topic: STRUCTURES

Standard:

Process structures: concatenations of instructions normally involving no transfer of control within the structure, for example, MOVEs, arithmetic, I/O.

Exception conditions (like AT END, ON SIZE ERROR): If dealing with this condition is part of the module's function, insert the necessary code. If the function should be dealt with by one of the calling modules, set a flag; or better still, use the normal output data parameters to return exception information.

A concatenation of structures normally can be treated as a simple process structure, except when it is under control of a conditional statement (such as, IF, READ . . . AT END); and the concatenation of structures must contain an imbedded period. In this case, the process structure is written as a separate paragraph and PERFORMed.

Decision structures: normal layout is

```
IF    condition-1
         imperative-1
ELSE
         imperative-2.
```

Where the logic demands a nested IF (that is, an imperative is replaced by another IF), the structure, wherever possible, should be rewritten linearly:

```
IF          condition-1
                imperative-1
ELSE IF    condition-2
                imperative-2
ELSE
                imperative-3.
```

NEXT SENTENCE should be revised out of the code wherever possible, even if it means introducing a NOT. Avoid mixing AND and OR in a condition; if you must do so, use parentheses to avoid ambiguity.

Where the code implements a decision table, include the decision table as comments.

Where IFs must be nested, each level of IF should be indented and its corresponding ELSE aligned with it. An obvious exception is the ELSE-IF chain on the previous page.

As far as possible, the code for a condition should follow the usage of normal speech; if a condition is not comprehensible when read aloud, recast it.

CASE structures: situation in which one variable may take more than two values, with a different procedure performed depending on each value.

For *non-numeric variables,* use the linear chain of ELSE IFs; for example,

```
IF        CODE = A
                PERFORM PROCEDURE-A
ELSE IF   CODE = B
                PERFORM PROCEDURE-B
ELSE IF   CODE = C
                PERFORM PROCEDURE-C
ELSE
                PERFORM ILLEGAL-
                CODE-ROUTINE.
         .
         .
         .

PROCEDURE-A.
         .
         .

PROCEDURE-B.
         .
         .
```

PROCEDURE-C.
.
.

ILLEGAL-CODE-ROUTINE.
.
.
.

For *integer variables,* it is permissible to use a GOTO . . . DEPENDING ON within a section; for example,

```
CASE-STRUCTURE SECTION.
SET-CASE-SWITCH.
        GOTO PROCEDURE-1 PROCEDURE-2 PROCEDURE-3
            DEPENDING ON CODE.
PROCEDURE-1.
        .
        .
        .
        GOTO CASE-STRUCTURE-XIT.
PROCEDURE-2.
        .
        .
        .
        GOTO CASE-STRUCTURE-XIT.
PROCEDURE-3.
        .
        .
        .
        GOTO CASE-STRUCTURE-XIT.
CASE-STRUCTURE-XIT.
        EXIT.
```

This whole section is PERFORMed from an appropriate place in the program.

Never contrive code just to use a GOTO . . . DEPENDING ON . . . . Unless the code arises naturally in the data representation, use linear ELSE IFs.

Loop structures: for multiple executions ending on a condition (zero or more times),

```
PERFORM loop-proc
    UNTIL condition.
```

For multiple executions ending on a condition (one or more times),

```
PERFORM loop-proc.
PERFORM loop-proc
    UNTIL condition.
```

For multiple executions on a counter value (zero or more times),

```
PERFORM loop-proc
    VARYING counter-name
    FROM     initial-value
    BY       increment
    UNTIL    condition.
```

Alternatives Rejected:

> PERFORM THRU: This leads to confusion and implies that a functional entity can be addressed to points inside itself. If you need to write PERFORM PROC-A THRU PROC-C, write a "sandwich" procedure, consisting of

```
SANDWICH-PROC.
    PERFORM PROC-A.
    PERFORM PROC-B.
    PERFORM PROC-C.
```

> Then PERFORM SANDWICH-PROC as needed.

> PERFORM n TIMES: This encourages the use of literals. Use PERFORM . . . VARYING instead, as this will show the exit point more meaningfully.

Discussion:

> Note that there are three uses for the PERFORM statement:

1) to invoke a submodule, which performs a complete function and returns (procedure call)

2) to invoke a process block, which cannot be written in-line (group)

3) to invoke a loop body zero or more times (loop)

> Therefore, not all paragraphs may be complete functional modules in the sense of structured design; some may be groups or loop-bodies, that is, sequentially or even procedurally bound modules.

Topic: LOOPS THAT READ SEQUENTIAL FILES

Standard:

```
MOVE YES TO RECORDS-LEFT.
READ the file
    AT END MOVE NO TO RECORDS-LEFT.
PERFORM the loop
    UNTIL RECORDS-LEFT = NO.
```

At the end of the loop's code, READ again to get the next record.

Rejected Alternatives:

```
MOVE YES TO RECORDS-LEFT.
PERFORM the loop
    UNTIL RECORDS-LEFT = NO.
```

As the first step in the loop

```
READ the file
    AT END MOVE NO TO RECORDS-LEFT.
IF RECORDS-LEFT = NO
    body of loop
        .
        .
        .
```

Discussion:

From the design point of view, it is preferable to carry out an initial read and set a flag, since the executive module can deal with the condition straight away of an empty file. The alternative puts the body of the loop as a series of clauses within the positive branch of an IF statement.

Topic: EXPLICITNESS

Standard:

> Arithmetic — Do not write a COMPUTE of more than three variables or constants: Break any more complex equation into intermediate steps.
>
> Notation — Do not use > < : People find them confusing, and some print chains do not have them.
>
> Format — Align all related verbs. Align all PICs (col. 32 is suggested). Align all VALUEs (col. 44 is suggested).

Topic: COMMENTS

Standard:

Use comments (* in col. 7) to explain code that is not self-evident, or that is not directly related to function. This usually occurs where the pseudocode cannot be converted directly to COBOL, for example, in a swap. Consider rewriting any code that needs explaining.

Include any decision tables you develop as comments to be placed immediately before the decision structure that implements them.

If the gross function of the macromodule is not clear from reading the highest-level micromodule, describe the macromodule in terms of pseudocode and include as comments at the beginning of the Procedure Division.

Include a comment wherever a variable is modified whose values have level-88 condition names, or wherever data are modified by more than one micromodule (unless the data is in COMMON-WS).

Use comments to explain *what* code is doing, not *how* it is doing it.

In general, to determine the need for comments, imagine that someone else is writing this code, and that, in the middle of the night next week, *you* will have to change it under pressure of time.

Moral: Write unto others as you would wish to be written unto.

Topic: FORMATTING

Standard:

1) Only one statement or procedure name per line.

2) UNTIL, AT END, ON SIZE ERROR, VARYING, and similar qualifying clauses should be indented two spaces from the verbs they qualify, for example,

    READ CARD-FILE
      AT END MOVE NO TO CARDS-LEFT.

3) Each ELSE should be directly under the IF to which it refers, except in the case of linear ELSE IF sequences.

4) In the case of a too-long statement, break it at a word such that it is obvious that the statement must be continued.

APPENDIX B

Suggested Standards for Structured Coding
in PL/I

Introduction

The objective of this style guide is the production of readable structured code from a structured design of independent functional modules. The standards are not intended for mechanical enforcement, but to serve as a point of departure for each software development group in deciding what will and will not be acceptable in code reviews.

YOURDON is delighted to advise on the adaption of these standards to a particular set of circumstances.

PL/I code for which YOURDON takes responsibility will conform to these standards.

Topic: BASIC MODULAR UNIT

Standard:

> The basic modular unit is an EXTERNAL PROCEDURE.

Rejected Alternatives:

> 1) Basic module is a PROCEDURE, either INTERNAL or EXTERNAL.
>
> 2) Basic module is possibly a portion of a multi-entry PROCEDURE.

Discussion:

> The intention of the standard is to create modules that can be compiled, tested, modified, and maintained independently of one another. In PL/I, this is best accomplished by using EXTERNAL PROCEDUREs. Considerations of packaging and efficiency may require moving some modules in-line into others; that is, making them INTERNAL PROCEDUREs. This can be done with great ease late in the project provided that all identifiers have been explicitly declared (with no exceptions); in particular, built-in functions should be declared BUILTIN, and ENTRY and RETURNS attributes should be declared in full.

Topic: ENSURING MODULAR INDEPENDENCE

Standard:

Any dependencies, inheritances, side effects, or shared assumptions between modules should be (a) eliminated if possible or (b) explicitly documented.

Discussion:

1) Declarations of EXTERNAL ENTRYs should specify all parameter and returned-value attributes, such as:

```
DECLARE  SUBROUT  ENTRY(FLOAT,CHAR(*))
RETURNS(FLOAT);
```

Parameter attributes can be verified by the compiler if given in ENTRY declaration, and if the programmer reads the attribute-and-cross-reference listing.

2) Shared assumptions, such as the possible range of a parameter, or the meaning of flags, can be described in narrative comments, which form the interface documentation. The most standard place for such documentation is at the beginning of the called module. Defensive programming, or anti-bugging, should be adhered to wherever such assumptions can be explicitly tested. In production, a section of anti-bugging code can be put into a comment frame if it takes too much execution time.

3) On-units intended to be shared among several modules must be mentioned in a comment in each module. On-units *not* intended to be shared should be established (via ON statement) and reverted (via REVERT statement) close to the affected statements so that they aren't inherited by subroutines.

4) EXTERNAL storage must be subject to system-wide controls; a pair of programmers could create tricky maintenance problems by a private agreement to pass information through EXTERNAL storage.

Topic: STRUCTURED CODING

Standard:

> Programs will be constructed from the basic control structures (SE-QUENCE, IF-THEN-ELSE, DO-WHILE) augmented by the multi-way conditional (or "CASE") and the loop termination (or "LEAVE"). Any exceptions to these rules have long-range maintenance implications and require project-wide agreement on the need for and implementation of the exception.

Rejected Alternatives:

1) No restrictions on control structures.

2) Dogmatic restriction to SEQUENCE, IF-THEN-ELSE, and DO-WHILE only.

Discussion:

1) DO-WHILE: Loops should conform either to the simple iteration form

    DO J = start TO finish BY step ;

or the general DO-WHILE form

    DO WHILE (condition) ;

2) CASE: The recommended, most general form of the CASE construct is this:

```
/* CASE:  alert the reader */
IF          case-1-condition THEN
            action-1;
ELSE IF     case-2-condition THEN
            action-2;
ELSE IF     case-3-condition THEN
            action-3;
            . . .
ELSE
            action-default;
/* END OF CASE */
```

3) LEAVE: An early loop termination, such as GOTO LEAVE$LOOP, can be allowed, provided that the GOTO goes to the point just past the loop being terminated, that a comment before the loop alerts the reader to the loop exit, and that there is no simpler way to write the code without the exit.

Topic: AVOIDING HIDDEN ERRORS

Standard:

> A PL/I programmer must adhere to a strict set of rules for avoiding surprises of PL/I syntax and semantics. The most important thing is to follow a consistent style, but there is room for individual selection of the exact style used. The discussion below lists one set of possible rules.

Rejected Alternative:

1) *Ad-hoc* approach to each potential hidden-error situation, for example, encountering a nested IF, the programmer asks "Hmm, should I use a DO-END here, or maybe a null ELSE, or restructure, or . . . ?"

Discussion:

1) Each IF-THEN-IF nesting must have a DO-END around its action clause.

2) All type-conversions should be done explicitly, preferably by assignment to a variable.

3) Multiple-closure END statements should not be used. Each END should be visually matchable with its DO.

4) Use aggregate assignments only for initialization of an aggregate.

5) Perform data editing explicitly with VERIFY rather than using the CONVERSION condition.

Topic: PROGRAM READABILITY

Standard:

>   If a piece of code requires explana-
>   tion and can be recoded so as to re-
>   quire none, then recode it.

Rejected Alternative:

>   1) Detailed layout rules.

Discussion:

1) Use a page heading comment before each PROCEDURE.

2) Adopt a consistent style of spacing and indenting, or use a formatting preprocessor.

3) Use a consistent system of the following:
>   keyword abbreviation,
>   order of attributes and options,
>   precisions,
>   variable abbreviations,
>   name-choice conventions,
>   order of declarations in the listing,
>   order of identifiers in lists (e.g., al-
>   phabetical).

4) Good code is capable of being self-documenting at the detail level, but not at the overall concept level. Precede each PROCEDURE's executable code with enough narrative comment to enable reading the code without further explanation. Examples in programming texts can be misleading because the necessary narrative appears in the text, not in the programs. Some especially helpful narrative items are the algorithm

used and any creatively chosen data structures.

5) Design so that the average module's executable code can fit on one page. Design and recode a module whose executable code exceeds two pages.

Topic: MAINTAINABILITY

Standard:

Write code that can be maintained by someone with less PL/I experience than yourself.

Discussion:

1) Use the advanced features that are listed below only when you have project-wide agreement on their necessity and maintainability.

ENTRY variables,
GENERIC entries,
multiple entry points,
DEFAULT,
RECURSIVE,
multi-tasking,
compile-time preprocessor,
LOCATE-mode input and output.

2) Eschew magic numbers: Program constants should be assigned as IN-ITIAL values to named variables. The constants $\emptyset$ and 1 should be the only hard-coded constants in the program, and there should be very few of them. Strive to make it easy to change the specific numeric and character values used by the program.

Topic: AVOIDING NEEDLESS INEFFICIEN-
CIES

Standard:

When unsure of the efficiency of a
PL/I method, code a sample and
execute it; make use of experimental programs to avoid depending on out-of-date dogma about
efficient features. Devote the
most attention to critical areas of
code.

Discussion:

In general, hard-and-fast rules
about inefficient features in PL/I
create unnecessary burdens on
programmers doing non-critical
code (the major portion of most
systems!). Furthermore, the vari-
ability of PL/I implementations
and environments makes many absolute rules somewhat risky. The
following rules are fairly safe:

1) Wherever possible, declare the
    same precisions for arithmetic
    variables added, subtracted, or as-
    signed to each other.

2) Whenever time is more critical
    than space, try an experiment with
    DEFAULT RANGE(*) STATIC;

3) Require item-by-item scanning of
    each attribute-and-cross-reference
    listing to catch the warning mes-
    sages "data conversion by subrou-
    tine call" and "dummy arguments
    have been created." Both mes-

sages reveal time-consuming consequences of attribute-mismatches. Try declaring the variables involved with the same attributes.

4) Don't use a BEGIN block where a DO-group will suffice.

5) Search each module for inner loops, expanses of repetitive code, and item-by-item (or character-by-character) processing. Experiment with replacing these sections with code using PL/I built-in features.

Index